The Monocle Guide to Drinking & Dining

The Monocle Guide to Drinking & Dining

From where to eat around the world to how to host, cook or start a food business, a handbook for anyone who appreciates honest eating.

For more information, please visit *gestalten.com*

Bibliographic information published by the Deutsche Nationalbibliothek. The Deutsche Nationalbibliothek lists this publication in the Deutsche Nationalbibliografie; detailed bibliographic data is available online at *dnb.d-nb.de*

This book was printed on paper certified by the FSC®

Gestalten is a climate-neutral company. We collaborate with the non-profit carbon offset provider myclimate (*myclimate.org*) to neutralise the company's carbon footprint produced through our worldwide business activities by investing in projects that reduce CO_2 emissions (*gestalten.com/myclimate*).

Edited by *Josh Fehnert*
Monocle editor *Andrew Tuck*
Books editor *Joe Pickard*
Foreword by *Tyler Brûlé*

Designed by *Monocle*
Proofreading by *Monocle*
Typeset in *Plantin & Helvetica*

Printed by *Offsetdruckerei Grammlich, Pliezhausen*

Made in Germany

Published by *Gestalten*, Berlin 2016
ISBN 978-3-89955-668-1

© Die Gestalten Verlag GmbH & Co. KG, Berlin 2016

Contents

Tyler Brûlé: *thoughts on the importance of good drinking and dining*

There's a better than 80 to 90 per cent chance that at some point during your working life you've stood back from your current gig and thought about what might unfold if you shifted gears and pursued that long-harboured dream of opening your own bar in a sunny, busy patch of the Med. If not a bar then perhaps you have considered raising some goats and trying your hand at running a boutique dairy operation. Or maybe it was apples and pressing the best juices, with some exquisite branding. At the very least you spend a considerable amount of time plotting and planning where you're going to sample brunch next Saturday, archiving articles on the best *izakaya* in Fukuoka and snapping photos of wine labels that you need to add to your ever-expanding cellar.

Purveyors of fine drink, outstanding produce and hearty dishes have been a constant in MONOCLE since our first issue hit newsstands back in 2007. From the start we've been interested in chronicling the brewers who've challenged the multinationals and the corner shops that have forced grocery chains to rethink their methods. We've also thought about how our relationship to drinking and dining can shape neighbourhoods, inspire a new breed of entrepreneur and transform the reputation of entire cities thanks to smart people who know their way around a market hall, kitchen and restaurant floor. Along the road we've also stumbled into the food-and-beverage business ourselves with the launch of a café in Tokyo and, later, fresh outposts in London and good coffee in Singapore and Merano. Running our own café operations has taught us that it's considerably easier to turn out a magazine 12 times a year, run a 24-hour radio station and publish a range of books.

This book is also a tribute to the people who've hosted us well into the wee hours with the tastiest Italian dishes and taken us on tours to buy fish in some of the biggest markets in the world. We also acknowledge those that have inspired us with their approach to retail design and proven that there's always room to improve the experience for the chef, shopper, diner and producer.

Over the next 300 or so pages we'll reveal why the Thais, Japanese and Swiss understand how to create world-class food halls, how to get up and running with that vineyard and what some of the world's most celebrated individuals would tuck in to for their last meals. There's also a comprehensive list of all the utensils and crockery you need for a perfectly stocked kitchen and an essential list of restaurants to sample over the years to come. In amongst all of this there's a straightforward selection of recipes that we've road-tested to give you a nice repertoire of dishes to pull together for any number of occasions. *Guten appetit, itadakimasu*, enjoy. — (M)

How to make the most of your food *plus where to drink and dine...*

At its best good food is a simple, fulfilling pleasure but too often "taste" itself can seem like a loaded term: something that people have or are harshly derided for lacking. But there's hope. After all, complexity isn't a recipe for success when it comes to cooking, hosting a dinner party or starting up your first restaurant.

If MONOCLE were a restaurant it would be a place where good produce is effortlessly prepared, where great wine is served without fuss, formality or reserve and where the maître d' has been around for years (and knows how to read the room). It would be a place where everyone is welcome, which anchors its neighbourhood and feels part of the community. It would also know that quality design and sharp branding help its cause. It would give a helping hand to young, aspiring chefs. It would never serve foamy dishes and nobody would worry if it had a star or two from Michelin. As you can see, we know what we think about fine food and its power to shape people and places.

This world of slow-ish food, fun and easy pleasures informs the book you're holding. It works on two levels: firstly to advise readers about everything from the best food market in Helsinki[1] to the finest coffee shop in Auckland[2]; and secondly it's aimed at anyone wishing to enter this world by taking over a forlorn vineyard or stumbling corner shop. Its message speaks to a generation who may have an MBA but may also think that an exceptional motorway restaurant business could be the way ahead.

We invite you to forget food that's preoccupied with fancy, frothy distractions, meagre portions and adjective-addled menus. To forego the bluff, bluster and snobbery that can surround that ever-so-human need to eat. Instead we're championing the humble pleasures of eating well and knowing where your food comes from[3].

For the past decade we have scoured the globe for businesses and individuals in the industry who have sincerity in spades and favour a homely, honest and hospitable approach to their trade; we meet the chefs and producers setting the table for success and discover how to stock a kitchen or rev up a food truck, bar or bistro[4]. Plus there are a few famous faces sharing tasty stories over supper[5], some food for thought from a range of writers, chefs and raconteurs[6] and a sprinkling of recipes to try your hand at[7]. MONOCLE's seasoned editors have prepared a spread of stories intended to make eating a nourishing experience once again.

Hungry for more?
We thought you might be.

How to use the guide

Part 1.
Food For Thought

Inspiring success stories from proud producers and expert tips on a new career in the industry. Plus a few essays worth savouring and reflections from some of our favourite people over their 'last meals'.

Part 2.
Stocking Up

A survey of the world's finest food markets, freshest retailers and on-point packaging. The best ingredients for an honest meal from around the world.

Part 3.
Roll Up Your Sleeves

All the kitchen kit you'll ever need, how to host a delightful dinner party, plus a range of recipes for any occasion (from need-to-impress lunches to an indulgent snack alone) courtesy of our favourite chefs and our own repertoire of tried-and-tested dishes.

Part 4.
The Directory

We offer a rundown of the best restaurants, cafés and bars from Adelaide to Zürich. A comprehensive compendium of proven stop-ins who pride themself on simplicity, hospitality and charm. Bon appétit.

PART I.
Food For Thought

I.
Inspirational Producers

The growers and showers

We meet the people who have foregone comfortable careers in favour of more fulfilling vocations in food. Some, such as the apple-brandy company whose fine product warmed George Washington's spirits on the battlefield, have been at it for centuries – while others are more recent arrivals. From developing a more sustainable method of harvesting salt along the Kanawha River in West Virginia to pioneering cocoa production in Vietnam, it's often a risk that leads to reward. Never before have we as diners been so concerned about the origin of the food on our plates. And while phrases such as "farm to table" and "locally sourced" are overused by chefs and market-savvy grocers, rarely do the farms and factories behind the world's most interesting produce get the kudos they deserve. Our favourite ones will tell you that making a good go of it takes courage, patience and grit. Decent branding plays its part too, but for these firms the gold is truly in the goods and producing them is seldom easy. As you take a tour of the fields, vineyards and factories in this chapter we hope you will source some inspiration to grow a business of your own.

Salt
JQ Dickinson Salt-Works, *USA*

The roots of JQ Dickinson Salt-Works go back to 1817 when William Dickinson set up a salt factory along the banks of the Kanawha River in West Virginia. For more than a century its furnaces boiled brine down into crystals until its closure in 1982. Thankfully, seventh-generation descendent Nancy Bruns and her brother Lewis Payne (*both pictured*) have resurrected the family business.

It was Bruns' husband's interest in American history that first triggered the revival. "His research revealed the Dickinson family was once one of the country's largest producers," says Bruns. "I had an 'Aha!' moment, called my brother and here we are."

While occupying the same land as the original facility, the fresh incarnation of JQ Dickinson Salt-Works called for a more sustainable manufacturing process. Today the company draws seawater from deep underground, then dries the liquid in three sun-houses. "We let the sun and mountain breezes do their work then hand-harvest the remaining salt," says Bruns. While most companies choose to purify their products to the extent that its component parts are only sodium-chloride and anti-caking agents (granules that keep the salt from clumping together), JQ Dickinson's approach allows their final product to retain natural minerals, imbuing it with a unique taste.

The subtle savoury flavour of the firm's haul has made JQ Dickinson an unsung hero of many US restaurants. It also justifies Bruns' and Payne's decision to give up their original careers. "With our family legacy in the industry, the same land as our ancestors and the current movement towards high-quality, natural food, we saw a great opportunity to fill a niche market," says Bruns.

jqdsalt.com

**JQ Dickinson Salt-Works
in numbers**

Founded: 1817 (revived in 2013)
Staff: 8 full-time
Family members on staff: 3
Purity level of salt: 94 per cent
Sun-houses used to crystallise salt: 3

Avocados
Barham Avocados, *Australia*

Based in the Australian town of Barham in southern New South Wales, husband-and-wife team Tim and Katrina Myers (*pictured*) have gained a healthy following for their pesticide-free avocados. The business offers monthly subscriptions sent directly from the family farm and from June onwards, customers in three Australian states can enjoy a box of the buxom fruit delivered to their door until the season ends in February. The most popular of Barham's four varieties of avocados is the reed, a creamy specimen that can grow as big as a bowling ball. "The beauty of the delivery box is that you can ripen the avocado yourself and you also know that no one has touched them, unlike in supermarkets, so they won't be bruised," says Katrina. The fragility of the product, rise in domestic postage costs and quarantine laws between states has meant Barham Avocados' market

remains restricted. The seasonal nature of the bounty complicates managing the budget. "We have to work out where to spend the money, whether to expand, how much to spend on marketing and developing sustainable fertilisers," says Katrina. To help maintain consistency in cash flow, the duo began making avocado oil in 2013. Their golden-hued oil, rich in vitamins, is now sold nationwide. And there's little sign that this energetic couple in the harsh Aussie outback plan to slow down. Production has expanded since the firm opened in 2011, seeing the farm grow from the original 7.7 hectares to 14.9 hectares, featuring 3,900 trees and counting. "We love the challenge of keeping the trees healthy and maximising production and quality," says Katrina. "We love running our own business and coming up with innovative ways to develop and sell this beautiful fruit." *barhamavocados.com.au*

Barham Avocados in numbers

Founded: 2011
Staff: 6
Avocado subscribers: 300
Avocados picked each season: 500,000
Furthest distance a Barham Avocado travels to a customer: 1,700km

Nougat
Scaldaferro, *Italy*

The first thing you notice walking into the Scaldaferro factory in the village of Dolo, near Venice, is a saccharine smell with hints of vanilla. There are bags of almonds from Puglia, hazelnuts from Piedmont and honey from Sicily, Trentino and the Venetian lagoon. The focus on ingredients has long been of paramount importance to the nougat-maker – which is why Scaldaferro's sweets are among the most sought after in Italy.

The laboratory is a relic and many of the machines and processes have been used since the company started in the early 1900s. It made biscuits at first, then hard sweets and panettone, but in the late 1950s decided to focus on the *torrone* (nougat) for which it has earned a formidable reputation.

The nougat is special because each piece is moulded by hand to retain the air bubbles that keep it brittle. It's this care that gives each piece the satisfying flakiness that has become a signature. It's also a source of pride for many who work here, not least because few firms still pledge themselves to this labour-intensive manner of production. Scaldaferro's recipe dates back to the 1700s and remains a mix of egg whites, honey, vanilla and nuts, the latter of which makes up just over half of the final product.

It's not a case of simply mixing the ingredients: combining them has to be carefully timed to ensure the nougat doesn't turn hard too quickly. "You have to taste it," says Pietro Scaldaferro, the brand's production manager, by way of explaining the nature of this attention to detail.

The brand often experiments with newer concoctions of rare honey but it is the well-established products that are the highest-selling ones, with Scaldaferro proving that there's plenty of business left to confect in confectionery. *scaldaferro.it*

Scaldaferro in numbers

Founded: 1919
Staff: 14 full-time
Start time on a production day: 03.00
Percentage of the mixture made up by nuts: About 50
Age of the original recipe: More than 300 years

Olive oil
Olisur, *Chile*

Before Chilean fruit and wine impresario Alfonso Swett decided to start Olisur in 2004, he and Tomás Eguiguren hit the road. "We travelled 1,500km over a year, looking for land," says business director Eguiguren, seated in a room at the company's plant in San Jose de Marchigue. The window behind him reveals thousands of olive trees swaying in the breeze. "We thought this property had the right mix of soil, climate, water and sunlight to give our oil a special character."

Olisur harvested its first crop in 2009 and is building a reputation for its sustainable product. It employed a technique of high-intensity planting, growing 1,750 trees per hectare to increase yields and reduce the time from planting to first harvest. The firm adheres to a stringent time limit between picking the fruit to the extraction of its oil, which ensures the utmost freshness. Olisur is also committed to maintaining the region's ecosystem. Workers have planted about 3,000 native vines to mitigate converting pasture to monocultures and left islands of native woodland throughout for eagles and foxes.

In production, little is wasted: leftover pulps are turned into fertiliser, while pits are made into biofuel.

The sensitivity to the environment continues through the Guillermo Hevia factory; the building's structure, for example, relies on laminated pine beams. Inside, climate control is mostly geothermal, using the stable subsoil temperature for summer cooling and winter heating. Skylights minimise the need for lighting.

Olisur's approach has won the brand fans across the Americas, with its reach growing into Brazil, the US, Canada and Chile. "The first harvest was at the beginning of 2009," says Eguiguren. "That was 200,000 litres, a tenth of what we do today." *olisur.com*

Olisur in numbers

Founded: 2004
First crop: 2009
Olive trees per hectare: 1,750
Hectares of olive trees: 1,550
Litres of olive oil produced annually: 2.5 million

Chocolate
Marou, Vietnam

Marou co-founder Samuel Maruta says people called him crazy when he ditched his job in finance in 2011 and jumped on his motorbike to find the best Vietnamese cocoa beans to fuel a chocolate factory. But the Frenchman, along with fellow expat Vincent Mourou, recognised the potential of a product that would tell another side of the "Made in Vietnam" story to the world. "Nothing was being done with cocoa in Vietnam," says Maruta. "We could see the appeal of something being made out of it in a very grassroots way."

Today Maruta and Mourou oversee a major chocolate production facility on the outskirts of Ho Chi Minh City. In 2016, they established Maison Marou, a downtown chocolatier where customers can experience the bean roasting, chocolate tempering, and bar-wrapping firsthand.

Marou's six core bars differentiate themselves by the unique origin of their beans and the varying richness of the cacao. Maruta's favourite is Treasure Island, a 75 per cent cocoa bar that showcases beans sourced from family-owned farms on the island of Tan Phu Dong. The bar's intensely satisfying flavour, low acidity and aromatic whiff have won it fans from Stockholm to Sydney. The addictiveness of the product and Marou's good intentions to elevate farming practices in Vietnam have proved important, as too has smart marketing with the aim to stand out from the pack. "We had our business heads screwed on from day one," says Maruta. "We want to export an intense, pure dark chocolate, not a crowd-pleaser."

Marou invested heavily in branding and packaging to draw attention to the brand's unique story. Maruta says the reaction from buyers across the globe was simply: "If it tastes half as good as it looks, we'll take it." Luckily for Marou, it does. *marouchocolate.com*

Marou in numbers

Founded: 2011
Staff: 53
Time until trees bear fruit: about 4 years
Tonnes of chocolate produced annually: 36
Highest cocoa percentage in a bar: 85

Butter
Ploughgate Creamery, USA

Marisa Mauro has always loved working on the land: she took her first job milking sheep at age 14. Through the years, Mauro honed her skills on farms across the US, eventually collaborating on her own cheese with the cheese-makers at Jasper Hill in Vermont. When a creamery fire halted production in 2011, she took the opportunity to switch paths.

"I wanted to try something new so I decided to focus on cultured butter," she says. "I saw a hole in the market – not a lot of people were doing it. It was hard to find equipment but it was a good challenge."

In 2013, Mauro purchased 20 hectares at Bragg Farm in Fayston, Vermont. She was assisted by the Vermont Land Trust, an organisation working to conserve rural Vermont by helping young farmers obtain land at affordable prices.

Using cream from nearby St Albans Creamery, Mauro cultures her butter for 48 to 72 hours, depending on the season, a process she says is reminiscent of her days as a cheese-maker. "This helps develop the aroma, flavour and texture," she says. "It's a more interesting product than sweet cream butter."

Mauro may have a passion for the pasture but she's not without business nous. "I loved working in the fields more than the creamery, but through working at farms I saw the only way to make it in dairy farming was to add value to your product," she says. "You can create high-quality products and have more control over the price that you're receiving." She also has a keen sense for smart packaging.

Mauro worked with Burlington designer Andrew Dernavich on her streamlined label. Each slab of Ploughgate's velvety butter is lovingly wrapped in butcher's paper by Mauro herself and sealed with her logo. "I think the presentation is as important as the flavour of your food." *ploughgate.com*

Ploughgate Creamery in numbers

Founded: 2015
Staff: 2
Cream processed each month: 1363 litres
Butter produced each month: 300 kilos
Time butter is cultured for: 2 to 3 days

Applejack brandy
Laird & Company, *USA*

Ups and downs are bound to befall a company that has endured for more than 300 years. Today Laird's direction is very much upward, with its applejack (apple brandy cut with neutral grain spirits) becoming a cocktail-bar staple that is in demand for its dusky taste, versatility and heritage. The company's Virginia distillery is a weathered 1930s throwback outside Charlottesville. For an industrial site it is remarkably bucolic, perfumed with the intoxicating aroma of smashed apples. The lawn is crisscrossed with pipes connecting a mill, fermenting tanks, stillroom and barrelhouse, all overseen by distiller Danny Swanson (*pictured*).

Laird & Company's state-of-the-art fermentation tanks are recent additions but much of the distillery's machinery has been doing the job for two generations. The density-determining hydrometers, alcohol-measuring equipment and dispensing nozzles all date from the 1930s. "Why replace this?" says Swanson. "It still works wonders."

One or two times a day, up to 25,000kg of gala, granny smith, winesap and pippin apples are tipped into a container to be washed before distillation. After being fermented and condensed, the alcohol is separated and turned into apple brandy. It is a meticulous process and every 65,000 litres only yields 5,000 litres of brandy.

Started in Scobeyville, New Jersey, by Scotsman William Laird in 1698, the company today produces 20,000 cases a year. That's slight by industry standards but its unusual spirit is holding strong. A key component of its recent success has been a careful global-expansion plan, headed by vice president Lisa Laird (*pictured*). With typically stoic management it is still winning over new customers in Canada, Europe, Singapore and Australia. *lairdandcompany.com*

Laird & Company in numbers
Founded: 1780
Staff: 35
Cases produced annually: 20,000
Apples needed for one barrel of apple brandy: 3,175kg
Countries supplied: 9 (and growing)

Dairy products
Nakahora Bokujou, *Japan*

In Japan's dairy industry, Tadashi Nakahora is an outsider. Since the early 1980s he has raised a growing herd of Jersey and Holstein cattle outdoors – not in a barn – in the mountains of Iwate, northern Japan. All year round his animals roam 80 hectares of pastures and forestland, grazing or eating the hay he harvests from his own property. Because he doesn't supplement their diet with feed or antibiotics, his cows produce milk that has less fat than at most other farms, a fact that prevents him from selling to the local agricultural co-operative. Nakahora practices a type of small-scale animal husbandry that's at odds with the methods of nearly all of the country's dairy farms. He came upon the idea as a university student in the late 1970s after hearing a pioneering botanist's talk about the sustainability of raising cattle in the mountains. It made perfect sense in a country whose land is 70 per cent mountainous; it also fitted with Nakahora's belief that profit-driven mass-production methods were hurting an industry that had become dependent on government subsidies for survival.

For Nakahora, figuring out how to sell his products to consumers without going through a farming co-operative was the hard part. But now, with the help of 13 staff, he turns nearly 100,000 litres of raw milk at a facility on his farm into Nakahora Bokujou milk, yoghurt, ice cream and curry that is sold online and at a handful of shops in Tokyo and Nagoya. It's a growing business and Nakahora has become a minor celebrity, writing books, giving lectures and passing on his knowledge to hundreds of first-time farmers. *nakahora-bokujou.jp*

Nakahora Bokujou in numbers

Founded: 1984
Staff: 13
Litres of raw milk produced annually: 100,000
Size of free-range herd: 80 cows
Property size: 80 hectares

Coffee
Allpress, *New Zealand*

Back in 1986, before Auckland became the far-flung frontier for in-the-know food folk that it is today, Italian-style espresso coffee in the city was difficult to come by. Michael Allpress (*pictured on left*) helped to change that when he gave up his career as a chef and turned his hand to coffee with a simple cart that served espressos at two locations. At first he used beans bought from elsewhere but he quickly decided that to create the flavour he wanted, he would need to source and roast his own. From its humble beginnings, Allpress became a speciality coffee roaster. These days Allpress staff train baristas at, and supply beans wholesale to, a few hundred New Zealand cafés, restaurants and offices – and that's not to mention the brand's growing international business (The Monocle Café in London is one grateful recipient). In 2000 it ventured across the Tasman Sea and set up a roastery in Sydney; in 2010 it made its first foray into the northern hemisphere with a roaster and café in London's hip district of Shoreditch; then four years later came a similar set-up in the Kiba neighbourhood of Tokyo. In almost all cases, Allpress moved into former industrial buildings.

Allpress buys its Arabica beans directly from farmers, small estates and co-operatives in Central and South America, Southeast Asia, Oceania and Africa. The company's signature espresso blend, Redchurch, goes some way to illustrating the diversity of the beans' origins, being a mix of Brasil Santa Alina, Colombia Pescador, Guatemala Huehuetenango and Sumatra Mandheling. Allpress staff regularly visit their suppliers, often staying with them, learning about the growing process and seeing how the above-market prices the farmers receive go back into their communities. Not to mention making a mean cup of the black stuff. *allpressespresso.com*

Allpress in numbers

Founded: 1989
Staff: 218
Espresso shots supplied annually: 62 million
Countries available: 5

Beer
Forst, *Italy*

Previously governed by the Habsburg empire before being ceded to Rome after the First World War, the mostly German-speaking province of South Tyrol in the Alps is an anomaly of sorts when set against Italy's other regions.

Central European influences are still seen everywhere, not least the trains that run with Teutonic precision. Cellina von Mannstein, the fifth-generation owner of Forst brewery, embodies these virtues. Her hard work has been rewarded to the tune of about €110m in annual sales and the company logo, a trio of Alpine trees set on a field, is as unmissable as the mountain peaks. Signage big and small in cafés, hotels and restaurants; kit deals for various sports clubs: the Forst crest is emblazoned wherever you turn your gaze.

"We have become part of the scenery," says Von Mannstein. From the window there's a view that looks out on the village of Forst, the company's home since its inception in 1857.

Forst is responsible for 5 per cent of beer sales in Italy so it has been a successful effort – the *Heidi*-like lands of South Tyrol account for the lion's share of its business.

"We have never looked at what the others are doing in our industry," says Von Mannstein when asked about the decision taken by rival Italian beer brands to cash in on deals presented by foreign buyers. "Our history is rooted in this place; we've had families working in the plant for generations."

"Our heritage is quite unique," she says as she removes a photo from the wall. It's an early advertisement for Forst from the 1930s featuring a rugged Alpinist mid-sip, a glass to his lips. "It's authentic. It's not something to just give away to the big multinationals." *forst.it*

Forst in numbers

Founded: 1857
Annual turnover: €110m
Share of beer market in Italy: 5 per cent
Varieties of beer: 6

Cheese
Molke 7, *Switzerland*

"Switzerland is well known for its emmentaler, gruyère and sprinz cheeses and I wanted to explore the craft," says cheesemaker Peter Limacher, who co-founded dairy business Molke 7 in 2014. Good fortune brought him to Bäch in the vicinity of Zürich, where he met farmers Hans Peter Jost and Thomas Bucher. Shortly thereafter the trio decided to buy and bring new life to a derelict creamery near Lake Sempach in central Switzerland.

The business has established decent rural and urban clienteles thanks to its devotion to traditional dairy practices, paired with strong design-minded branding. Its range of cheeses (including Limacher's aged chällermeister, salvatore and blüemlichääs), whey drinks, butter and yogurts made with homemade fruit and berry preserves are available from Molke 7's factory shop. You can also get them at regional open-air weekend markets, as well as the Zürich and Lucerne-based branches of Swiss department store Globus *(see page 160)*. "We value organic growth and only produce as much as we can sell," says Limacher, who every week collects jugs of milk from nearby farms, minutes after the cows have been milked.

The milk is still warm when the cheese-making process begins. First it's heated in copper vessels; then an enzyme thickens the milk before it's divided, dried and pressed into moulds. At the end of the days-long process, the cheese is stored in the cellar for nine to 12 months. "For me quality begins with the ground, which grows healthy food for the cows," says Limacher. "In summer there's fresh grass; in winter, hay. The cows that produce Molke 7's milk literally live on Wolke 7." Cloud Nine to you and me.
kaeserei-molke7.ch

Molke 7 in numbers

Founded: 2014
Staff: 8
Types of cheese produced: 7
Litres of local milk used each day: 800
Stockists in Switzerland: 40

Snails
Fereikos Helix, *Greece*

The idea for a heliciculture (snail farming) venture in the ancient city of Corinth in Greece came to the Vlachou sisters over a plate of €37 escargots in Zürich. For years Athens-born Maria Vlachou had been working in Brussels as a translator but longed to return home and join her sister Penny, whose teaching job had become increasingly precarious as the country teetered on the brink of financial collapse. The garlicky gourmet molluscs presented a new start. "There are so many unexplored opportunities in farming that can be a pillar for Greece to help its people stand back on their feet," says Maria, standing next to stacks of snail-filled pallets. "We saw that the market [for snails] was huge and the potential was great, especially in a country like Greece with favourable climate conditions."

Soon after the meal they set about cultivating snails on their grandfather's patch of land 90km west of Athens. Fereikos Helix (ancient Greek for "carry my own house") has incorporated 215 family franchises across four countries into its supply chain and plans continued growth. Beyond harvesting their snails, which they sell fresh, frozen and tinned, the sisters expanded their line of work to include farming consultancy and packaged ready-meals. The pair offers would-be farmers the chance to attend free seminars on snail-rearing in the hopes of expanding their network of producers.

The work is paying off: these exemplary gastropods have attracted a diverse clientele, ranging from Spain's El Corte Inglés department store to the UK designer Vivienne Westwood, who in 2014 made use of the sisters' snail shells for a typically outlandish jewellery collection. Business is anything but slow. *fereikos.com*

Fereikos Helix in numbers

Founded: 2007
Staff: 8 permanent, 5 freelancers
Snails per 1-acre farm: 100,000
Farms in collaboration: 215
Countries exported to: 11

2.
How To...
Make a life in the food world

Packing in the day job and starting up a food business is a reliably common reverie. Who wouldn't want to indulge in a passion and get back to the land? Or launch a bold new business that turns out honed plates and crisp cocktails, or cultivates great produce? Many of the best businesses were once daunting prospects. They were deliberated over and delayed before ever coming to fruition; even the most confident start-ups needed advice and learnt a few lessons along the way. So as a push to the ponderous and a nudge to the nonchalant, here are a few individuals and ideas to spur you on to start your own venture. From setting up a retailer or a vineyard to becoming a restaurant magnate or a food-truck impressario, here's how to take your first steps towards founding a food firm, along with some advice to keep you on the straight and narrow as you go.

Open a restaurant

Advice and inspiration to help turn your fondness for food into a livelihood.

Case study 1
The serial restaurateur

Andrew McConnell
Supernormal, *Melbourne*

With a stable of smart restaurants that includes Supernormal, Cumulus Inc and Cutler & Co, Andrew McConnell is the doyen of Melbourne's culinary scene. Over the past 15 years, the chef and restaurateur has opened some of the city's finest venues, which serve everything from European (Cumulus Inc) to pan-Asian (Supernormal) to meat-centric (Meatsmith) fare.

It all started with Diningroom 211. Having cooked abroad for 10 years, McConnell returned to Melbourne and opened the place in 2001. "I wanted to be the master of my own destiny," he says. "I'd known for a long time that I wanted to open my own restaurant and had been collecting ideas."

The first thing that McConnell thinks about is where he would like to eat. "Cumulus Inc came about because I wanted a place where I could go to relax at any time of the day – and not have the restrictions of service times," he says. "So I created it."

There are some key things to consider while converting these visions into reality. "When the restaurant opens I want the space to feel like it's already had a life," says McConnell. He also stresses the need to think about things such as service and prices.

But the most important element is finding the right people. McConnell began considering Supernormal's 80-strong team of chefs, sommeliers and front-of-house staff two years before it opened. "No matter how good your idea, without the right team you won't get off the ground." *supernormal.net.au*

MONOCLE COMMENT
When putting your restaurant vision into practice, spend time finding a team with a good dynamic before sweating the setting, menu and pricing.

Case study 2
The all-rounder

Rimpei Yoshikawa
Pignon, *Tokyo*

Rimpei Yoshikawa's realisation that he wanted to open his own restaurant came about through working at several restaurants over the course of 10 years. He opened Pignon in the peaceful Kamiyama-cho neighbourhood of Tokyo in 2010 and quickly captured a loyal fan base with his hearty menu featuring Amakusa pork *roti*, Moroccan salad and a crisp quiche Lorraine.

Yoshikawa was at university when he got his first job in the food industry, cooking at a *yakitori* (barbecue) restaurant. "I was studying economics but I didn't want to be a salaryman," he says. One day a customer took him to a French restaurant. "It was delicious. I thought, 'This might be something I want to do.'"

He got a job in the same bistro but was initially disappointed. "It was a traditional master-and-apprentice relationship," he says. "I got told off all the time. Throughout my six-and-a-half years there I wanted to quit every day." Today he laughs about it and is willing to concede that it was a great proving ground.

Next he worked for a year in a restaurant in Bordeaux before returning to cook in two more bistros in Tokyo. "I was always complaining. I realised that if I do everything myself, I only have myself to blame, so I decided to make everything my responsibility." Thus Pignon was born.

Despite years of learning French cookery, Yoshikawa's style is more simple. "The most important thing is that the food tastes good," he says. "When I cook I'm making a meal, not a work of art. I want people to be able to tell what they have on the plate." *+81 (0)3 3468 2331*

MONOCLE COMMENT
Working in restaurants saw Yoshikawa hone his concept. The result is a relaxed contemporary bistro that borrows elements of French cooking.

Yoshikawa's tips:

1.
Fall in love
'Keep looking for the perfect place – you'll know when you've found it. The right space is the one you fall for immediately.'

2.
Strengthen the team
'Invest time in hunting for great staff. Your team doesn't have to be big; it has to be strong.'

3.
Be yourself
'You need to have your own style. At the beginning you will have to give everything to the business. Sure, customers are important but it's your restaurant. Build your style and live it; the customers will follow.'

Case study 3
The career switcher

Q&A

Tannis Ling
Bao Bei Chinese Brasserie,
Vancouver

In 2010, bartender-turned-restaurateur Tannis Ling christened her Asian joint Bao Bei Chinese Brasserie after a childhood nickname (*bao bei* means "precious" in Mandarin). Her fresh take on Chinese cooking, and chef Joël Watanabe's indomitable culinary finesse, are the key ingredients that make Bao Bei stand out in a crowd of generic Chinese restaurants in Vancouver's Chinatown.

Why start Bao Bei?
What prompted me was a feeling that I had reached the end of my bartending career. The next step was to either start all over again in a new career or continue along the path I was on but in a different direction. I decided to take a risk and open Bao Bei because I trusted in the concept.

What was unexpectedly difficult and what came easily?
While I was fairly familiar with all aspects of service, I had a lot of difficulties with the administrative side: the taxes, profit control and inventory. It's still a weakness but I've taught myself to understand it with greater confidence. Staffing is always one of the hardest things about restaurants but I've somehow been able to find interesting, funny, smart and hard-working people who stay on for long periods of time. bao-bei.ca

Three things Ling learnt:

1.
Put the time in
'In the 11 years I was working in restaurants before opening my own, I worked almost every position, including a stint in the kitchen. Having that knowledge is crucial to the success and longevity of your business.'

2.
Create a positive environment
'Be kind and generous to your staff. If you provide a positive and fun work environment you'll find that people are happy to work hard for you.'

3.
Laugh about it
'Have a sense of humour. I wouldn't have lasted this long if I wasn't able to find the humour in every situation, because shit will happen all day, every day.'

1.
Andrew McConnell's Supernormal, Melbourne

2.
Inside the restaurant

3.
Rimpei Yoshikawa at Pignon, Tokyo

4.
Kitchen at Supernormal, Melbourne

5.
French wines at Pignon reflect Yoshikawa's time spent in Bordeaux

6.
Pignon's streetfront outlook

7.
Bartender-turned-restaurateur Tannis Ling

Grow a restaurant group

A road map for transforming a single restaurant into a mini empire – while staying fresh and unique.

Case study 1
The visionaries

Ronald Akili and Jason Gunawan
PTT Family, *Jakarta*

The Indonesian founders of hospitality group PTT Family combine lessons from their heritage with sensitivity to global expectations, trends and tastes. This reflects their backgrounds too: Ronald Akili grew up in Hawaii, while Jason Gunawan spent many years in Australia.

Since 2010, the group has opened three restaurants and a housing project in Jakarta, the internationally lauded Potato Head Beach Club in Bali, a clothing boutique, a free-wheeling entertainment, drinking and dining venue in Hong Kong, and two restaurants in Singapore. In 2016 they returned to Bali to open the stunning Katamama Hotel.

"Good hospitality is something that you can't fake," says Akili. "Authenticity has to be present. The soul needs be present."

One of the biggest lessons he has learnt is that you can never do too much research. For the Katamama Hotel, his team laboured over every detail, both in understanding their consumer and knowing the character of the destination and the local culture. The resulting 58-room stop-in uses 1.5 million Balinese temple bricks, follows traditional architectural cues and provides furnishings by the island's best artisans.

"We want to showcase a contemporary interpretation of Indonesian culture," says Akili. "The traditions of old are well preserved but we look at it in a modern way." *pttfamily.com*

MONOCLE COMMENT
PTT Family balances style and substance by celebrating heritage. It highlights Indonesian craftsmanship on its home-soil destinations and takes inspiration from the neighbourhoods of its restaurants opened further afield.

Case study 2
The magnate

Justin Hemmes
Merivale, *Sydney*

Some of the world's best chefs ply their trade in Sydney and are spoilt by the country's unrivalled produce, from fruit and vegetables to succulent beef and fresh fish. Competition for the city's discerning diners is therefore intense, and new restaurants seem to appear and vanish on a daily basis. So to set up a successful restaurant group here takes something special.

And Merivale is something special. The company's outposts – now comprising more than 60 restaurants, bars and pubs, and a hotel – repeatedly transition from being the hottest tables in town to becoming venerated staples that still keep picky Sydneysiders enthralled.

"It's about really understanding your demographic and tailoring the product to suit them," says CEO Justin Hemmes, who took over and transformed his parents' business in the late 1990s. "You need to create something your customers may be missing and that, once it's available, they won't be able to live without."

What impresses about Merivale venues is that each has a different aesthetic, ambience and inspiration, yet there are always telltale signs that you're sitting in one: the atmosphere will be relaxed, the decor well thought out, the food good quality and unfussy, and the service top-drawer.

As Hemmes's empire grows, he is recruiting employees and investing in training, from new hires to senior veterans. "One of the greatest assets in our business is our staff, so training is vital," he says. *merivale.com.au*

MONOCLE COMMENT
Turning one successful restaurant into a thriving hospitality group is about approaching every new project without a set formula. Also, as you grow, make sure you pick people you can rely on.

Hemmes's tips:

1.
Know your consumer
'Always have an insight into the customers and demographics for which you're catering. This takes time so avoid rushing headlong into a place.'

2.
Love what you do
'The hospitality industry is hard work – it's not your regular nine-to-five. You need total dedication.'

3.
Hire the best
'We choose staff who believe in giving the best customer service possible. That feeds through to all our venues, ensuring our customers have consistency.'

1.
Jackie Grant and Scott
Brown of Hip Group
2.
Potato Head, Singapore
3.
PTT Family's Ronald
Akili (left) and
Jason Gunawan
4.
Palmer & Co cocktail bar
in Sydney, one of Justin
Hemmes's many venues
5.
Merivale CEO
Justin Hemmes

3   4

5

Case study 3
The gamechangers

Q&A

Scott Brown
Hip Group, *Auckland*

Scott Brown and Jackie Grant, the duo
behind Auckland's Hip Group, can
take a lot of credit for turning their city into
a food-lover's paradise and debunking the
tyranny-of-distance myth. What started
with a humble space (Café on Kohi) in
2004 has become a hospitality group with
a stable of the best restaurants in town,
synonymous with excellent food and
relaxed and well-designed spaces.

Why start the business?
Auckland has always had great raw
produce but it lacked operators paying
homage to these fabulous resources.
Friends and family would visit from
other international cities and mention
the wonderful countryside, the lovely
people and the easy lifestyle – but also
how difficult it was to get a decent coffee
or a glass of wine.

**What was unexpectedly difficult and what
came easily?**
People are reluctant to change. We set out
to change Kiwi eating and drinking habits,
and met with resistance. We knew we'd
win them over but it was a hard slog. By
contrast, it's easy to set up a business here.
The barriers to entry are low. *hipgroup.co.nz*

Three things the pair learnt:

1.
Put passion before profits
'Early on we focused on revenue but
halfway through realised that was not –
and shouldn't be – the driving force. We
decided that the experience was more
important and our direction since then
has been about self-sufficiency.'

2.
Work with like-minded people
'Find landlords who are sympathetic to the
way you want to run your business. Our
business is about the experience so I don't
want to work for a landlord who doesn't
appreciate what we are trying to do.'

3.
Keep control of your brand
'Don't rely on anyone else. We diversified
into a supermarket on a grand scale. It
was a joint venture so we didn't have
complete control. We spent two years
and a lot of money on that project before
bailing out, at a huge cost.'

Set up a bar

Part alchemist and part agony aunt, a great barman needs skill and tact in equal measure. Here's what else.

Case study 1
The conversationalist

Rachelle Hair
The Baxter Inn, *Sydney*

Sydney is well known as a capital of gastronomy but few outside the worldwide bartending industry are aware of its credentials as a drinker's paradise (lock-out laws notwithstanding). The Baxter Inn is one of the city's top watering holes, not for its eccentric cocktails that use liquid nitrogen but for its intimate atmosphere, classic speakeasy decor, selection of more than 300 whiskies and talkative bartenders.

Rachelle Hair decided to give up her career as a music-event manager in 2012 to pursue the bartending profession and joined the Baxter Inn team in 2014. She reckons her previous job gave her the skill of being able to develop a rapport quickly. "I love talking to people and hearing their stories," she says. "Understanding you can make someone's night by treating them well, that came easily to me."

But it's not exactly easy work. Hair is often on her feet for 12 hours straight, working through to early morning. At the end of the night it's taking care of the regular customers that "makes my job", she says.

One of her top tips for excelling as a bartender is to leave your ego behind. "Some bartenders say, 'Oh, you don't want to drink that,' and prescribe what their guests should and shouldn't drink," says Hair. "That's not ideal service." Neither, though, is simply being smiley, she points out. You need encyclopaedic knowledge of the classics, a lot of energy and a knack for charming the regulars. *thebaxterinn.com*

MONOCLE COMMENT
Knowing how to shake and stir is essential but the difference between a good bartender and a great one is the ability to strike up conversations and have a rapport that will leave a pleasant aftertaste.

Case study 2
The mix master

Christian Heiss
Kronenhalle, *Zürich*

Kronenhalle (*see page 325*) is an iconic restaurant that has served James Joyce, Einstein, Picasso and Chargall (whose art adorns the walls). Founded in 1924, it is known for its German-Swiss cuisine and beautiful bar.

For many years the restaurant bar was run by Peter Roth, inventor of the gin-based Ladykiller cocktail that won him the 1984 World Cocktail Championship. Now his deputy of seven years, Christian Heiss, has taken over. The highly lauded South Tyrol native has served in Munich's top bars and hotels, and ranked first in numerous cocktail competitions.

Many of Heiss's guests have been loyal patrons for years and he has long memorised their favourite drinks. One of his first cocktails for the Kronenhalle was the Dürrenmatt (a sophisticated concoction of Scottish whisky, Lillet Blanc and Grand Marnier), in honour of the Swiss author Friedrich Dürrenmatt.

Heiss is eager to carry on Roth's legacy. "Continuing his work will be my greatest priority but I'll also introduce my own style and pay close attention to the patrons of tomorrow."

The secret to bartending at such a beloved address is experience and practice, knowing one's guests and treating them like old friends. "From my experience, the best barkeepers are those who are passionate about their job," he says. "It's that desire for perfection, passion for spirits and the creativity to invent and mix the most diverse cocktails." *kronenhalle.ch*

MONOCLE COMMENT
Forget the dry ice and theatrics. In venues such as Kronenhalle, what drinkers really want is consistency, a familiar face behind the bar and a friendly "willkommen".

1

Heiss's tips:

1.
Become an expert
'Acquire a knowledge of spirits, just like a sommelier has of wine.'

2.
Know your ingredients
'A bartender needs to be able to mix ingredients like a master chef does in the kitchen.'

3.
Be the perfect host
'Last but not least he needs to make his guests feel welcome, as though they were his own family.'

2   3

4

5

1.
One of the cocktails on offer at The Baxter Inn

2.
The Baxter Inn, Sydney

3.
Kronenhalle's Christian Heiss

4.
The Baxter Inn's speakeasy-style interior

5.
Rachelle Hair says a good rapport with customers is all-important

Case study 3
The innovator

Q&A

Tony Conigliaro
Drink Factory, *London*

Tony Conigliaro is the bartender behind some of the best drinks venues in London, including 69 Colebrooke Row and the bar at the Zetter Townhouse hotel. He also founded the Drink Factory, a forum for experimenting with drinks, and published a cocktail guide titled *Drinks*, in 2012.

Why did you start Drink Factory and what inspired you to become a barman?
I've always been intrigued by the science of taste. I draw my inspiration from art, science and design, and am inspired by everyone from chefs to perfumers. I started the Drink Factory to talk to these people and bring together like-minded creatives in an ongoing discussion.

What was unexpectedly difficult and what came easily?
The hardest part was changing people's habits. Twenty years ago it was difficult to get anyone to even drink a martini. In the first year I bartended, only one person asked for a martini and he was American. People wanted sickly, sugary concoctions and there was no interest in the classics. Now the classics are some of the biggest sellers. People's palates have become more sophisticated and they're open to trying new things. The laughter and fun have always been easy – it's important to have a sense of humour about what you do. *thedrinkfactory.com*

Three things Conigliaro learnt:

1.
Never settle for mediocrity
'The key to success is in the detail. If you don't have the details, the chances are it's been done before and people won't be interested.'

2.
Don't rush to get to the top
'You learn a lot from working your way up and it will make you more respectful and understanding of people from all walks of life.'

3.
Your own unique style will come
'But it won't come straight away. Be patient; you'll find it develops over time.'

Open a food shop
Supermarkets can be depressing strip-lit affairs so how about starting a neighbourhood grocery shop?

Case study 1
The relationship builder

Jerome Batten
Sourced Grocer, *Brisbane*

There's no lack of quality produce coming out of the lush region of Queensland. What Brisbane did lack, for many years, was a decent shop to make that produce available to time-poor customers. That changed in 2011 when Jerome Batten rolled up the shutters at Sourced Grocer. Here a vertical garden climbs the walls of an open fit-out that encourages interaction around the food on display.

The business is split between a grocery and a café, and many of the ingredients gracing both the plates and the shelves have been ferried from producer to door by the Sourced Grocer team. Batten notes that much of his business's success comes from bonds he has formed with small Aussie businesses. "A lot of them are the same suppliers we've been working with since day one. They are relationships we have been able to grow as we've expanded our operation, and we pride ourselves on being that link in the supply chain, connecting them with the community."

Located in Teneriffe, Brisbane's most densely populated inner-city corner, Sourced Grocer provides everything from Tasmanian-grown quinoa to honey farmed on a nearby rooftop.

"Retail is a sensory experience," says Batten. "We're constantly experimenting with the visual merchandising. Our customers are busy people and our aim is to fit naturally into their everyday lives." *sourcedgrocer.com.au*

MONOCLE COMMENT
Relationships with regional producers and suppliers are crucial. Offer customers a novel way of experiencing the quality products by having a café on-site that takes inspiration for its menu from the shop shelves.

Case study 2
The local favourite

Mike Zupan
Zupan's Markets, *Portland*

In 1975 a produce manager in Oregon set out on his own, establishing Zupan's Markets. The next decades saw John Zupan's venture nourish the city's culinary landscape and today, residents, food-lover's and chefs alike know it as the first destination for decent food.

"Portland is a food Mecca in the US and we are blessed to be in the Pacific Northwest with easy access to a bounty of great farms for fresh produce," says the founder's son and president of the family-run business, Mike Zupan. More than 75 per cent of the perishables are sourced from 30 to 40 regional producers. "Our role has been to be a place to find new products and present the latest trends in food," he adds.

Zupan consults with chefs, reads trade magazines and travels frequently to stay on top of the fast changing industry. The brand's four outposts across the state are designed simply, and lightly accented with wood finishes. The purpose is to shine the spotlight on the vegetables, fruit and fresh cuts. Don't be surprised to find heirloom tomatoes next to bottles of olive oil and fresh herbs – ingredients that might go well together in a recipe are intentionally placed in close proximity. The 100 or so employees at each location are trained to deliver customer service to match the quality products. As Zupan puts it, "All these ingredients are essential to the great shopping experience." *zupans.com*

MONOCLE COMMENT
When it comes to product display, the model in supermarkets worldwide is focused on profit and upselling. Zupan has shown that rethinking the shop's layout can make shopping more fun and still be financially viable.

1

Zupan's tips:

1.
Pick your spot
'Find the right location. Healthy footfall is vital when selling fresh produce.'

2.
Recruit wisely
'Hire the right management staff. Every employee is a brand representative so needs to be trained well and knowledgeable about the products.'

3.
Set high standards
'Never settle for second best. We take pains to ensure only the best-tasting products reach our customers. It may be a more expensive process but it's what adds value to the brand.'

1.
Jerome Batten

2.
Zupan's Markets

3.
Sourced Grocer's well
stocked aisles

4.
Zupan's Markets are piled
high with produce

5.
Schweitzer Project CEO
Bernhard Schweitzer

6.
The Sourced Grocer café

7.
Zupan's Nob Hill outlet

8.
Mike Zupan

9.
Goods at Sourced Grocer

Case study 3
The shop fitter

Q&A

Bernhard Schweitzer
Schweitzer Project, *South Tyrol*

Family-owned Schweitzer Project is one of
the world's leading shop-fitting companies.
It develops made-to-measure solutions
for retailers, whether they want one
perfect shop or to roll out a design around
the world. Bernhard Schweitzer is the
company's third-generation CEO.

**When you're asked to design a new shop,
what is the first thing you do?**
Before we start we want to fully understand
our client's business model and how they
work. Who are their customers and what
needs do they have? Then we sit together
with the client and work out the vision and
strategy. Our aim is always to translate the
vision of our client's brand into a unique
live retail experience. To do so it is always
important to observe new trends in store
design and consumer behaviour.

How has the design of food shops changed?
The focus is more on the retail experience.
With the growing online food market, retail
spaces are becoming smaller and are used
in a different way than maybe 10 years
ago. Staging of products is becoming more
important. You can also say that food has
become the new fashion. Concepts like
the one at Jelmoli in Zürich, where fashion
is mixed with food, are an interesting
development. Also, the integration of online
tools into traditional trading is a big topic.
Carrefour Belgium is a good example
for such an integration, implemented
already in two hypermarkets in Mons and
Koksijde. *schweitzerproject.com*

Three things Schweitzer learnt:

1.
Try to stand out from the competition
'Offer something special: a format,
products or services, or even different
opening hours to your competitors.'

2.
Innovate and be seen to innovate
'Create something new, which is also
perceived as such by customers. Give
people a reason to come into your shop
in the first instance, then to come back.'

3.
Remember: the competition is very tough
'There are already a lot of food shops; you
have to question and review your business
model regularly.'

Found a fishmonger
There are few delights to rival that of fresh seafood and there's business in bringing it to the city.

Case study 1
The designer

Rick Toogood
Prawn on the Lawn, *London and Padstow*

As a designer with a keen eye for handsome spaces, Rick Toogood was in a privileged position when starting his fishmonger. "It was always lino flooring and stainless-steel worktops," he says. "I thought we could offer something different."

What followed, in 2013, was Prawn on the Lawn (POTL): a fishmonger-cum-restaurant in the north London borough of Islington that combines slick Corian countertops and exposed-brick walls with friendly service, late-night opening hours and, of course, the freshest seafood around. About 90 per cent of the produce is sourced from day boats operating off Cornwall in southwest England, and it was there that Toogood set up a second outpost in 2015, in the port town of Padstow.

It hasn't all been smooth sailing, however. The biggest hurdle was trying to find an appropriate space in which to open shop. "Drainage is always an issue; if there's a flat underneath you, it's not great when putting your case forward [as a tenant]," says Toogood. "Landlords are worried about the smell."

Toogood's fishmonger has proved a hit with Islington's well-heeled clientele. He attributes the success partly to a shift in mentality, from "buying from supermarkets to supporting fishmongers". More surprising has been the popularity of the restaurant. When POTL opened there were eight stools next to the fish counter; that soon expanded to a downstairs room that seats 16. *prawnonthelawn.com*

MONOCLE COMMENT
Just because the prevailing design standard is unimaginative, doesn't mean something more ambitious shouldn't be attempted. Toogood raised the bar and has seen the punt pay dividends.

Toogood's tips:

1.
Source the best suppliers
'Whether wholesalers, co-operatives or individual fishermen, if you've got suppliers who you know are going to deliver the best fish – even if you have to pay more for it – customers will taste the difference.'

2.
Find the right space
'You'll need room to house all your equipment and be in an area that has – or will soon have – good footfall.'

3.
Budget
'You need to make sure that you can survive for at least six months. The business is seasonal: in winter, sales can be very quiet.'

Get a food truck on the road
Bricks and mortar can be expensive so why not invest in a mobile set-up to test out the neighbourhood first?

1.
Prawn on the Lawn's restaurant in London has been a big hit

2.
A venue with good footfall is key

3.
Toogood's customers expect the finest-quality produce

4.
Prawn on the Lawn's Islington shop

5.
Van Leeuwen Ice Cream expanded quickly to serve drinks

6.
Laura O'Neill

7.
The ice-cream truck

5 6

7

Case study 1
The trucker

Laura O'Neill
Van Leeuwen Ice Cream, *New York*

When it was set up in 2008, Van Leeuwen Ice Cream was responding to a gap in the market: while there were plenty of ice-cream trucks on the streets, none used high-quality ingredients.
Laura O'Neill and her co-founders, brothers Pete and Ben Van Leeuwen, settled on a simple business principle: make great ice cream without fillers or stabilisers, using ingredients such as Tahitian vanilla, Sicilian pistachios and organic peppermint from Oregon. "We came up with what we thought were the best ingredients," says O'Neill. "They became the original 10 flavours."
The trio began testing recipes in their home kitchen before buying their first 1988 Chevrolet Stepvan, placing large windows on all sides and the company's butter-yellow hue on the exterior. Initial location scouting was trial and error but success came in Manhattan's Soho, and in sticking to locations so customers knew where to find them. The product inspired loyalty, and bricks-and-mortar shops soon followed.
Van Leeuwen's fleet of trucks now operates on both coasts; the ice cream is produced in the company's Brooklyn factory, allowing them to experiment with more flavours. "In the early days we did really simple flavours and it would be a celebration of one great ingredient," says O'Neill. "We still have the same ideals – but now we're able to make new flavours to our standard." *vanleeuwenicecream.com*

O'Neill's tips:

1.
Manage expectations
'Be sure that, whatever your product, you can truly achieve high quality on a truck – choose a simple product that can be done perfectly in a small and often challenging space.'

2.
Be patient
'Your team members will need licences so give yourself plenty of time to apply for permits.'

3.
Take care of your truck
'Find a good mechanic.'

MONOCLE COMMENT
A truck gives a fledgling business the flexibility to try different districts in a city. Take advantage of this and explore before fixing on a few locations.

Revamp a vineyard

Three winegrowers share the secrets of getting your business blooming and the joy of getting back to the land.

Case study 1
The reformed perfectionist

Karl-Friedrich Scheufele
Chateau Monestier La Tour, *Dordogne*

As co-president of Swiss watchmaker Chopard, Karl-Friedrich Scheufele needs to be something of a perfectionist. His working life revolves around precision and detail, so when he and his wife bought a vineyard in 2012, he was in for a surprise. "Working in industry and craft, the human factor is important – and you can correct human errors," he says. "But if there's a major problem with a given vintage, there's no way to correct it. That's just it."

The most anarchic factor is, of course, the weather. "We learnt that in a brutal way in 2013, when a major thunder and hailstorm destroyed half the harvest," says Scheufele. It was a difficult but necessary lesson, a stark reminder that, when it comes to winemaking, you can only be in charge of so much.

For the past 20 years or so, Scheufele has run a small chain of wine shops across Switzerland. "It was a natural development to dream about making wine myself," he says. Having spent years looking for the right vineyard the chance arose to purchase the Chateau Monestier La Tour in the Dordogne.

Since 2012 the Scheufeles have invested in new equipment, built two new cellars for storing and maturing, and restored one 18th-century building. Crucially, they have begun using natural techniques to create fewer bottles of better wine. "We want more quality and less quantity," says Scheufele. "For us it's about solid distribution with smaller players and quality points of sale in a wider range of countries." *chateaumonestierlatour.com*

MONOCLE COMMENT
You have to be a bit Zen when starting a vineyard. It's crucial to find a balance between embracing the relative unpredictability and controlling the details.

Case study 2
The cousins

Matteo and Camilla Lunelli
Ferrari winery, *Trento*

Fifty years after Giulio Ferrari founded Ferrari winery in 1902, he passed it on to Bruno Lunelli. Today, Bruno's grandchildren – cousins Matteo and Camilla – have been running the Ferrari winery for more than a decade, helped by Camilla's brother, Alessandro, and the estate's oenologist, cousin Marcello. And when producing a great reserve wine can be a 30-year investment, keeping it in the family is an advantage.

"Ageing a good wine increases a brand's quality but has no short-term economic gains," says Camilla, Ferrari's first female head. "It's a luxury we're permitted because our business plan spans generations."

Ferrari's wine is a Trentodoc, grown in mountaintop vineyards that produce distinct chardonnay grapes which release their complexity in *méthode champenoise* bottle ageing. The vineyards are farmed with a system of sustainable agriculture and "green manure" (using plants, not chemicals). "The territory defines and enriches the wine," says Matteo. "Protecting it is crucial to our long-term vision."

In 1952, Ferrari produced 8,800 bottles of wine; today the number is about 3.5 million, still painstakingly produced with hand-picked grapes and artisanal methods, and aged for two to 10 years in an underground cantina.

"Fine wine is the result of every small step being done with passion and care," says Matteo, who has increased his staff numbers. "The key is we are all driven by a love for our wine and our terroir." *ferraritrento.it*

MONOCLE COMMENT
Expansion doesn't have to mean cutting corners. The owners of Ferrari have proved that quality is paramount for long-term sustainable success.

Matteo and Camilla's tips:

1.
Pick your location well
'Territory is the most important factor in a great wine – the soil, the climate and the altitude all affect the flavour of your grapes.'

2.
Look after the land
'Excellent wine requires years – even decades – to make and you need to be able to depend on the health of the land for a very long time.'

3.
The devil's in the detail
'Manage every step of production, from the vineyard to bottling. Details such as how vines are trimmed and grapes are picked are crucial.'

1

3

4

2   5

Case study 3
The vintner

Q&A

Tomofumi Fujimaru
Papilles, *Osaka*

Tomofumi Fujimaru opened his first wine shop in Osaka in 2006. Four years later he planted Muscat Bailey A grapevines on idle farmland on the city's outskirts; today he owns a two-hectare vineyard and looks after 15 other small vineyards around Japan. His business now includes two urban wineries in Tokyo, two in Osaka, and five wine shops, nearly all of them sharing space with a restaurant or deli.

Why start making wine?
I wanted to become a winemaker but I was starting from scratch. With my first shop I set out to develop Osaka's wine market. After saving up enough money I planted grapevines on a tenth of a hectare. I set out to make affordable table wines. I had worked at a winery in New Zealand but I'm mainly self-taught.

What was unexpectedly difficult and what came easily?
Waiting years until I could turn my grapes into wine was hard. Making enough to invest in the vineyard was a challenge; so was obtaining a licence to start the Osaka winery. I had to prove that I could meet the minimum volume requirement without having made wine before. Getting a second licence was easy. *papilles.net*

Three things Fujimaru learnt:

1.
Community outreach
'Before opening a winery in central Tokyo I was worried about a backlash from neighbours. My staff and I visited 100 homes and apartments to explain our plan, which helped to win them over.'

2.
Try something new
'Most wineries are located near vineyards. People assume shipping grapes to a big city doesn't make sense; we have found that it's very convenient because we look after farms in surrounding prefectures.'

3.
Don't follow the crowd
'Wineries here tend to copy those in warm European climates but why not experiment with Japanese grapes? Delaware is a common Japanese table grape variety. It has a light flavour that's great for our wines.'

1.
Ferrari winery employs 'méthode champenoise' bottle ageing

2.
Ferrari vineyard

3.
Fujimaru's bottles

4.
Tomofumi Fujimaru (right)

5.
Inspecting the vines at Chateau Monestier La Tour

6.
Ferrari production line

7.
Karl-Friedrich and Christine Scheufele

8.
Chateau Monestier La Tour now makes natural wines

6

7   8

Make it in a market
Lessons on starting a fledgling food venture, from picking your produce to getting the word out there.

Case study 1
The modern classic

El Mercat Central
Valencia

Valencia's El Mercat Central hums as 400 stallholders vie for trade under its glass dome. This is one of Europe's largest food markets, sitting in a 1920s structure resembling a cathedral.

Residents have been flocking here since it opened in 1928 looking for fresh produce that's grown nearby. "Uncompromising quality is key in any food business," says market president Francisco Dasí.

El Mercat has always held a healthy ground between tradition (regional delicacies such as *pastissets* – jam-filled cakes – are always stocked) and modernisation. In 2012, chef Ricard Camarena took over the central cafeteria, serving typical regional dishes with a modern twist. Meanwhile the fish market was the first in the world to computerise orders and offer home delivery, aiming to facilitate business from Valencia's restaurateurs as well as residents. "Catering to typical Valencian tastes, while staying abreast of the changing gastronomic world, is crucial to our success," says Dasí.

But an excellent product must be coupled with an understanding of your audience. One of the market's many unique qualities is its friendly atmosphere. Traders often know their customers by name; initial pleasantries are as important as the final transaction. It all comes down to how you deliver the product. "It's a question of knowing what works and what doesn't," says Dasí. "Be professional, be passionate and maintain a positive mindset." *mercadocentralvalencia.es*

MONOCLE COMMENT
For a stall that's built to last, do the simple things well – smiling service and the best produce – but also embrace technology and innovation.

Case study 2
The design lovers

Fantastic Market
Osaka

Japanese design firm Graf might never have organised an urban market had the company not been hired to build a farm hut. The commission, in 2009, came from the editor of an Osaka-based lifestyle magazine, *Meets Regional*. "We went from building the hut to working alongside the magazine's staff in their vegetable patch," says Mari Kawanishi.

Kawanishi and her Graf colleagues had experience making furniture, designing interiors and running a canteen but growing vegetables brought them a new appreciation of farming. They decided to organise an event in Osaka to promote regional food producers: Fantastic Market.

It launched in autumn 2010 with more than two dozen farmers and food producers. "We chose people who were good communicators and who had a product that was special," says Kawanishi.

With every event the market expanded and now includes designers, artisans and artists. Today it's staged about three times a year around central Osaka and draws from about 100 small farmers and food producers, shopkeepers, bakers, fashion brands, speciality coffee roasters, patisseries and cheese-makers.

It has become a launchpad for start-ups and a chance for small-scale producers to connect with a wider community. In 2016, Fantastic Market went on the road with 25 of its regular members, setting up their own corner at a major music and food festival in Aichi, central Japan.

MONOCLE COMMENT
A farmers' market can be more than just food. Graf has turned a simple one into a community including artists and designers.

Kawanishi's tips:

1.
Know your stuff
'Eat what is sold at the market and familiarise yourself with the flavours. Think about recipes and ways for consumers to prepare the food.'

2.
Be discerning
'The market is only as good as the vendors and the food and products they sell. You must select those who will be able to convey their passion to consumers.'

3.
Be consistent
'The key to continuity is having the trust and confidence of producers and vendors.'

Case study 3
The baker

Q&A

Daniel Leader
Bread Alone, *New York*

Daniel Leader, a chef by training, began Bread Alone bakery in the Catskill Mountains, New York State, in 1983. Leader set up stands at a handful of food markets in New York City, and today his loaves have become a staple in the city, available in just shy of 20 markets every week.

Why did you start Bread Alone?
My inspiration and role models for opening Bread Alone were small artisan bakers I met while travelling in France. I'm a trained chef and I was working in New York at French restaurants. I would go to France every August to visit colleagues. Everywhere I would go I'd meet a baker. I was in Paris and this baker said to me, "I bet bread like this is really popular in New York." I said, "Actually, no," and he said, "I bet it will be." It planted a seed in my mind.

What was unexpectedly difficult and what came easily?
While there is nothing easy about baking bread from scratch, the easy part is the reaction from our customers who appreciate our products, and the enthusiastic response from people who like great bread. A restaurant opens and closes but a bakery runs 24 hours a day. It's a little bit more hectic but we're really organised. If you came here it would seem more like a Swiss watch factory than an artisanal bakery. *breadalone.com*

Three things Leader learnt:

1.
Consider what you're selling
'Have unique products at fair prices.'

2.
Make sure you present well
'Put together an engaging stand that's well organised and easy to shop at. People spend more money when the products are attractively displayed.'

3.
Don't forget good service
'Have knowledgeable staff and give out lots of samples.'

1.
Sample of Fantastic Market's fresh food

2.
Small producers have a chance to shine

3.
Bread Alone founder Dan Leader (**right**)

4.
Fantastic Market, Osaka

5.
Warm welcome at Fantastic Market

6.
Fresh fruit at El Mercat Central

7.
At El Mercat Central, pride is taken in offering superior products

Get it on page

Fresh content with an editor, photographer and author who are making an impression in print.

Case study 1
The photographer

Simon Bajada
Food stylist and photographer, *Stockholm*

Simon Bajada, an Australian based in Stockholm, worked as a chef before turning to food styling. "I was always intimidated by the technical side of photography but working [with photographers] as a stylist, I realised I was capable of doing it," he says.

It may have been a logical progression but that doesn't mean his photography took off at once. "Like any freelance work, the cold calling and putting yourself out there is hard to do. It takes persistence." The trick, he says, is to "work out your look or your niche and find out who is publishing that".

Bajada loves shooting travel stories but making a living requires both editorial and advertising work. "If you did editorial around the clock you might compromise the quality, because you need to give it a lot more time. You can earn three times that in half a day with an advertising shoot."

The first thing Bajada focuses on when shooting a plate of food is natural light. He then decides on the composition before choosing what to draw the viewer's eye to: "It could be the garnish or it could be a liquid that's getting a beautiful highlight." The key, however, is experimenting. "For me the fun is all these variables together. Can you mess the food up a bit, can you change the direction of the lighting? You can play for hours really." *simonbajada.com*

MONOCLE COMMENT
When trying to get your name out there, target publications that fit your style; also bear in mind that, no matter what your passion, you will likely need to balance editorial and advertising work.

Case study 2
The editor

Martina Liverani
'Dispensa' magazine, *Faenza, Italy*

Before journalist-turned-editor Martina Liverani started her magazine *Dispensa*, food journalism in Italy was stuck in a rut. "The content was always the same: recipes, reviews, praise for the great chefs. What was missing was a different way of talking about food."

Dispensa was created in 2013 and soon gathered a loyal following for its insightful long-form features published in both English and Italian. Its biannual issues are themed around topics such as the ethics of eating meat, or the relationship between humans and food.

"My family owned a food shop so I spent a lot of time there as a child," says Liverani. "It taught me how to look at the world through food; you can tell a lot about a person's character from the food they buy."

Liverani's plan never involved advertising: leveraging her editorial rather than sales talent, she instead created a collectible. "If you make a print magazine in this digital age you need the paper to be the protagonist," she says. "Ours is made from repurposed food waste."

To beat distribution costs, new issues can be ordered online; she approached select stockists in Italy individually. But *Dispensa* is unique for its commitment to storytelling. "We had to be an antidote to the digital binge, to tell stories nobody else would," says Liverani. "We may have had difficulties but it's not true that people don't read anymore. People recognise quality." *dispensamagazine.com*

MONOCLE COMMENT
'Dispensa' has shown that in the Italian market there will always be a place for food journalism and photography, provided they're done with heart and soul. Check out the shelves of your local newsstand and spot the gap.

Liverani's tips:

1.
Know your market
'I had been writing about food for 15 years so I knew the sector. We worked to make a magazine for readers, not advertisers.'

2.
Work with good writers
'Journalists can have a great deal of freedom in interpreting the issue's theme but must be able to tell the story in the best possible way.'

3.
Consider print costs
'There are unavoidable fixed costs so you need to keep the big picture in mind. Everything must be co-ordinated, from PR to page structure.'

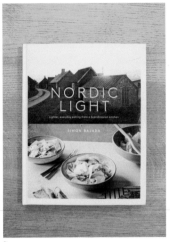

1.
'Dispensa' magazine

2.
'Nordic Light', one of the cookbooks Simon Bajada has authored and shot

3.
'Dispensa' was founded in 2013

4.
Author Anissa Helou

5.
Food stylist and photographer Simon Bajada at work

Case study 3
The writer

Q&A

Anissa Helou
Cookbook author, *London*

Anissa Helou worked in the art world before she turned her collector's eye to the cuisine of the Middle East and the Levant. Born in Beirut to parents from Lebanon and Syria, she is the author of eight books about cooking, and now lives in London and Trapani in Sicily.

Why did you start writing cookbooks?
I wanted to record my mother's recipes, which I knew would disappear once she died. I started my first book in 1992, after the end of the Lebanese civil war, and I knew the kids who had emigrated from Lebanon during the war did not see what I saw when I was growing up: the preserves being made, animals being prepared at the butcher. These were aspects of food culture I had absorbed naturally that were being lost. I had young Lebanese people from the US tell me they appreciated my book because it allowed them to cook like their grandmothers and mothers.

What was unexpectedly difficult and what came easily?
The easy part is producing food everybody loves – it's a very convivial occupation. There is something about food everybody connects with. The unexpectedly difficult thing was that my mother was an amazing cook but not a precise one in the sense of saying you need 100g of this or 500g of that. For almost all of her recipes, it was a handful of this or a coffee cup of that or 'cook until it's done' – instructions that were totally useless to me as a cookbook writer. *anissas.com*

Three things Helou learnt:

1.
Connect with the subject
'It's essential to have some link to the food you want to write about – either through a spouse or having worked in the country or travelled there a lot.'

2.
Choose your publisher well
'Hold out for one who will do a good job with the final product.'

3.
Test and retest your recipes
'There are lots of cookbooks where you can tell that hasn't been done.'

Brand a product
So what makes us plump for a particular item?
Here's some advice on creating a product with pull.

Case study 1
The legacy

Johanna Händlmaier
Händlmaier's mustard, *Regensburg*

The sausage is one of the true staples of German cooking but it would be nothing without its near-constant companion: the sharp and slightly sweet Händlmaier's mustard.

It began in 1910 when Johanna Händlmaier and her husband Karl opened a butcher's in Regensburg, a Bavarian city on the Danube. Shifting sausages turned out to be far less lucrative than selling the wurst's favoured accompaniment; Johanna's homemade mustard was an instant hit and by 1965 the business had grown exponentially, with more than 400 markets in the region carrying the now-famous condiment.

Today the company is in the hands of fourth-generation owner Franz Wunderlich, who has added new flavours and products to the range, including a super hot mustard (Superschafer Senf). Convenient packaging solutions have been created too, such as squeeze tubes and sachets for barbecues or picnics. The product has since arrived in the US.

Despite these innovations, the recipe for the classic creation by Wunderlich's great-grandmother has not changed and is safely stored behind the steel doors of the company safe. Meanwhile, the trademark design of the Bavarian condiment has remained true to its origins. The red label, the early 20th-century typeface and the logo featuring the beaming face of Johanna Händlmaier are all hallmarks – now the world over – of quality Bavarian mustard. *haendlmaier.de*

MONOCLE COMMENT
Händlmaier's proves that good branding is sometimes about sticking with a look that works and allowing the humble product (and the wurst with which it shares a plate) to speak for itself.

Case study 2
The patriot

Geoff Dillon
Dillon's Gin, *Beamsville (Canada)*

Browse the gin section of any Toronto liquor shop and bottles of Dillon's Gin stand out for their sleek shape and sharply designed labels. When Canadian Geoff Dillon started his eponymous distillery in 2012 he tapped Burlington-based designer Barry Imber to tell his brand's tale. The two quickly decided that it was essential to capitalise on the traits that make Dillon's Gin unique.

Ontario's Niagara region is known for its wineries, making Dillon a very rare gin-maker indeed. His distillery sources ingredients – from grapes to botanicals – from the area, which is renowned for its fertile soil and relatively temperate climate. Dillon is proud of this emphasis on using produce solely from his neighbours. "The point is to show off the ingredients," he says.

It's also what drives the company's brand aesthetic. "It's all about transparency," says Imber. "You need to create a brand that reflects authenticity so there's no fear of replication." Dillon's sports a clean colour palette; from the bottles to the website – even the production facility – everything feels simple and effortless.

Before settling on the final look, Imber discarded countless drafts because they were generic. Certain elements of the final outcome – such as the clearly listed ingredients and the nods to the copper stills used in the distillation process – stand out. As he puts it, "Being in the Niagara region, using specific ingredients and equipment – you can't copy that." *dillons.ca*

MONOCLE COMMENT
Getting cut-through in a highly saturated market such as small-batch gin is tricky. Branding will play its part but it can only work with the product and the narrative you've created.

1

Dillon's tips:

1.
Be clear
'Find the elements that distinguish your company from others in the industry and make design decisions to highlight them.'

2.
Be consistent
'Great branding is seamless across all platforms. A great website might lure curious customers to your shop but if the in-store experience is a letdown, they won't come back.'

3.
Be honest
'Branding only goes so far. If you're bottling moonshine, no amount of fancy packaging will make up for a sub-par product.'

Case study 3
The designer

Q&A

Grigoris Tsaknakis
Mousegraphics, *Athens*

The forte of Athens-based design studio Mousegraphics is honest and unfussy designs for food packaging, from lobster caught off Prince Edward Island in Canada to premium Greek-thyme honey.

How did you start Mousegraphics?
At first, 90 per cent of my design work with Mousegraphics came from one big Greek company, until suddenly that work stopped. I thought it would destroy my business but it ended up being the beginning of my relationship with design. Specialising in packaging came via the clients we worked with, and 30 years on I still think the best aspects of our designs come from the product. The job of a designer is to reach the truth of a product, then say only one thing about it.

What was unexpectedly difficult and what came easily?
It's hard to convince a client when the studio is young; you need to establish a sense of authority early. Sixty per cent of your job success is in the presentation. In the past six or seven years, finding clients has got easier, if you're willing to think openly about a global market.
mousegraphics.eu

1.
Händlmaier's shop
in Regensburg

2.
Geoff Dillon, creator
of Dillon's Gin

3.
Trademark branding of
Händlmaier's

4.
Barry Imber (second from
left) and his design team

5.
At work on the designs for
new Dillon's releases

6.
Selection of products
bearing the distinctive
Dillon's branding

7.
Dillon's Gin

Three things Tsaknakis learnt:

1.
Be ready to be tested daily, and not quit
'This is not a straightforward commercial business where you just sell a product and find a market; this is a daily examination of your practice. A client will not be satisfied with something mediocre.'

2.
Specialise in a certain area of design
'For us, food packaging was an opportunity because it's tied closely to mass print and the production line, and therefore businesses will spend more to create a perfect design.'

3.
Think about cross-promotion
'We've worked with small companies and new start-ups, and noticed that by sharing our designs online, their products have attracted international orders. The design creates opportunities for global expansion of the product and, as its profile grows, the product can do the same for your design.'

Distill a spirit or brew a beer
The drinks business is ripe for reinvention so how can you perfect your porter or join the gin market?

Case study 1
The hiker

Stephan Garbe
Gin Sul, *Hamburg*

Inspiration struck Stephan Garbe in 2012 while hiking Portugal's Vicentina coastline. He noticed white-flowering gum rockrose bushes growing alongside the windswept juniper trees. "I've always been a gin aficionado but that's when I knew I wanted to make the first Portuguese craft gin," says Garbe. "I bought books about gin, spirits and distilling, and started developing the project."

Now the former advertising copywriter is at the helm of a thriving business that employs six workers. Although the distillery is located in Garbe's hometown of Hamburg, Portugal is the heart and soul of Gin Sul, which translates as "Gin South". Garbe tried to establish his business in Portugal but, after months of struggling with red tape, turned instead to Germany's second-largest city.

Gin Sul's popularity comes from its unique blend of ingredients. Each week, Garbe receives 20kg to 50kg of untreated lemons. Their zest, blended in a 100-litre copper still with the usual botanicals – juniper berries, coriander and rosemary – provides a distinctive citrus kick, while gum rockrose (*Cistus ladanifer*) brings a delicate sweetness.

The process of setting up his distillery may have been longwinded but Garbe continues to live and breathe gin. After distilling for eight hours every day he scours bars to see what's on offer; he even travels abroad to gin-making masterclasses. "It really is a great job – the best thing I've done in my life." *gin-sul.de*

MONOCLE COMMENT
The gin industry is small but you should find your niche to set you apart from the increasing number of craft distilleries that are popping up.

Case study 2
The revivalist

Cesco Amodio
Staibano, *Amalfi*

Staibano's tale starts on the lemon groves in the southern reaches of the Sorrentine Peninsula in Campania, Italy. In the 1930s, landowner Don Vincenzo Staibano gained a reputation for the parties he threw among his plantations, and the home-brewed lemon liqueur that became synonymous with his name.

About 80 years later, Staibano's London-based great-grandson Cesco Amodio hatched a plan to relaunch the tipple. Funding the product was the first step, then it was time to find the perfect supplier. "My uncle introduced me to the De Riso family, which has the best lemons," says Amodio.

The lemons he buys – straw-coloured sfusato amalfitano with thick waxy skins – are grown on what were the family groves, before Amodio's great-grandfather lost them to gambling. The lemons thrive on volcanic soil and the breeze blowing in from the Tyrrhenian Sea. Pickers collect the fruits one by one before carrying them to the factory in the small fishing village of Minori, 45 minutes away on the coast.

The 1,000 bottles Staibano produces each week bear attractive dark blue-and-yellow labels. "Having a beautiful, eye-catching bottle helps but that's only a small percentage of the game," says Amodio. A focus on quality, heritage and gutsiness have ensured Staibano's take-off. "There are only so many measured decisions you can make. Sometimes you have to risk it and hope for success." *staibano.com*

MONOCLE COMMENT
Staibano is a product with a story that isn't manufactured to fit a concept. The lesson to be drawn: however overcrowded the market, you can stand out with the right level of commitment (and the right dose of courage).

1
Amodio's tips:

1.
Perfect your recipe
'Before you get into larger production, make sure people like your product. Sample it with friends and family, as well as experts within the industry.'

2.
Work with people
'Having the expertise of others around you is reassuring and calming, especially during the difficult initial phases of building a business.'

3.
Be patient
'Sadly things do not happen overnight. Alcohol companies are expensive to run and it requires time for brands to grow.'

Case study 3
The pump attendants

Q&A

Jos Ruffell
Garage Project, *Wellington*

Garage Project brewery was set up in 2011 by Jos Ruffell and Pete Gillespie and is housed in a disused petrol station in Wellington's Te Aro Street. Ruffell runs the business side while Gillespie runs the brewing, inspired by Michelin-starred chefs rather than other brewers. "There are more cooking books here than books about beer," says Ruffell.

Why did you start Garage Project?
The inspiration was to bring brewing back to Wellington, which at the time had a great beer culture but no independent breweries. The craft brewers in New Zealand were producing excellent generic beers so we wanted to try something new and focused on being more progressive. Art, music, dance, cooking – our inspirations have come from all sorts of weird and wonderful areas.

What was unexpectedly difficult and what came easily?
Unfortunately we were not eccentric millionaires so starting up was a huge leap of faith. We both quit our jobs and worked on the brewery full time for almost eight months before we produced our first drop. We also decided to start brewing at a level that we knew was not economically viable – just 50 litres per batch. But it seemed the only way that we could begin immediately on our relatively small savings. What came naturally was a willingness to try something new. We wanted to be unlike the other brewers, not from a lack of respect but so we felt we were making our own contribution. *garageproject.co.nz*

Three things Ruffell learnt:

1.
Cash flow is paramount
'With brewing being so capital-intensive and with long production times, this is especially important.'

2.
Have a real point of difference
'You need something unique and special. Quality is the most important thing.'

3.
Be in it for the right reasons
'Get experience in the industry. Take your time, get the knowledge you need and then make your move.'

1.
Gin Sul distillery

2.
Garage Project, Wellington

3.
Harvesting lemons
for Staibano

4.
Jos Ruffell (left) and Pete Gillespie from Garage Project brewery

5.
Cesco Amodio with his lemon liqueur

6.
Adding juniper berries to the mix at Gin Sul

7.
Bottling at Garage Project

8.
Stephan Garbe of Gin Sul

3.
My Last Meal

Our favourite people's final feasts

Despite the everyday nature of eating, meals themselves are often linked with life's most important moments: break-ups, catch-ups, reunions and proposals; singular encounters and overdue rendezvous. They're times to reflect on the rituals and emotions we attach to food, from our earliest childhood memories to exotic flavours encountered on travels and much-missed dishes while we're away. With this in mind we have corralled some of our favourite film-makers, actors, musicians and more to impart their food-related stories and – without being morbid – where and what their last ever meal would be, as well as who they would invite to join them. Pull up a chair for a little after-dinner conversation and a few tasty tales.

Alison Goldfrapp
Musician

VENUE: Toff's of Muswell Hill, *London*

Fried haddock, chips, mushy peas and gherkins. Close at hand: plenty of tomato ketchup, vinegar (both in glass bottles, of course) and salt

"I grew up in Alton, Hampshire, and I guess I'm a country girl at heart. My dad was obsessed with the countryside. When there was a full moon the family would all get in the car and drive to the beach, about an hour away, rain or shine. He'd insist that we be quiet – we weren't allowed to speak, just listen. He was really big on listening and I think that had a huge influence on me.

My dad was a creative person. There were art books everywhere and he was always playing music – he took it very seriously. He'd make us listen to a piece of music and then have a discussion about it. From a pretty early age I knew I wanted to have a career in music. I started singing professionally when I was 20, with a Belgian dance troupe. I did that for about two years, touring the Netherlands, and was introduced to a lot of music I didn't know such as Yma Sumac and Steve Reich. People elsewhere in Europe seemed so sophisticated.

When I came back I wasn't sure about the music thing so I went to art school [at Middlesex University in London]. Eventually I met Will [Gregory, Goldfrapp's collaborator]. We recorded some songs and sent them to Mute Records and then producer Daniel Miller rang me – I nearly had a heart attack.

We've been so lucky to be able to keep doing whatever we like, for better or worse. I'm always amazed when I perform. I think, 'Oh, we're doing another one of these. Brilliant.' But it's the writing where you can really delve into being creative. I write out in the countryside in my cottage near Bristol.

I crave isolation. I have this vision of me sitting on a roadside, with a brolly and a little table, in a bikini with everything hanging, seriously brown, selling pots of honey or something. It's a weird kind of freedom. Thinking about my last meal – the end of things – it's a bit abstract.

My mum's cooking, bless her, wasn't great. She came from the school of thought where you had a joint of meat and you'd make it last the week. We'd start the week with steaks and on Fridays we'd have gristle. I'm not a very good cook either but I do love food.

So fish and chips. I see it as comfort food. I hardly ever eat it but I have fantasies about it: sitting on the beach, eating fish and chips. I always feel slightly ill afterwards – but I enjoy it at the time. I have memories of fish and chips from my childhood or in the pub as a teenager. For my last meal I'd also have a nice glass of English champagne. It elevates it to a slightly more glamorous meal. It's a good combination.

I'd invite my girlfriend Lisa, Maus – our whippet – and all my friends. And we'd be dancing with everyone playing their instruments. That would be great. It would be at home – even more comfort. But I don't think I could say goodbye. I'd be convinced we'd see each other again." — (M)

Wim Wenders
Film-maker

VENUE: **Florian**, *Berlin*

1. Matjes (soused herring) salad with red and yellow beetroot
2. Franconian pork roast with a potato dumpling and gravy
3. Chocolate mousse

"My first memory of food is sitting on the back of my dad's bike. My mother was on a bike as well. We were cycling out of Düsseldorf, which in 1948 was just bombed ruins. We took a ferry to the other side of the Rhine and rode for a couple of hours to meet some farmers. My father traded jewellery for a bag of potatoes, which ended up on the back of his bike and meant that I had to ride on the front bar between his knees. I was crying because I was so uncomfortable. But we ate those potatoes for weeks. I was three years old.

I've had an office and apartment in Berlin since the early 1970s, even when I lived in the US. The culinary aspects of the city were pretty grim then. There were Prussian places where the main food was greasy sausages and heavy German things; they've disappeared.

Florian serves southern German cuisine from Franconia, a region in northern Bavaria. Their speciality is *rostbratwürstchen* [small roasted sausages] and sauerkraut. When friends visit from far away I bring them here because they don't know German food. The *tafelspitz* [boiled beef] is amazing.

I don't even look at the menu: I know what I want. I lived around the corner and for 20 years I ate here almost every day. I now live in Mitte so I only come once a month or so.

I don't like fancy cuisine much. White asparagus is my favourite food in Germany; it grows next to Berlin but also in the Rhineland.

We always had it when I was a kid, with potatoes and melted butter. Later, when the *wirtschaftswunder* [postwar prosperity] came, we had it with ham.

I've taken pictures since I was six. My father gave me a camera; he was a surgeon but also an amateur photographer. I wanted to become a painter so photography was nothing special. I only took it seriously from the early 1980s. It was spring of 1983 when I was travelling a lot in the American southwest and I had to get used to these bright colours; I wanted to lose my fear of this light. Until then I'd only photographed in black and white.

Photography doesn't coincide with my film work anymore. As a film-maker I'm a social animal and have been adventurous with digital production and 3D. But as a photographer it's essential that I'm alone and shoot analogue. There's nothing retouched. On a long day of shooting I'll travel with a Thermos; most of these places are lonely and I can't get a coffee. Now and then I'll bring a *stulle*: a small sandwich.

Independent film is shrinking and can only survive if a need for narrative remains. Every second blockbuster is a seventh sequel. Like with food, it's a matter of what you're offered. The more you get a certain food, the more you depend on it. Slow food is a luxury, fast food is not. And that's the same with blockbuster films. They're fast food for the eyes." — (M)

Rossana Orlandi
Gallerist and curator

VENUE: **Larte,** *Milan*

1. Macelleria Giacobbe pancetta
2. Mezzi paccheri pasta with aubergine, tomatoes and provolone del Monaco cheese
3. Silver garfish with spinach, prawns and smoked provolone cheese
4. Lemon crème anglaise with almond biscotti and ricotta gelato

"My first memory related to food is that I couldn't wait to grow up so I wouldn't have to eat spinach soup anymore. I wanted to eat chicken wings like my brothers. But my first truly pleasurable memory of food is a lunch with my husband, a very difficult person who spends very little time at the table. We spent four hours in a French restaurant and we were disappointed when it came to an end. It was marvellous; an old house in Brittany and plate after plate of food. We could have stayed there forever.

I adore simple food that respects the ingredients it's made with; I love dishes that make good use of herbs and elevate their basic flavours. The more a dish is simple and flavourful, the more I appreciate it. I'm very curious when it comes to eating. I like to go to cheap restaurants sometimes because you eat more authentic food and often you eat very well. I'm a big fan of tripe, which is really a poor man's dish in classic Italian cuisine. And I adore cassoulet – another humble dish made with pork and cabbage, and served with polenta.

I opened a charming little restaurant next to my gallery in Milan called Pane e Acqua [now called Marta]. I did it because it is absolutely necessary to have a place where you can welcome clients. You work, you live – and food is at the heart of all of it. It's our space with our flavours, our warmth, our way of

being. Something that brings me pleasure is to feel at home, especially with a chef on hand.

To inaugurate the gallery [Spazio Rossana Orlandi in Milan] I organised an exhibit entitled *Tabula Rara*. We invited friends, artists, designers, fashion people and regular people to create artistic visions of dinner tables. There was a table made of make-up and one made out of a bed. There were so many ideas.

Food is eaten first with the eyes. Even something very simple – a nice slice of salami – is a joy if the table is set up in a certain manner. It's like a warm embrace. Another thing that is very important to me is the atmosphere. If everything is done with a smile, with love, it's wonderful.

I do really envy people who are good in the kitchen. To make a dish well is not difficult; the difficult part is to enjoy making the dish. Cooking gives me a stiff neck; too much nervous tension. I'm capable of burning boiling water. Fortunately my husband believes that chefs are dangerous people because they know how to handle fire and knives.

The meal, for me, is truly the moment when people enjoy life: there's conversation, there's intimacy. It can be a tête-à-tête, it can be a friendly dinner but it's always distinct from the rest of the day. When you speak from behind a desk you're not the same as when you speak at the table. Being at the table brings out your human side." — (M)

Cecil Balmond
Architect and engineer

VENUE: Bombay Brasserie, *London*

1. Palak patta chaat and sev batata puri
2. Paneer tikka, tandoori lamb chops, Goan fish curry, masala sea bass and dal tadka
3. Naan bread and steamed rice

"My first memory of my mother's cooking is of witchcraft in the kitchen. She would throw in ingredients and say, 'This is good for your eyes, this is good for your spleen,' and she believed it. She was an amazing cook; I fell in love with the entire process as a boy of three or four. You can't beat your mother's cooking but I keep trying.

When I was 13 my father got a Fulbright scholarship to visit the US so I left school for six months. He wisely decided to go around the world to complete the circuit; I went through Spain, England, the US, Fiji, Tahiti, Australia, Malaysia and back. I remember the street-food vendors in Singapore and eating from the riverboats in Bangkok.

I left Sri Lanka when I was 20. We were a Christian minority and my father was pushed out of a top job because he wasn't a Buddhist. I was living with my grandmother in Colombo and thought, 'What am I doing here?' I wrote to my father and said, 'I'm leaving,' took luck into my own hands and just went.

I ended up in Nigeria for three years – the most hedonistic period of my life. Then I came to England to study. London was awful eating; the cooking was banal and very basic so we ate mainly Indian or Chinese food. I used to sing and play guitar in clubs and I travelled around Northumbria and the Lake District before I realised what a great dish fish and chips is with a pint of ale.

I discovered Bombay Brasserie when my wife and I had just had our children. There were wonderful pictures on the wall and a great frieze of Bombay. It was lovely, very Raj and slightly opulent. It was the place where I found relief at the end of a hard day. It became a place of celebration. We'd come here for every birthday and anniversary in the family; if someone won a prize or John, my eldest, joined a rock band, any excuse, we'd come.

One last meal would be hard; I'd need to make a day of it. Breakfast is easy. It sounds crazy to say the Hilton hotel but everyone in Sri Lanka knows it. They have a delicate curry that is lime yellow and made from fish caught around the island, which is like halibut but tastier. Then you have a potato curry, which is like satin; there's no other word to explain it.

Lunch would be in Düsseldorf, Munich or Berlin, where I've had the best Italian food: *aglio e olio*, which is spaghettini with garlic and chilli. I'd have two espressos to keep moving and then I'd fly to Japan to my favourite sushi place. It's just six tables and the prices are truly ridiculous because they serve *fugu* [pufferfish]: you pay for the privilege of risking your own life. I don't know the names of everything but the food just keeps coming and you keep eating it along with the wonderful saké. I have it warm but I'm told you should have it cold. Since it's my last meal I'll have it the way I want it." — (M)

Donna Hay
Writer, TV presenter, editor

VENUE: Berowra Waters Inn, *Sydney*

1. Tasting plates: scallops, corn and foie gras; truffle and kipfler tortellini;
trout, dashi and smoked milk; duck, grapes and parsnip;
beef, onions and tarragon; beetroot and goat's cheese
2. Rice pudding

"Food has always been important to me. When I was a child I'd spend holidays with my grandparents. We'd be in the vegetable garden in the morning and in the afternoon we'd pod peas or string the beans together. I am the youngest of three girls, which was great because as the youngest you get to do adventurous things above your age.

I'd like my last meal to be theatrical; it needs to be about much more than the food. I'd want it to be an adventure – and a long one; a lunch to ensure that we'd have plenty of time. I'd start with a flight in a seaplane. I'd pile my two sons and my friends in. The plane would dock at Rose Bay in Sydney and fly across the harbour and the city, along the coastline. The flight would take you over sea cliffs and past beaches to a spot called Berowra Waters, nestled in the bush.

The restaurant is legendary. It is only accessible by water. All the great Sydney chefs have cooked here. I love the isolation. The water, a wall of bush in front of you; it's peaceful. That said, the fact that it's so isolated means we could make plenty of noise and be as badly behaved as we liked. I'm sure all of my friends would jump off the jetty into the water.

It is hard to believe that *Donna Hay* magazine is in its second decade. I never really had a full-time job until we started it. I was freelancing, creating about 30 pages of food a month for *Marie Claire*, as well as cookbooks.

It wasn't glamorous. I spent years figuring out ways to make food look great, from stopping a pea from wrinkling to fluffing ice cream for so long that my nose froze. I didn't know until then that I could be precise, that I had enough attention to detail to look through 700 ice-cream cones to find the perfect one.

When I was in my early twenties I went to Paris. Every day I'd go out for lunch and in the evening I'd have just a crêpe. I'd watch the crêpe vendors fold them. Some rolled the crêpe, some folded it into a square, others a triangle. I had my epiphany there: I needed to find ways to make familiar ingredients look different on a plate.

I looked elsewhere to find ways to do that. Working with editors with different motivations helped. Jane Roarty, fashion and style editor on *Marie Claire* in those days, would encourage me to research what was happening in fashion, to be inspired by colours and textures. That was long before food was about fashion. I started using colour: blue because most food is brown and white, and I love its freshness. Lots of white, lots of light and ingredients on a plate with minimal props; it became my style.

Often when I travel people tell me that my books reflect Australia. I think that is the light. When I was promoting my book in Europe and I didn't see the sun for nine days, I wondered why I was feeling odd. In Australia we never go that long without the sun." — (M)

Nobuyuki 'Nobu' Matsuhisa
Chef and restaurateur

VENUE: Nobu Miami Beach at Eden Roc, *Miami*

1. Yellowtail sashimi with jalapeños
2. Black cod with miso
3. Squid pasta with garlic sauce and rock-shrimp tempura with spicy ponzu
4. Shave ice with condensed milk and yuzu sorbet

"I lost my father when I was young and I've always missed him. Looking through a photo album I saw a picture of him in Palau with some natives; I wanted to be just like him and leave Japan. Going to another country was my dream – that and I always wanted kids.

When I was training in Tokyo in the 1970s some Japanese-Peruvians came in and asked me to come to Peru to open a restaurant. It had the Amazon, natives like those in my father's picture and Lima right by the ocean so I thought, 'I'd like to go there.' After four years in South America I went back to Japan but I couldn't stay. I was young, just 28 years old. So I went to Alaska because someone offered to open a restaurant with me. Alaska has indigenous people so I said, 'Let's go.'

After eight months of building, my restaurant in Anchorage finally opened in 1979 and it was a big success. My first day off was Thanksgiving; I stayed at a friend's house and celebrated. Then my colleagues called me and said, 'Hey Nobu, you should come to the restaurant: it's on fire.' It wasn't a joke. Anchorage is a small town and soon after the phone call I could hear the sirens and see the smoke outside.

It was a big shock. I had no insurance and I lost a lot of money. I almost tried to kill myself because my dream was gone. I'd gone from Peru to Argentina and back to Japan; Alaska was my last chance and there was a fire less than two months after opening. I saw no future but my wife and two little daughters supported me. Every day for a week I sat at my table, didn't eat or drink and thought about jumping into the ocean. I didn't and that's why I'm here [laughs]. My wife told me it would all be OK and the kids were happy because I stayed at home. Smart people learn from mistakes and bad experiences. I like to think positively – like how I could learn from this accident.

When I was a kid my mother worked and my grandmothers would cook simple food every day. In the morning I'd have steamed rice, miso soup, pickled radish and grilled fish. I was born in 1949 so my generation started to watch more American TV. I'd never had a steak so I asked my mum if I could have one. I don't remember the taste but I do remember seeing it on the table and realising Japanese people didn't use silverware. So I asked my mum, 'Where's the knife and fork?' That's a strong memory.

When I was nine my brother took me to a restaurant. Sushi is very popular now but then it was very high-end and expensive. My first thought was, 'Wow, I want to be a chef.' It was a feeling of *irasshaimase* [welcome] when the doors slid open. I try to recreate this feeling in my restaurants.

For my last meal I would like to be with my family: my wife and kids. I appreciate my life because I've been able to spend all of it cooking. I'm very happy right now." — (M)

Isabel Allende
Novelist

VENUE: Insalata's, *San Anselmo, California*

1. Cataplana: clam, chorizo and tomato sauté
2. Lamb kofta, fattoush salad
3. Duck breast, bulgur pilaf, sautéed leeks, chutney
4. Banoffee tart

"If I had to choose my last meal, what would I want? Kindness. Who cares what you eat? As for whom I'd have with me, well, I hope a lover. Friends and family, they're boring, I know them so well but a new lover – that would be great.

The food at Insalata's reminds me of the places I have lived: the clams of Chile and the fattoush salad of mint, coriander and cheese of Lebanon, where I lived as a child. I like to go to restaurants because I hate washing dishes. There are lots of high-end places around here that I could have chosen – especially in San Francisco – but this is where I feel at home. Insalata's is a 15-minute drive from my house and I often eat here. I know everyone here; I'm taken care of.

I worked as a journalist until the coup in Chile on 11 September 1973. President Salvador Allende – my father's first cousin – died on that day and a regime of repression and terror began immediately. Thousands of Chileans were killed or disappeared; others fled. I was the last member of the Allende family to leave the country because I didn't think the dictatorship would last. But eventually I also fled, with my then husband and two children. I went into exile in Venezuela.

In 1981 I got a phone call saying that my grandfather was dying in Chile but I couldn't return due to the dictatorship so I started writing a sort of spiritual letter. He died and never got to read it but I kept writing and knew from the first couple of pages that it wasn't a normal letter. Although it was based on his life, my family and my country, it was fictionalised.

By the end of the year I had 500 pages, all of them filthy because I was working in the kitchen. I didn't know if it was a memoir or a novel but an agent in Spain was interested: *The House of the Spirits* was published there in 1982. A month later at the Frankfurt Book Fair every European country bought it. My life changed completely.

I love experimenting with food. I can't follow a recipe just as I can't follow a pre-ordained script when I am writing; I have to improvise. It was in that same Venezuelan kitchen that I used to cook for my then teenage children. I cooked mostly Chilean dishes such as *charquicán*, a peasant stew of potatoes, pumpkin, meat and vegetables.

I like the ceremony of food. My mother is a fantastic cook and wrote recipe books. After my daughter died I had writer's block and to pull myself out of the mourning and the heaviness I wrote *Aphrodite*, which is about food and love.

I never thought I would be successful; it happens to a few lucky ones. I love telling stories so when one book is finished I need to write another because I want to delve into a new story. It doesn't tire me because it's not work. It's a lifestyle." — (M)

John Malkovich
Actor and film director

VENUE: Le Fournil, *Provence*

1. Presse de porc with courgette and coriander
2. Brochettes de volaille (chicken skewers) aux épices douces with rice and vegetables
3. Lemon sorbet

"I'd want my last meal to be a happy occasion. I would invite my family, my movie-producing partners and probably a few of my really good friends. I just want it to be a normal night out. For the most part, for someone who has been as lucky as I have been, life has been incredibly, indescribably beautiful. When I die I don't want people to be unhappy for two minutes. Things went along well enough before I was born and they will go along well enough – let's hope – after I'm gone.

I have a house in Provence and I've been coming to Le Fournil for many years. The food is always good and it's one of the only places that's open in winter. The weather can be quite cold and a little grim here but inside it's very cosy. It's a cave. Bonnieux is one of those cliff cities with a lot of troglodyte houses carved out of the rock.

I don't like to be full when I'm performing. When I'm working on a movie, breakfast is just coffee and toast and then I'll have a light lunch if I have it at all. I eat at night – really that's the meal. If I can I like to set up a kitchen on set.

I can't remember well over half of the 70 or 80 movies I've done. The only meal I ever enjoyed on screen was in *Rounders* where I ate about 600 Oreo cookies. I think that's about 30,000 calories. They were Oreo classics, none of this double cream nonsense. I try not to eat anything in dinner scenes because you're going to be doing that for 12 hours. I remember when I did *The Ogre* and my friend – the film's director, Volker Schlöndorff – wanted me to eat some kind of jellied eel. Really not my bag.

My mother was not a cook, nor could she do the dishes. We ate whatever was fast and easy – essentially junk food – but she did a decent chilli con carne. One of her famous dishes was mashed potato with a dog food called Alpo for flavouring. Some people used horseradish; my mother used Alpo. My wife and daughter are spectacular cooks. When my daughter was seven she could bake without a recipe.

For my last meal I'd order a *presse de porc* – a Provençal pâté similar to rillettes but with less fat – and simple *brochettes de volaille* [chicken skewers]. A good eater makes a good cook. I think that's critical. But I don't know much about big chefs. I've only ever read one book on cookery. It was about this French chef called Bernard Loiseau, who committed suicide. There were a lot of theories about why he did it. He was afraid he was going to lose one of his Michelin stars.

Looking back there are things I should have gotten out of earlier, situations I should not have put myself into, movies I shouldn't have done, plays I shouldn't have directed, things I shouldn't have said, could have said or might have communicated differently. But what difference does it make? In the end we will all die and the sun will burn out eventually." — (M)

Lee Lin Chin
Newsreader

VENUE: Gowings Bar & Grill, QT, *Sydney*

1. French onion soup served with grated pecorino and gruyère
2. Seafood pie with snapper, ocean trout, prawns and scallops in a puff-pastry crust
3. Profiteroles dipped in Valrhona dark chocolate

"I prefer to socialise and conduct business over a drink rather than lunch or dinner. I am a beer drinker. I've tried to cultivate a taste for whiskey, gin and tonic, martini – but no dice. I am not an adventurous eater but I do have a hearty appetite. I don't cook either. I recently visited my family in Singapore and my brother was working late so I rustled up some dinner. As he was eating he said, 'I don't know how to say this but I like my food with a bit of taste.'

It is chance, my being here in Australia. I didn't come as an immigrant like so many people – I came for love. I was living in London and met an English butterfly collector who was fond of photographing them. He was at the British Museum one day when he got talking with a fellow collector from Melbourne who said, 'You must come to Australia – the light is totally different.' So we came.

I have lived here for decades but I don't feel like it is home because there are no emotional landmarks for me. I was born in Jakarta and grew up in Singapore. I like Indonesian-Chinese food; my favourite cake is the *kueh lapis* [layer cake].

I don't read a lot of contemporary writers but modernists – from James Joyce to Marcel Proust, TS Eliot and William Faulkner – I do. I identify with émigré writers; people like me who are suddenly transplanted from one place to another. Eventually there comes a point when one experiences a sense of homesickness that is almost spiritual. One leaves the country of their birth but never finds another.

The current obsession with devices bothers me – they make life boring. They shorten one's attention span; people are so caught up with this thing in their hands and the paraphernalia in their ears.

Perhaps it all started with television but I prefer films to television. I love the last great period of American cinema, which begins with *Bonnie and Clyde*. Just after the Hollywood studio system collapsed you had these wonderful films being made, such as *Five Easy Pieces*, *Night Moves*, *The Godfather* and *The Parallax View*, and the likes of Bob Rafelson, Hal Ashby, Francis Ford Coppola and John Cassavetes were in their prime. They made sociopolitical films that were inspired by the turbulent times for thinking audiences. The way they were constructed would not be of interest in the age of the short-attention span.

I love Hong Kong. It's somewhere where I feel at home even though the cuisine doesn't grab me because of the absence of chilli. If I could split my last meal I would have southern fried chicken on the grounds of Rowan Oak in Mississippi, my last drink would be a beer at the Phil – the Philharmonic bar in Liverpool in the UK – and high tea at the Goodwood Park Hotel in Singapore, in the company of childhood friends, partaking of childhood favourites." — (M)

John Pawson
Architect

VENUE: Sake no Hana, *London*

1. Green-tea soba salad
2. Braised aubergine, duck and rib-eye beef tataki, and sesame dressing

"I grew up in Halifax in the north of England and remember my mum's Yorkshire pudding and my dad serving Romanée-Conti wine. I went into my father's textile business after school but, when I was 23, he said the company was failing. I was basically fired but then, by chance, I was offered a discounted First Class ticket around the world at a party. I was going to stop in Japan for a week but ended up staying four years.

I was interested in architecture from an early age. I was introduced to *Domus* magazine where I saw Shiro Kuromata's work; it was the first time I had seen something I really liked. When I moved to Tokyo I rang Kuromata and asked if we could meet. It was the early 1970s and there weren't many foreigners knocking on his door so he agreed and got architect Masayuki Kurokawa to come too. They were design aristocracy and introduced me to people like Issey Miyake and Rei Kawakubo. Eventually Kuromata got fed up with me hanging around and made me enrol at the Architectural Association in London as I hadn't studied architecture.

I like the iconic 1960s Smithsons' building here at Sake no Hana. It has a beautiful piazza, gorgeous Portland stone and inside, Kengo Kuma's screens are exquisite. The owner Alan Yau and I came up with the idea of communal tables for his restaurant Wagamama in 1990. He was initially resistant to people sitting together but I was used to it from Japan. My schoolboy dream would be to have a Japanese chef at home. As it's not practical to go to Tokyo for my last meal, I like that I can get a table here. Other Japanese places are a nightmare. My wife says I shouldn't be annoyed and that I should congratulate restaurants on being full.

I often get frustrated about small things and my children make me see how ridiculous I am. In 2002 I was in a car crash in India that killed my friend. Very few look death in the face and I felt so elated to be alive. I realised life is short and decided to only do projects that I really want to do. At my age you don't think about ideal projects but the monastery in the Czech Republic was the project of a lifetime – monks are the ultimate minimalists.

What's important to me is the idea rather than the decoration. It was the same with my own house. When my son Caius, who works in the music industry, came home with friends once before a concert, they couldn't believe how minimalist it was. For me there's still too much furniture – that's why I was happy in Japan.

Eating is like reading: there just isn't the time to indulge. My wife is a great cook, mostly with fish as I don't like meat much. It's important for me to eat at home with the family, just like the memory of my mum's Yorkshire pudding served whenever I came home from school." — (M)

Ruth Rogers
Chef and restaurateur

VENUE: The River Café, *London*

1. Mixed-leaf winter salad
2. Taglierini pasta with slow-cooked tomato sauce
3. Chocolate tart with a dollop of crème fraîche

"I was born in upstate New York and there was real excitement about the fresh corn in the summer and pumpkins and squashes in the winter so I grew up appreciating seasonal food. I came to London in 1967 as a student and had very little money. None of us were really spending on restaurants so we'd eat in ethnic places. There was a place called Jimmy's that was a Greek restaurant in Soho and a place called the Dumpling Inn that we used to go to. It was really budget but great fun.

The food scene in London has changed so radically. When I first came here people used to say, 'Forget food, you can't even get an espresso here.' You couldn't even buy olive oil except for a few shops in Soho.

Moving to Paris was an influence on my cooking. I lived above a market in Le Marais and learnt to never go there with a shopping list. I'd go to see what was there and then decide what to cook. The idea that we've gotten into with supermarkets is that you can get any ingredient from anywhere any time of the year.

I remember those meals in the 1970s when my husband [Richard Rogers], an architect, was building the Pompidou Centre. Every cheque in my cheque book was made out to restaurants and we explored Paris. We went to grand ones like Le Grand Véfour, where we got to know the waiters, and very simple ones around the corner from the site where the Pompidou was being built.

I also remember the first meal with Rose [Ruth's former business partner and co-founder of The River Café, who died in 2010] where we discussed the restaurant in 1985. She had been a chef in New York and my husband had just bought these warehouses and wanted to open somewhere to eat. The two of us went into this little café called Drummonds on King's Road and I remember sitting there and showing her the plans for this tiny little restaurant with enough room for 12 tables and wondering how we'd do it. I remember that meal as a turning point.

My last meal would be with my family and the people I work with. It would be a big table. I suppose my comfort food is pasta with tomato sauce and that's probably my last dinner. There are so many different sauces, sophisticated sauces but when it comes down to it, there's nothing better than pasta with tomatoes.

My other comfort food is chocolate. I crave chocolate. I'm a fan of Tuscan wine because that's what I was brought up on. My husband's family come from Tuscany and so I'd probably have a bottle of the Sassicaia merlot.

Every summer we go to Val d'Orcia, which is this beautiful part of Tuscany where there are big skies. It's an almost brutal landscape with few houses. I like southern Italy as well as Naples and the Puglia area but I'm happy when I'm in Tuscany." — (M)

George Lois
Creative director and graphic designer

VENUE: The Four Seasons, *New York*

1. Risotto with white truffle shavings
2. Sautéed Dover sole topped with parsley and key lime sauce
3. Chocolate velvet cake

"At lunch this place usually has five or six billionaires. The Grill Room is where the 'power lunch' happens. I coined that phrase while working with [restaurateur] Joe Baum. He was leading a personal crusade to elevate eating in America to a theatrical experience. He hired me in 1960 to do the advertising for The Four Seasons but I realised he was creating restaurants so I became creative director. I did that until 2000. I've had lunch here about 8,000 times over 40 years.

Decades ago I was sitting here with [graphic designer] Jean-Paul Goude when Andy Warhol came in. He had just gotten a Polaroid camera and he said, 'Oh, you're both so good looking, my first shot's going to be of you.' He took the shot, signed it with a 'W' and gave it to me. I shot him drowning in a can of Campbell's tomato soup for an *Esquire* cover. Till the day he died he called me up and tried to get the original art. He said, 'I'll give you a dozen Brillo boxes.' I said, 'Andy, I can go to an A&P [supermarket] and there are Brillo boxes out in the street.' Today his 'Brillo Box' costs about $100,000.

At 19 I got drafted for the Korean War. When I went I weighed 84 kilos; when I came home I weighed 65 kilos. When my wife – she's an amazing cook – saw me she started cooking. I picked up the 19 kilos within two months.

In 1962, Harold Hayes, editor of *Esquire*, asked me to do a cover. I had never done a cover in my life. They had a terrific photograph of Floyd Patterson, heavyweight champion of the world, and Sonny Liston. They had an upcoming fight. Patterson was the favourite but I knew he was going to get shattered. So for the next cover I photographed a guy built like Patterson lying face down in the ring.

Only problem was I didn't know what colour trunks Patterson would wear. So we flipped a coin. Heads it's black, tails it's white. Heads. Black. We do the cover. Everybody said, 'This is going to kill *Esquire*,' which was deep in the red. Few days later I was watching the fight. Liston gets in the ring. He's wearing white [and Patterson did wear black]. Sometimes things like that happen and you say, 'Maybe there is a God.' Liston destroyed Patterson. *Esquire*'s circulation went from 400,000 to two million.

All my career I left the house at 05.30 every morning. My wife would wake up with me and bake a dozen corn muffins. I would bring them, piping hot, to the agency. I had the most incredible kitchen there. When clients would come we served them food. I would walk around keeping the coffee cups full. To me that was an important part of hospitality.

I'd like my last meal to be a big supper with my family and all my pals. I play basketball with some of my best friends and we'd get a game in afterwards. Make a lot of noise. Yell and scream. That's the way to go out: in action." — (M)

Laurie Anderson
Contemporary artist, film-maker and musician

VENUE: Russ & Daughters Café, *New York*

1. Kippered salmon and Scottish smoked salmon spread with waffle-cut crisps
2. Smoked whitefish chowder with dill, espelette pepper and matzo (flatbread)

"I was forced to play the violin. Not at gunpoint or anything: we had a family orchestra and we needed violins. We were eight kids and we all played – flute, cello, clarinet, piano and violin. It was like the Von Trapp family. We wore matching outfits: red turtleneck sweaters, with navy pants for the boys, navy skirts for the girls.

I grew up in Chicago and didn't appreciate it like I do now. It's a generous place and the people are genuinely friendly. But I like New Yorkers; people are very awake here.

My mother was a terrible cook – and by terrible I mean monotonous. Sometimes we had liver, which we would scrape off the table onto our laps and down into our shoes, and then we would squish out to the woods to get rid of it. Have you ever had liver in your shoes? It's not a good feeling.

I played the violin until I was 16 and then stopped for a decade. When I was 26 I was really lost and I decided to stay in bed until I could think of a reason to get up. I stayed there for a year. It was near here, between Avenues B and C. I wasn't depressed, I just decided I didn't know what I was going to do so I was going to wait until I did. I made the same food every day that year: a pie. I would go out after I'd taught night class and buy the same things: cornmeal, black beans, broccoli and cheese. At the end of that year I had a lightbulb moment: I wanted to make singing sculptures.

I moved to New York in 1966. When I began as an artist in the 1970s it was still idealistic. I was part of a group. I did a lot of street stuff, a lot of operas and I did sculpture. I was in Soho; it was messed up. We kept our lights off at night because we lived there illegally.

I met my husband [Lou Reed] at a music festival based on Kristallnacht that [composer] John Zorn did in Munich. It was wonderful to meet someone who was never boring. We loved the Russ & Daughters shop [around the corner on Houston Street] and Lou would have loved it here at the café but it opened a year after he died. Have you had the horseradish cream cheese? They take something really sharp and put it into something humble.

I've done too many things in prisons to think about a last meal. But I can talk about my best meal. Who would be there? Lou, his cousin 'Red Shirley', John Zorn; people who would enjoy this food. Socrates might have been good to have there. I'm interested in the Socratic method and would ask him if he imagined Plato naming that concept after him.

I'm not that ambitious; I'm not someone who wants to open the Munich office. I just don't care. I've asked myself if that's just a bullshit thing that I say as I've said it so many times. I love working and I love making stuff – I'm doing some things now that I have no idea about." — (M)

Subodh Gupta
Artist

VENUE: His family home in Gurgaon, *India*

1. Aubergine, spinach and okra pakora with various chutneys and chapati
2. Lamb curry with white rice mixed with peas and carrots
3. Dal tadka (yellow daal)

"If I had not become an artist I would have been a cook. As a child, whenever my mother was in the kitchen making food I wanted to be by her side. I wasn't interested in helping so much as wanting her to teach me how to cook. It was with her and my three sisters that I discovered just how much of a foodie I really am. The very first meals they taught me to make were vegetable dishes that came from the region where I was born and raised: Bihar in eastern India.

Even after childhood my passion for food and cooking found its way into my art. When I first started working I was quite experimental. Because I spent a lot of time in the kitchen cooking – looking at pots and pans – I thought, 'Why not do something with it?' Especially because I am so close to it.

Since becoming an artist I have seen the Indian contemporary-art scene evolve but it still has a long way to go. While there are a lot of people now working in the industry, all the artists – even those in different cities such as New Delhi, Mumbai or Kolkata – know one another. In the Indian contemporary-art scene today, people tend to talk about money more than art. I think that is quite sad. I do believe if that changes and people start focusing more on the art then everything else will follow.

Growing up we had a lot of customs at home, one of which was every Saturday we used to eat a daal and rice dish called *khichdi*.

Not only was it for sustenance but it also had a powerful spiritual element to it. In Hinduism we have many gods and goddesses. It is believed that the Saturday God can be quite dangerous. And so to calm the gods, as well as ourselves, we would eat *khichdi*. In India, it was a once-accepted practice to let men eat first and women later. This was the case for my mother's generation. Now, this practice has for the most part gone. In my house we all eat together.

Of course, this is just one of many things changing in the country. Today, everybody in India eats everything. All over the country, from east to west, food is completely transforming. And the middle class keeps on growing fast. You can see it from the number of cars, how hard people are working, five-star hotels and the way cities are growing. Yet despite all these transformations, the reality is that most of us prefer to eat at home. I don't think this will change soon.

Sitting at the table for my last meal would be those who are so important to me: my family. My children love food and they are very honest about how a dish tastes. I would want us to talk about the two things in my life that are most dear to me: art and food. All of us eating together is one of the most enjoyable aspects of my life. I like to live with art and I want to die with it too. I couldn't think of anything more pleasurable than if I was surrounded by it while eating my last meal." — (M)

Martha Stewart
TV chef and media entrepreneur

VENUE: Martha Stewart's kitchen with help from Toshihiro Uezu, *New York*

1. Sushi with endive-and-watercress salad
2. Baked potato topped with crème fraîche and a portion of American Royal Transmontanus caviar
3. Scrambled eggs from Stewart's own hens
4. Hot fudge sundae made with homemade vanilla ice cream and peanut brittle

"If I were to have a last meal – which I am not planning to any time soon – it would definitely include sushi prepared by Uezu-san [Toshihiro Uezu] of Kurumazushi restaurant in New York. I've been eating his food for a very long time. He is a perfectionist of the first order and my daughter and I used to be able to eat a wardrobe of his sushi. Instead of going shopping for clothes we'd go there together.

I've always eaten the same way. There are ways to get into places and I found that out early on [laughs]. There was always a boy or a man who also loved good food who would take me to Masa or one of those great places.

I first had sushi on a date with my husband-to-be when I was 18 years old; back then there were only two restaurants in New York that served it. One was called Aki; it was uptown and we ate there a lot. It was very unusual in 1960 to eat sushi.

You always remember the best date you had with the best meal. That was at Lutèce, the old one in Manhattan. That was a very fun meal, a very fun date and a very fun evening. We had duck – I remember having the most delicious duck *bigarade* [bitter orange] with dark cherries – and a lemon soufflé for dessert.

When I first met my husband we ate in exotic places all the time. I always lived at home because I went to college at Barnard, which was near my house, so we ate the most amazing food all around Manhattan.

Chinese food was one of my favourites – it still is – and we ate a lot in Chinatown. What made it special was the carefulness of preparation and the unique kinds of food from different parts of China. Today it is more homogenised.

But Japanese is becoming more and more exotic in the US and someone like Uezu-san is now famous for his raw fish; he doesn't do cooked food. I like my sushi buttery with perfectly cooked rice that doesn't mask the taste of the fish. It has to be the way Uezu-san cooks it: it's sticky but it falls apart.

A baked potato with caviar is my comfort food. That or my beautiful scrambled eggs. I raise my own hens so I know what they eat and how good the eggs taste and look. They're my go-to food.

For dessert I love vanilla ice cream and really good homemade hot fudge with salty peanut brittle. It's not fancy; it's simple but it's also fun. If the hot fudge doesn't solidify when it hits the ice cream, it is not hot fudge. And you need a lot of it. I like it with a dollop of whipped cream too.

For my last meal I'm not sharing with anybody; I'm going to savour every bite by myself. I might want to have it in my house in Maine. I have a very beautiful dining room from where you can see the sun rise in the east and set in the west, with windows on three sides. There's also a raging fire in the fireplace. It's heavenly." — (M)

Nick Jones
Hospitality entrepreneur and Soho House founder

VENUE: Cecconi's, *London*

1. Cherry tomatoes with basil and zucchini fritti
2. Veal Milanese with lemon salt
3. Lobster spaghetti

"My mum was a keen 1970s housewife. I was brought up on chicken fricassée and brandy snaps, and roasts on a Sunday. My parents used to entertain a lot and I loved going to the butchers and food shopping with my mother.

My mum was an alright cook; she had some horrors though. Her gravy was like blancmange. Because she's no longer with us I can say this: she put me off Brussels sprouts but now it's one of my favourite vegetables. Overcooked Brussels sprouts remind me of home. That and the smell of scampi in a basket at the pub.

My first experience of cooking was at the French Horn restaurant in Sonning, Berkshire, when I was 16. The only thing I made was a lemon meringue pie – and not very well. Then I became a chef and worked at St George's Hotel as part of the training course I was on. Next I went to Paris for six months and worked in a kitchen. I embraced it.

I hate fussy eaters and have brought up my children to try everything. I'm always thinking about what I'm having for my supper; I'm always one meal ahead. That's the pleasure of food: it's legal, it's three times a day, it's creative and it's interesting.

I think people got interested in food in the UK when good chefs came over and people started to care about ingredients. I remember being slightly ashamed of saying I worked in a kitchen but now people are proud of it.

When I went into catering it was because my careers master really felt there was nothing else I could do. So I did but was surrounded by people who weren't passionate about food, who weren't passionate about drink – it was just that they couldn't get a job anywhere else.

My first restaurant, Over the Top, was shocking. I'm allowed to say that and it was, ask anyone. The food, design, service: everything was appalling. I started my first restaurant when I was too young – 23 or 24 – but it taught me a lot: that if I did everything in the opposite way I might succeed. I raised the money from banks and family friends, and it was a disaster. But I still run the same company that started Over the Top all those years ago.

I love Cecconi's but my last meal could easily be a summer lunch at the River Café. It'd be with my wife Kirsty and our four kids. Eating and drinking by water is the best; on the sea, by a river or by a lake. We'd have all the bits they put on the table while we're having a drink, then starters, a pasta course, a main, cheese and pudding. Then I'd be asked to leave because people have arrived for their evening table. A long lunch is my favourite meal.

My favourite food moment of the week is Sunday lunch. We always have people around for a roast with undercooked sprouts. Some people want to play golf or mow the lawn on Sunday – I like cooking lunch." — (M)

Pam Ann
Alter ego of comedienne Caroline Reid

VENUE: Nobu Berkeley St, *London*

1. Tuna tataki with ponzu, yellowtail sashimi with jalapeño and steamed broccoli with shiso salsa
2. Black cod den miso, soft-shell crab karaage with ponzu, lobster karaage with spicy lemon garlic
3. Chilean sea bass yasai zuke, dragon rolls and rainbow rolls
4. Lollipops selection, Nobu chocolate tart, banana split and numerous espresso martinis

"I was first introduced to Nobu by the fashion designer Julien Macdonald. He designed the British Airways uniform and is a great friend – and a total pisshead. If you want really good Japanese food, nothing beats Nobu unless you're in Tokyo. The flavours, the presentation – it's flawless and I'm into perfection. What's great is that I travel so much and they have them all around the world. The yellowtail is one of my favourite dishes. Everything is a taste sensation and nothing has been missed. But I have to say, never order soy sauce in this restaurant because they'll come down on you like al-Qaeda.

For my last meal I'd invite Barack and Michelle [Obama] because they can get me on Air Force One and I really want to know what that's like. I'd also invite Julien Macdonald because we'd enjoy it together, Nelson Mandela just to freak everyone out and The Weather Girls to give it some disco. Plus Kim Kardashian and Kanye [West]. They can sit on another table trying to get into our party like they did with the *Vogue* cover.

If I had to have my last meal on a plane I must say the food and service on Air New Zealand is amazing. I can't remember what I ate because I was so high on Xanax and red wine but it tasted good. I think. Qantas has Neil Perry and the food is clean and nice. Marc Newson designed everything from the cutlery to the cups.

The most consistent airline in the world though is British Airways. I love the Britishness, the no-nonsense 'Get on board, sit in your seat, here's your champagne and macadamia nuts, now shut up and don't bother me.' Air France also has a certain style that no one can ever take from them. They really do look you up and down and say, 'You are *so* fat,' with their eyes. It's so chic.

I don't believe the Golden Age of travel is over, not if you have the money. Lufthansa has an S-class Mercedes that comes and meets you at the wheel of the plane at Frankfurt Airport – not even at the gate. The other people have to get a bus. It's still the Golden Age of travel, there are just more economy passengers. I wish they wouldn't ruin it for the rest of us.

What could an airline like Easyjet learn about service at Nobu? They could never do it. They don't have plates, they don't have cutlery and they wouldn't know how to use chopsticks. All they can do is heat up a panini. Virgin is a bit too kitsch; get rid of your airplane salt and pepper shakers, up the ante.

If you want to ruin the palate of someone from the ghetto, take them to Nobu. They won't be able to afford it ever again and they'll have to have cheap Japanese when you drop them like a hot potato and say, 'Go and eat in Chinatown.' My ex-boyfriend claimed that I had ruined his palate because nothing can beat Nobu. And he was right: nothing can." — (M)

Joël Robuchon
Chef and restaurateur

VENUE: Yoshi, *Monaco*

1. Salmon yuzu carpaccio
2. Sushi platter
3. Kudamono salad with shiso sorbet

"My first memory with food is of a day I spent with my parents in the countryside visiting an acquaintance, a butcher friend who had organised a barbecue. I can't remember what type of meat it was but he cooked it *saignant* [rare] and it had lots of taste and a particular, extraordinary perfume.

I didn't start cooking passionately until I was in my early teens, when I attended the Mauléon-sur-Sèvre theological school in the Deux-Sèvres region. I was always helping out in the kitchen; it was an obligation but a relaxing activity too. The food wasn't great; I remember a pastry with boiled egg inside and pasta with minced meat being on the menu, nothing special.

The first important recipe I ever cooked was *lièvre farci* [stuffed wild hare] for a national competition, which I won. I treated it with respect; you can't destroy your ingredients just for the sake of creating something different. You have to keep in mind that you're killing an animal and that requires respect.

In 1976 I visited Japan for the first time after [French chef] Paul Bocuse sent me to do a French cuisine demonstration at a congress. I now go four times a year, always for one week. The chefs have a great admiration for the flavours, seasons and presentation – even the crockery changes depending on the time of year. Japanese cuisine has influenced me enormously; it's simple and healthy.

My favourite restaurant is in Ginza. It's run by sushi master Jiro Ono, who serves the best and freshest fish in the world. Today Jiro's restaurant has three Michelin stars. When running a kitchen we don't have time to eat and when we do, it might just be a sandwich. My favourite fast food is a baguette with mustard and butter, seared beef, tomatoes and lettuce. I used to eat that when I was behind the kitchen counter [Robuchon retired in 1995]. It is said that 'the cobbler always has the worst shoes'; we don't have time to enjoy what we do.

Restaurants today lack charm and they don't have good service; they should be like temples, not a place where you go to be fed. I don't put pressure on my staff when it comes to setting up a table but rather on greeting people nicely; I don't care if the cutlery is aligned as long as my staff are always smiling.

It's difficult to choose whom to invite to your last meal. A friend is great to eat with but a romantic dinner has to be with the person you love most. I'd like to have mine in a *ryokan* in Japan or here in Monaco, at Yoshi, where we serve food like they do in Asia. The place is as important as the person you're sharing the meal with; these are very romantic spots where you can let go of any issues and focus on the food. I would have a salmon carpaccio with herbs followed by black cod and a selection of sushi. No matter what, the rice has to be warm." — (M)

Gay Talese
Writer

1. Mussel soup with sautéed leeks, white wine and cream
2. Sole fillet with almonds and lemon, served with boiled potatoes and sautéed spinach
3. Lemon sorbet

"When I was 11 years old and in my hometown of Ocean City [Maryland, US], I'd go to the drugstore to buy a milkshake. Sometimes they'd give me the shaker and there would be an extra drop inside. Some restaurants do the same with a martini but not many. What I get when I come to Le Veau d'Or is really a martini and a half. The owner, Catherine, knows that I like a little extra, just like when I had a milkshake as a boy.

I'm not a demanding food connoisseur; I'm more interested in the atmosphere and being comfortable. If I'm going for a meal I usually know where I'd like to sit before I leave the house. Sometimes I even know the numbers of the tables. The table I get here is a good example of what I like because it's enclosed. It's like a little apartment: a room with a view.

When I was a boy my mother and father worked late so we went out every night. At the age of three I was in a high chair in some of the best restaurants in Atlantic City. My town, Ocean City, was a dry town but my father liked his wine and a bit of whiskey before dinner so we went [to Atlantic City]. Now I still do the same thing I did at three years old. I'm not in a high chair anymore but I have a good seat.

I am alone during the day by choice while I work. I never have lunch and I have breakfast on my own so I don't engage with anyone during the day. But by 6 o'clock I'm ready to go out. I'm not saying I'm ready to have a party – although sometimes I am – but I'm ready to see people. Seeing is what makes restaurants special; it's like theatre. There are people interacting: some are beautiful, some not so beautiful; some old and some young; some are talking about getting a job; some are talking about getting married; some are engaged in sexual overtures. Restaurants are show businesses.

I indulge in my curiosity from afar. I want to see people in their scene but I don't always want to talk to them. I am an eavesdropper and a voyeur in restaurants – and in life. When I wrote [lauded *Esquire* article] *Frank Sinatra Has a Cold*, in the beginning there was no dialogue. I didn't talk to Frank saying, 'Hello Frank, how are you doing?' I sat back. How could I have a question for Frank Sinatra? We were in a supper club in Los Angeles. I sat across the room and saw him at the bar with two women. I was too far away to know what they were talking about but not too far away to see the gestures, how they were dressed, what he was looking at when he looked around. Frank didn't want to talk to me. If he had, I couldn't have written that article. He would have nullified it with his boredom.

I was a scene-watcher and he was a scene. I love seeing, whether in a restaurant or watching Sinatra in a studio session. I'm just an aspiring chronicler. It's what I do." — (M)

Olafur Eliasson
Artist

VENUE: Eliasson's studio, *Berlin*

1. Barley salad with celeriac and lovage
2. Steamed broccoli and roasted sunchokes
3. Broccoli salad
4. Beer bread

"When my parents divorced and I was really small, my mother fed me tinned baked beans. You can eat those white beans in tomato sauce straight out of the can with a spoon. My father was a cook on a fishing boat; my mother was alone. They were 19 when they had me and sometimes we had to do with very little, which was a good learning experience. I came to treasure a good meal – and I mean *treasure* it.

My father was a chef, my sister is a chef – she's here today – and my uncle is also a chef. If you are surrounded by people who are good at cooking you end up like me: being a bad cook. I can pan-fry a fish and cook a chicken but the truth is I don't cook a lot. I find making food stressful.

I'm more interested in fishing, agriculture and gardening – if I became more involved in food I would grow vegetables. This [a broccoli stalk] is actually a type of battery. There's solar energy in here. If I eat it, I get energised. In turn we manufacture the Little Sun [Eliasson's portable solar LED lamps]. If this really were my last meal I would be eating the sun.

I would have my last meal here in my studio with my staff and family. Eating is social; it's about the relationships you have with people and the things you do. Interdependence and consequence – cause and effect – are important. Everything we eat here is environmentally considered. It might have a carbon footprint but it's close to not having one. My kitchen thinks about this a lot. The lunches are organic, vegetarian and sometimes even vegan.

The communal lunches here allow the departments to see each other. I depend on people's commitment to the studio and the food is an opportunity to express my care for the team – and their health. We keep the flu rate low: in the winter we serve a lot of vitamin C; in December we serve more foods with vitamin D and even do anti-depression exercises.

The studio has grown a lot. We have about 80 people working here and 30 or so more on Little Sun and our architecture projects. It's taken 20 years to cultivate our idea of art as well as a sense of civic patronage and trust. For someone walking by it seems like the same atmosphere as a techie start-up but it's unique: we have 21 languages in the building; we have friends in all continents; and we're involved in projects in China, North America, South America and Africa. We take the environment seriously so we take food seriously.

What I'm focused on in art is where you can find real authenticity, real people and real responsibility. Kitchens should be about fun and good times but also about dignity, respect and inclusion. It's about being sophisticated without being arrogant or ignorant. The space between ignorance and arrogance is so small – one step and you're already in one of the two categories." — (M)

Nancy Pilcher
Australian fashion laureate and former magazine editor

VENUE: The Apollo, *Sydney*

1. Taramasalata mullet-roe dip with pitta bread
2. Oven-baked lamb shoulder, lemon and Greek yoghurt
3. Saganaki cheese with honey and oregano

"I hate tricky food that has foam on it. The food here at The Apollo is delicious because it's not tricky. The slow-cooked lamb is to die for and the taramasalata is mind-boggling. You can't book so you have to come early.

My family has always been into food. My grandfather was a German chef who moved to Pittsburgh, Pennsylvania, where I grew up. I always remember him coming to our house. He would spend a week with us and cook the most amazing dishes. But quite German: beautiful *latkes* – potato pancakes – or beef.

Before I came to Australia I'd never had a piece of lamb; in the US it was always beef or pork. My family still lives in Pittsburgh but I moved to New York and went to fashion school. That's where I met my husband: he was a waiter in a restaurant. A few years later we travelled in and around Europe in a camper van. The best food we had was spaghetti out of a can and sardines that we could find on the beach in Morocco. That was it. We never ate in restaurants and my husband used to say, 'Every restaurant we eat in is another day that you can't stay in Europe.' We had great fun.

I went back to New York then came to Australia for work in 1973. I studied to be a fashion buyer and I thought we were only going to stay in Australia for a couple of months. One day I was walking along the street with my husband and we saw a newsstand. There was a copy of *Vogue* and I said, 'There's

something wrong here: I've got the latest *Vogue*.' You know how Americans think that everything that happens is in the US. He said, 'No, there's an Australian *Vogue*.' And I thought, 'Oh, that's interesting.'

I started as a secretary for the marketing director in 1973. I worked my way up to fashion editor, executive editor to fashion director and then eventually, years later, I became the editor.

I cooked a lot when I first got married. I didn't in the US at all because I lived in New York – why cook? I went to a different restaurant every time and my husband would pay. But when I came to Australia I had more time and a house of my own. I bought editions of Elizabeth David's cookbooks and started to dive in and out.

I think eating and cooking in Australia is a pleasure because the produce is so beautiful. I don't shop in a supermarket: I go to my greengrocer, I go to my butcher, I go to all the specialist health-food shops to get different things. You can make food that tastes beautiful without having to put too much into it.

For my last meal I might cook. It might be at home, with my family. I could include close friends and I'd have it here in Sydney. This city has come into its own: food is very important. It used to be fashionable to say, 'I'm a stylist' or 'I'm a model' – but today chefs are the stylists of the world." — (M)

Yuichiro Miura
Mountaineer

VENUE: Chaco Amemiya, *Tokyo*

1. Salad of lettuce, tomato, cucumber, carrot and purple cabbage with thousand island dressing, French dressing and garlic bread
2. Boneless rib-eye and fillet steak, charcoal-grilled then served with carrots, sweetcorn, green beans and a baked potato

"I've been coming to this place for more than 10 years. Basically I love a good steak. If I come with someone else we'll usually share a rib-eye and a good bottle of wine; I can eat nearly a kilo of steak on my own. I like eating a lot and preferably with other people. We had 16 people over for New Year at our house in Hokkaido: children, grandchildren and friends.

I have climbed Everest three times now. The altitude sickness at 8,000 metres is bad and I lost 10kg in the final week the last time. I was still thinking about food though. Before the final ascent my Japanese team – which included my son [former Olympic skier] Gota – ate noodles, *mochi* [sticky rice cakes], canned sea urchin, salted squid and salmon. We even made temaki rolls from seaweed and rehydrated rice. When I came back to Japan the first thing I wanted to eat was sushi.

I come from Aomori but I've lived in Sapporo for years. The snow is great there. People call me a climber but I think of myself as a skier. Most of the time I climb mountains so I can ski down. I've been skiing since I was three; then, you had to walk to the top.

When [Edmund] Hillary and Tenzing [Norgay] climbed Everest in 1953 I was at university in Hokkaido and it made a big impression on me. I later became friends with Hillary. He said skiing down Everest was a crazy idea but that if he'd been younger he might have done the same thing.

I did so many things when I was a young man that when I hit middle age I realised I'd lost my motivation. It was my father [legendary skier Keizo Miura] who inspired me. He skied down Mont Blanc when he was 99 and for his 100th birthday we went to the Snowbird Ski Resort in Utah. One hundred and twenty friends and family came from Japan and we all skied down, with him leading the way.

I've been lucky. I was caught in an avalanche in Antarctica once and I crashed into a rock when I was skiing down Everest. I broke my pelvis and thighbone a few years ago and the doctors said I might not walk properly again but I healed quickly. I've been told I have the bone density of a 20-year-old.

My weakness is my heart. I have arrhythmia and a blocked artery. I've had seven operations but no open-heart surgery yet. I'm an optimist.

What I always say to people is that you need a goal; it doesn't matter how old you are. When I'm training in Tokyo I wear 5kg weights on each leg, carry a 25kg pack and walk for an hour or two. I also have a hypoxic chamber in my office; it can replicate the altitude at 6,000 metres.

I don't dream about climbing but if I close my eyes I can still see the final approach to the summit of Everest. Nothing beats the view from the top: it's the gateway to the universe." — (M)

Margaret Howell
Fashion designer

VENUE: The beach, *Suffolk, UK*

1. A poached kipper, caught in nearby Lowestoft and smoked locally, with brown bread and butter, cheese, a pear and fresh cafetière coffee brewed in situ

"I came here to Suffolk for a holiday when my children Miriam and Edward were young and we stayed in a pretty little cottage for a week. All the time I was daydreaming about having a cottage here, a traditional cosy one. The house I bought was designed in the 1960s by Rudy Mock – it came up for sale later, at a time when I was becoming interested in mid-century design. I bought it as a second home, from a schools inspector from Croydon, when the children were older. She [the previous owner] had good taste in furniture but it had bright-blue ceilings and geriatric handles everywhere. My son said, 'You should hang on to those, mum.'

Having a picnic up here on the coast is much more meaningful to me for my last meal than a restaurant. I'm good at making tasty picnics from the leftovers of the previous night's supper. I'm not really one for a sandwich. I take lunch to work in London as well; I'd hate to buy food every day that someone else has made. I'm not one of those people who won't cook just because it's for one. I cook a proper meal and enjoy a glass of wine with it. For this picnic I'd poach the kipper in water with a bay leaf for about five minutes. They've a very strong taste, kippers. That's why they're nice with just lemon and bread and butter. I like the simplicity of it.

We do most of our business in Japan. I've always presumed it's because of the quality of the clothes and the Englishness. The team of people there come over twice a year and our design team go there twice a year. It's through going to Japan so often that I've learnt to appreciate the simplicity of food; they'll serve just one vegetable incredibly well.

I have a smallish house in London and a smallish house here. I come up from London when I have gaps. I think that when you are away from your normal workspace you empty your head of all the everyday things you're doing and you get ideas. I do see myself as a country person, ultimately.

I was brought up in Surrey and moved to London when I was 19 to study fine art at Goldsmiths, University of London. I thought I'd never like London then. I lived with an eccentric old painter-landlord who liked having art students around. When my husband and I split up towards the end of the 1980s I moved to Lewisham [south London]. I have more friends up here than I do in London now but I don't feel ready to leave completely. I don't type and I can't do emails at work. If I was computer literate I'd be more likely to be based here.

I like to swim before breakfast though I do get numb fingers. There are tremendous waves but there's something so nice about battling against it and then finding a spot to take shelter for a picnic. When you're really hungry, that's when you appreciate the simple things." — (M)

John Simpson
Foreign correspondent and author

VENUE: J Sheekey, *London*

1. Chargrilled cuttlefish with soft polenta and red pepper
2. Fried fillet of haddock with chips and mushy peas

"My life is terribly unplanned. I do everything on the spur of the moment and long ago gave up booking restaurants in advance, so I usually wander in and hope someone will take pity on me – and they're inclined to do that here. This has a sort of 1930s or '40s touch to it and, the older I get, the more I like that period.

You can get decent fish and chips here. In 1992 I spent five months in Sarajevo during the siege; you couldn't get food, except in tiny amounts. At the Holiday Inn, where I stayed, we had one meal a day and that was very watery soup, followed by root vegetables and a small sliver of some kind of meat. And always for pudding – God knows where they got it from – a little slab of some sort of coconut chocolate. We had a rule that we couldn't talk about food but somebody always broke it, then you'd all start with your fantasies. They started out being quite elaborate but eventually I began to realise that all I wanted was fish and chips.

I spend part of my time in Paris. My wife and I have a tiny flat there and downstairs is a beautiful little restaurant. After about seven years they started to remember my name. Then President Sarkozy came to the restaurant so the prices went up. Then when Barack Obama came to Paris, Sarkozy took him there. We went about two months later, in all innocence, for the sort of Sunday lunch we've had so often; the price was £280 for three people.

My first wife and I always concentrated on having meals with our two daughters, from when they were little right through to when they were teenagers. Same with my younger son; the poor little bugger has to sit there and behave. And my wife is a very good cook, which I didn't know until some time into our marriage.

Mostly in conflict zones everything closes, so you're down to ghastly rations. I've tried to love the food in Afghanistan but I've had trouble with it. If possible, wherever I am, I prefer to try new restaurants. But I spend a lot of time in places where it's difficult to go out. In Iran – and Iraq and Lebanon too – eating can almost become a problem.

There have been some bad moments. I have this pathetic belief that I can talk my way out of anything because so far I have – but you've only got to get that wrong once. We were in a bomb explosion in Afghanistan. It was quite good, really: I undergo a lot of physiotherapy for injuries I got in 2003, one of which was that my neck got pushed rightwards out of alignment. And this more recent bombing happened on the right-hand side of the vehicle we were travelling in. The physio says it did me the world of good.

I eat out too much. It's my excuse for being overweight. But the real reason is that I'm not very disciplined. I don't like being disciplined. It's not how journalists are, is it?" — (M)

Paolo Sorrentino
Film-maker

VENUE: La Pergola, *Rome*

1. Egg gnocchi with scallops, asparagus, peas and broad beans
2. Fagottelli carbonara
3. Soya-poached fillet of beef with garlic dandelion and wasabi purée
4. Tiramisu

"On Sunday mornings my mother would cook gnocchi. From my bed I could hear her knife cutting the pasta into strips and we ate it with ragù for lunch with the whole family.

Today I love it when my wife makes pasta. Like me, she is from Naples. She comes from a family of restaurateurs and is a wonderful cook. I love dinners, I love good company but I have to say it's a recent thing. I used to be solitary and dark but my wife has forged me.

She makes a dish I like called *pesto alla trapanese*. It's not pesto but it has pine nuts. I never ask for the recipe because I truly could not care less. I am only interested in eating it. I am constantly begging for pasta but my wife is cautious because she says I am getting fat.

Everyone eats a lot if they work a lot. It depends on where you are. I remember I shot a film in the US and we were in godforsaken places so we ate terribly. When I came back my wife was shocked when she saw me. I had been away for months and I weighed almost 100 kilos. Thankfully I lost them.

On set I work while I eat but at night we go for dinner and relax. I went for dinner in Washington with Sean Penn. I was chasing him everywhere and I had to convince him to be in the film [*This Must Be the Place*, 2011]. We met at this hotel and he arrived late. When we finally ate my assistant director was translating as I didn't speak such good English and I remember this state of tension between us.

In the film he needed to be in drag and the character is quite elusive, so I had to ask him whether he understood. We had a lot to drink and then he had a strange reaction: 'Yes, I understand perfectly,' he said, and just started playing the character. That was beautiful. I remember another crazy meal with him in a hotel in New York. He was having a steak at 9 o' clock in the morning [laughs]. He drinks at night so the steak helps his metabolism.

I cook very little. I started when I moved [to Rome] some years ago. On my balcony there's a wood-burning oven so I learned to make pizza. I decided that when I age, I want to cook. It is my resolution but my wife and my kids make fun of me for it.

I was right when I said this interview would be sombre. I know we're joking but I would be really scared of my last meal. Before making *Youth* [2015] I was obsessed with mortality: how many years have I lived, how many years do I have left? It's something that seizes you.

I would share my last meal with my wife and kids and would definitely have a dessert: tiramisu. I am obsessed with sweets. With age it's got better but when I was young I was ready to kill for chocolate. My sister was beautiful and had a lot of admirers; she's in her 60s now but at that time courtship happened through chocolates. My brother and I always took the sweets she received. She would hide the chocolates but we always found them." — (M)

Alice Waters
Restaurateur and food activist

VENUE: The home of a close friend; ingredients from Union Square farmers' market, *New York*

1. Local spring greens with garlic, red-wine vinegar and olive oil vinaigrette
2. Green garlic soup with homemade chicken stock and toasted wholewheat sourdough bread
3. Asparagus drizzled with olive oil and served with boiled, freshly laid hen's eggs
4. Strawberries from Bodhitree farm

"The real roots of my love of food come from the vegetable garden that my parents had during the Second World War. They had a victory garden. I remember being sat out there in the strawberry patch, eating the berries warm off the plant. I was a very picky eater as a kid. I liked beans, corn and tomatoes and I probably liked those things because they came right out of our garden. I could see myself wanting to cook my last meal, feeling the ritual of it and wanting to be present in that way. But there's nothing like eating food cooked by somebody who knows you really well. I think my daughter could cook for me.

I always eat and cook with my friends and family so that's who I would have at the meal. I would buy the food at the nearest market and then put them to work in the kitchen. I used to love cooking at my restaurant Chez Panisse; I loved the puzzle of it and the demand to put together a menu that people are going to like. It was an intellectual stimulus for me. I still cook at home every day.

I think that the way people eat determines the way they think. Eating fast food means that your eating values are fast, cheap and easy and that you think that way. It means you want everything like that, from music, to art, to love. That's what is going on in the US. It's not only destroying natural resources and people's health but it's also destroying cultural diversity and potential.

I've never talked about health in food. I've done what I have for reasons of taste and it turns out it marries with health. We need to discover that convergence again. That's where I'm going with the idea of edible education.

Education and food go together like hand and glove. Food is a way to open up the senses and we get information through our senses. Eating with intention brings an awareness to children that is critical to understanding the world around them. I want them to fall in love with good food because then they are there for life. That is the ultimate in sustainability. I want to empower children to cook, open their eyes and their senses, and then let them choose for themselves.

I am impressed by parts of the UK as they have a history of farming and great chefs who are using the produce – and you need both. The more restaurants that depend on those little markets, the more likely that we are going to make some change. It has happened in the US in little pockets but we are such a big country. There are things happening in and around Washington. There is the Thomas Jefferson influence and we have also had Michelle Obama and her garden-planting.

We depend on nature even though we pretend we don't. It's a deeply satisfying pleasure to recognise that. Partaking in this precise moment." — (M)

4.
Essays

Thoughts on dining and drinking

Nostalgic nourishment
by Alicia Kirby

More often than not, comfort food provides a link to the flavours of childhood – so why not enjoy it in adult company or in a fancy hotel restaurant?

I.

Toast smothered in Marmite and honey, chunks of potato bobbing in leek soup, prawn tempura drenched in sweet soy *tsuyu* and yakisoba noodles sprinkled with flecks of dark-green nori. These foods weave a narrative of my childhood that was spent shuttling between England, where I went to school, and Japan, where my parents lived. These are the comfort foods that I turn to for a trip down memory lane and it is this hodgepodge of dishes from East and West that serve as happy reminders of countless family meals, gatherings and celebrations.

Serving as a gastronomical flashback to the blissful innocence of childhood, comfort foods offer a fix of nostalgia. The French have *brandade de morue* (salt-cod gratin), the English have shepherd's pie and the Japanese are no different. Infamous for a health-conscious food repertoire replete with fish and vegetables, Japan has a lesser-known bounty of stodgy and carbohydrate-laden delights that I have a particular weakness for. A far cry from its delicate *kaiseki* cuisine – a form of rarified cooking that is perceived as an impenetrable tower of spiritual and aesthetic elitism – Japanese soul food hails from the country's appealingly greasy underbelly.

Deep-fried breaded-pork tonkatsu, *karei raisu* (curry rice), *nikujaga* beef-and-potato stew, gyoza and ramen noodles are just some of the artery-clogging classics that form Japan's modern culinary lexicon. A hangover of the country's seven-year US occupation from 1945, each is a unique Japanese adaptation of Chinese and western classics and cooking techniques. Entrepreneurial military and restaurant chefs attempted to emulate the western diets of the occupying forces, influenced by the strapping physiques of American GIs who embodied affluence and modernity amid a backdrop of postwar poverty and famine. In turn, Japanese troops repatriated from colonies such as

China brought back with them a taste for Chinese noodles. Coupled with a surplus of wheat provided by the US military, these noodles became ramen, the food phenomenon we know today.

These comfort foods, which contributed to the increase in meat consumption, were created as an unconscious exercise in culinary nation branding. They were the result of the Japanese people conforming to attempts by the Meiji government, beginning in the 19th century, to westernise and therefore "enlighten" Japan. National cuisine was a cultural element that underwent a shift towards a more carnivorous and *yoshoku*-style (western) diet in the process.

My late mother was Japanese and my father is English so I grew up savouring the guilt-ridden riches of Nippon cooking – the prandial flip-side of sushi, tofu and miso soup. As a small child I remember the countless trips I would make with my grandmother as she delicately hobbled to the fishmonger in her kimono. After an indulgent (but essential) ice-cream pit-stop on the journey back, once home my job was to help her catch the straggling live prawns that would hop away in a frenzy around her overcrowded tiny kitchen, desperately trying to avoid ending up as the tempura we would eat kneeling on the tatami floor for dinner. Tempura, a recipe taken from Portuguese traders in the 16th century, was consequently tweaked to Japanese tastes and is a dish that forever keeps my long-gone grandmother close to my heart.

Currently comfort foods translate into big business and food corporations are capitalising on our collective hankering for a taste of nostalgia and the burning desire to recapture the feeling of a mother's hug on a plate. The menus of expensive hotels and restaurants around the globe have become increasingly infantilised in recent years. Gratingly twee basics such as ice-cream sundaes, chowders

and pies are on offer for grossly inflated amounts because, of course, you can't put a price on a memory.

For me, though, eating comfort food is a deeply personal affair and I simply cannot enjoy dishes imbued with the memories from my childhood in ornately designed five-star establishments where a heavy dollop of schmaltz is forced upon you. Comfort food is my vice; it is like a dirty little secret that can only be truly savoured at home, in private or in the company of a small handful of my nearest and dearest family and friends.

Unsightly, unsophisticated and largely uncolourful dishes: to me, comfort foods are the antithesis of the ferociously tweezered plates that grace the passes of the world's hippest restaurants. They are like the tattered pieces of clothing you would never be seen wearing in public but can't bear to throw away: the tracksuits that you don't admit to owning; the pockmarked Nirvana T-shirt from your youth. Comfort foods are your faithful friends when you're feeling blue; they have healing powers to mend broken hearts, put a smile on your face and ignite a warmth in your belly. They're a bit like parents or children: you love them no matter what and in times of need, it's them that you turn to for reassurance. — (M)

Alicia Kirby

A former member of the MONOCLE editorial team, Alicia is now a freelance journalist. She continuously makes a mess of her London kitchen trying to cook overambitious meals. In 2014 she had a (short-lived) stint as a commis chef at Soho's udon institution Koya Bar.

Comfort on the road

1.
For a punchy iteration of the classic chicken soup, turn to the Korean *samgyetang*.

2.
If you're looking for comfort in Naples, pasta e zucca is like a hug on a plate.

3.
A *tonkatsu* (fried pork cutlet) sandwich is one of the most effective and moreish ways of stymieing a Tokyo hangover.

Bloody locals
by Robert Bound

A seasonally changing menu of sustainably grown 'local' produce: sound familiar? Next time you go on holiday, don't be fooled by what the guidebooks tell you – regional specialities aren't always as they seem.

2.

So food became global and now these three abide: "seasonal", "sustainable" and "local". "Local" is the greatest lie. With apologies to 1 Corinthians 13:13, these are the contemporary culinary buzzwords you'll wish you'd bought the rights to, such is their border-busting ubiquity and corresponding hollowness. In terms of the produce on grocers' shelves, the words on chefs' menus and particularly the moveable feast that is the reputation of the "regional speciality" (that hoary old imposter), "local" isn't meaningless *exactly* but it is food's most disingenuously used adjective. I am recommending a way to travel and thrive precisely by mistrusting the locals.

Those lovable muggers, our never-off-TV cooks, might grab you by the eyeballs to present the Aragonese of Spain drinking cider bottled on the night of the winter solstice, or the Finns who only eat reindeer floored by shot packed with nettles and summer rain. But that's just TV. Producers in packs have scouted the region for any old crusty who maintains those most telegenic ancient traditions of animal husbandry while requiring to be art-directed toward uber-rusticality. "Trade those Diadora jogging bottoms for some breeches secured with baler twine and swap sleeping in the back of the Peugeot for a mountainside cabin and we'll put you on the box, my old son."

The tourism and the television are quite different to the truth: the local speciality isn't quite what you think it is. We have a case of "local" versus local. The former is the plate of show-food for tourists to upload to Instagram; the latter the stuff that the locals actually eat. Show me a regional culinary speciality that appears in the guides or on the dreaded bullshit aggregator that is Tripadvisor and I'll show you a casserole of spare parts, a fry-up of dubious renown and a bouillabaisse of broken promises (and bollocks and bums and hooves and eyes).

In Carcassone you can't move for cassoulet. Don't have it. Hearteningly, within the 12th-century citadel there is a kebab concession. In Marseille, every opportunistic maître d' will point you in the direction of the bouillabaisse, *bien sûr*. Avoid it like *la plage* (the beach in Marseille will show you why you shouldn't eat the bouillabaisse). Pizza, of all sorts and shapes and sizes, is the real food of the contemporary Marseillaise and it is wonderful there; fish stew of high vintage is just for the tourists. Get yourself to Chez Etienne and order a pizza *moitié-moitié* – half cheese, half anchovy – and save some room for the tentacular-spectacular fried squid for your main (a fish still fishable in the French Med). As you'll still have plenty of euros to spare, visit Le Souk, a great exponent of the other culinary elephant in the room: north African food. It is irresistible.

When you see fishermen eating mutton kebabs by the quayside you know the notion of authenticity is as tricky when it comes to food as it is when it comes to going places. When abroad, we often negotiate a menu with a sense of trepidation masquerading as adventurism. It is the same bit of inbuilt minor snobbery that makes us believe we're "travelling" rather than going on holiday. C'mon cats: they're the same.

We (I'm writing in London) aren't the only ones to have forgotten when the harvest is brought in or when strawberries should be in the shops. We might well sympathise with the shopper who feels a pang of guilt as he wipes his dirty carbon footprints all over the hallway rug on returning from the shops with Guatemalan beans, Kenyan cabbages and Peruvian blueberries.

So go *really* local. Go to Mykonos and order the hamburger that's travelled a fraction of the distance of the "local" frozen Norwegian squid; eat Italian in Tokyo (don't you feel sorry for a city of chefs constantly slicing raw fish for the rumbling tummies of a million smartphone cameras?). And the fish stew? *Bouillabaisse-moi*! — (M)

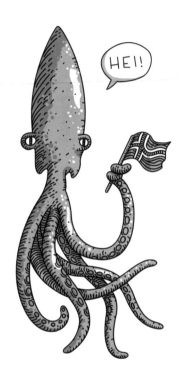

HEI!

Robert Bound

Robert is MONOCLE's Culture editor. He would like to write about food more often but, suspiciously, it keeps disappearing before his very eyes. In the kitchen, the Bound favourites begin with the letter "p": fresh peas from the pod; Jersey Royal potatoes; and most forms of plonk.

Three ways to spot an unreliable delicacy from a safe distance

1.
The Chinese restaurant rule: as in, are there any Chinese people in the Chinese restaurant? If not, neither should you be.

2.
Does the delicacy look a lot like leftovers from the rest of the menu? If so, it probably is.

3.
If the restaurant has a famous view or you have to take a lift to the entrance, don't touch it with a bargepole.

Raw ingredients
by Bill Granger

This self-taught Australian chef, businessman and restaurateur is known around the world for his no-frills restaurants and fancy-free recipes. In a rare moment of downtime, he profers some advice for aspiring restaurateurs.

3.

I've never been very good at being told what to do. It figures, then, that becoming my own boss was something that had always appealed. But, as I'm always telling my children, with great freedom comes great responsibility.

Truth be told, when I first started out I didn't really have a clue about how to run a restaurant: I was an art student who also studied architecture. But I knew that I loved cooking and I wanted to create a place that people would like so much that they'd want to come back time and again.

Cafés are a great way for beginners in hospitality to learn on the job and starting small definitely worked best for me. My first venture was a little café with just 24 seats in the Sydney suburb of Darlinghurst, which I opened in 1993, aged 23. A couple of years later I expanded to increase the covers to 36. The business gave me the opportunity to learn all the facets of the operation, from the finances and the kitchen to dealing with deliveries and waiting tables.

I was extremely lucky to have a fully supportive family. For the first few years my father lent a hand with the book-keeping and invoicing and in the early days my mother helped me get the place ready in the morning so that I was able to concentrate on my customers. Nowadays my wife and I work together and being able to share the ups and downs has been hugely beneficial. Having some kind of support network from the beginning is essential.

Restaurants are collaborative, physically demanding, highly social environments and to work in them you have to love them. My first piece of advice to anyone thinking of starting their own venture would be to dip your toe in first. Once you've gained some experience you'll find it easier to tap into the industry; those working in hospitality are usually hugely supportive of one another. Prior to opening my first place I worked part-time for a café that was only open for lunch: it may have been small-scale but the experience was invaluable.

The next important step is to recognise what type of person you are and where your talents lie. If you're a creative, bring someone in to help with the finances – a book-keeper or an accountant. Don't dream of starting without one: cash is king. Make sure you have enough money to pay the bills and yourself a wage for six months to a year, as it will take at least that long for you to start making money. Spend what you can afford to lose. If it doesn't work out, how long will it take you to pay off your debts? Whatever you do, don't think you can get by on daily cash flow.

Be prepared to put in the hours from the get-go: in the early days you'll need to eat, sleep and breathe your new business. When I opened the first Bills in my early twenties I was there six days a week, 12 hours a day, and was jumping (or crawling) out of my bed at the same ungodly hour that most of my friends were jumping (or crawling) into theirs. You need stamina and discipline and you can forget about holidays for the first year or so.

For me a good restaurant is not just about the food: it's equal parts food, environment and service. Creating a great environment doesn't have to mean spending a tonne of money. When I first started Bills in Sydney I painted the walls and sanded the floors myself, spending the little money I had on furniture and a coffee machine. It was a good investment but my parents thought I was nuts: why spend AU$400 on a chair when I could buy one for AU$100? But the big table is still going strong and the chairs continue to accommodate customers, with just the odd repair here and there.

One thing that all my favourite restaurants and cafés have in common is an owner that cares. Whether it's fresh flowers or a spotless bathroom – or preferably both – it's the little details that count. And there's nothing wrong with keeping the food simple: I recently went to a lovely café in Copenhagen that only served rye-bread toast, boiled eggs and tomato salad but it was perfect.

People – both staff and customers – are key to creating an inviting atmosphere so you have to take care of them. It can be a huge challenge to find a team you can trust to look after your "baby" so once you've found them, make sure you nurture them. When things go wrong, waiting staff who are genuine and charming towards customers can be your biggest asset.

It's rare for a new restaurant to stay exactly the same as the day it opened. Make sure there's room to move and adjust and that the fixed costs aren't too high. Customers will let you know what's working: when we first opened Bills we only served the famous ricotta pancakes on a Saturday morning but our patrons soon let us know that they wanted them to be more readily available.

One of the things I love most about restaurants is that, in a sense, they allow you to start all over again every day. I love being in a restaurant when it's busy, quiet or even empty at the beginning or end of the day. I can't imagine doing anything else. — (M)

Bill Granger

Bill is an Australian restaurateur and food writer with restaurants in Sydney, Tokyo, London, Honolulu and Seoul. He has published 11 cookbooks and writes recipe columns for magazines and newspapers worldwide. His favourite comfort food is fried rice with lots of sliced fresh chilli and a good squeeze of lime (for breakfast, lunch or dinner).

Bill's advice for budding restaurateurs

1.

Commit to a business plan: by writing it down you're more than halfway to making it happen.

2.

Love your customers: they are the reason you have a business.

3.

Nurture your team: this is a collaborative art.

Back to basics
by Josh Fehnert

Pea foam, anybody? Didn't think so. Food should be fuss-free and restaurants should be comfortable, their menus simple and their staff friendly. So no matter what the critics say, hold the jus – we'll stick to the gravy, thanks.

4.

Food is not art. Or at least, at its best it shouldn't pretend to be. Beyond a few fitting metaphors about consuming and being nourished by either, comparing the two is a dangerous game that risks misrepresenting and diminishing both. It sounds like common sense but you need only look at the libraries of books (and miles of column inches) devoted to tarting up tarts or over-egging an egg; they have turned us all into unquestioningly voracious consumers of fads that put food on a pedestal or, worse, a plinth. The tendency to label, overthink and over-style our edibles is at risk of alienating us from the thing that we're eating in the first place.

Think of the unsatisfyingly meagre portions of nouvelle cuisine or the dreadful worthiness that goes hand in hand with the foraging movement. Isn't it better to actually pay a farmer? Who wants to eat pissy nettles picked from an urban park anyway? Most disturbingly there's micro-gastronomy and the pretentious jumble of accompanying emulsions, veloutés, slimes and mists that it brings to the table. Critics and food writers seem obsessed with discussing degustation and raving about needlessly complicated tasting menus.

How much can you deconstruct a dish before it stops being the thing you ordered? How much dust, drizzle and paste can you adorn a plate with? All too often it's a finicky affair that leaves the diner hungry – and in so doing completely misses the reason that they visited in the first place.

So what's the remedy? First we must resist our instinct to treat food as art and instead acknowledge it for what it is. This isn't to say that food shouldn't be expressive like art. What – and even how – we eat betrays our culture, class and deepest predilections, after all. It represents our taste in a fundamental sense and can be a visual delight: it's pleasing to see pomegranate seeds sprinkled Jackson Pollock-style on a salad. However, the second a

decorative flower with no bearing on taste is added, things become a little more complicated. Our food stops being a simple pleasure and a matter of sustenance, simplicity and beauty to cross an invisible line and become something altogether more pretentious.

Just as surely as a dish shouldn't be treated as a canvas by highfalutin chefs, so a menu shouldn't read like a wordy novel littered with excess verbiage, adjectives and wasted phrases. Chef and restaurateur Fergus Henderson's blissfully simple dishes are rendered with a spare, wordless wonder that inspires confidence in his choices. It's a policy that other menu scribblers – sorry, authors – should look to. Keep it brief.

You shouldn't need a degree in catering (or literature) to read a menu. The addition of superfluous adjectives such as "juicy", "fresh" and "aromatic" are permissible but add little to proceedings and sometimes cover up for food that's lacking. The problem is that they're gateway phrases for the deeply unhelpful tripe that some restaurants insist on listing. Anyone for "hand-torn" pasta or a few "flame-blistered" tomatoes? These florid flourishes don't damn a dish but nor do they elevate it.

Finally, restaurants shouldn't be made up like art galleries. Too often they err on the spare side when it comes to decoration and feel all the chillier for it. Hard brick walls and polished-concrete floors make for unappealing acoustics and smack of formality. Likewise, vast glass walls, steel girders and LED lights are rarely features of our favourite places to unwind. Restaurateurs should aspire to create comfier places that impose themselves less on their diners, where lives and meals can unfold in cosy booths complete with flattering light and a few soft furnishings to dampen the din.

Also, plates should actually *be* plates, preferably with a lip to avoid spillages. Slates belong on roofs and chunks of wood are unsuitable for serving drippy burgers or chopping leafy salads.

So there are a few satisfying parallels between food and art after all: both are joyous human creations that fulfill us. Sadly though, our tendency to see the two as utterly interchangeable has led to an unappetising rise in adornment, abstraction, deconstruction, waffle and worse. Worse food, that is. — (M)

Josh Fehnert

Josh is MONOCLE's Edits editor, overseeing the magazine's coverage of food, drink and travel – plus the odd publishing project (including the one you're holding). Ever the Epicurean, he took to the task of amassing a book on the subject with gusto and particularly relished the restaurant reviews. The adage about free lunches was put to the test during the extensive editing and proofreading process but Josh is said to be regaining his appetite for food writing.

Three restaurants where simplicity is the best sell

1.
Toutant, Buffalo: Southern-style fare from upstate New York's best farms. *toutantbuffalo.com*

2.
Santa Lucia, Milan: old-school haunt presided over by white-jacketed waiters bearing Neapolitan dishes. *asantalucia.it*

3.
Stanbuli, Sydney: Turkish delights served behind a 1950s pink-and-purple façade in gritty Newtown. *stanbuli.com.au*

Table for one, sir?
by Tom Morris

Going to a restaurant by yourself is a daunting experience – and in some countries it's even considered a sign of bad luck. But order a drink and embrace it; you never know what you might learn.

5.

Eating out – or so we're told – is all about getting together, breaking bread and sharing stories. Dining has perhaps never been so sociable, especially with the glut of sharing plates and communal tables that define much of the contemporary food scene. Restaurants are not just venues at which to eat but places to gather, laugh gaily and be convivial with close pals – all the while suspiciously eyeballing the lone diner sat in the corner with a newspaper.

As early as our school days we're taught to feel sorry for the person sat eating alone. In Thailand, solo dining is actually believed to attract bad luck and although the taboo has certainly lessened over recent decades, it still exists and people go to extreme lengths to avoid eating on their lonesome. There is a Moomin-themed restaurant in Japan where you can sit across the table from a stuffed Finnish hippo to save yourself the dishonour of being seen alone. There is even an app called PlusBoys that allows you to scroll through a roster of boys that will virtually eat a bowl of noodles in front of you, chatting to you while you gobble. I'd sooner starve.

Please don't pity the solo diner in the corner of the restaurant – envy him. To many people, sitting alone in a restaurant is a punishment worse than death but I'm a firm believer in the joys of eating alone and it's something I treat myself to once every couple of weeks. Learning to love eating out alone takes time and is perhaps best practised on business trips. There is a slightly cruddy, eternally half-empty Chinese restaurant near Opéra in Paris (an underwhelming venue is, inevitably, elemental to solo dining) that I would visit regularly during fashion weeks as a young MONOCLE editor. I'd swipe a copy of the IHT from the hotel lobby and take the same table each time, pointing it out to the maître d' with the same singular index finger I'd use to show I'd be eating alone. I always found I'd feel self-conscious for about 30 seconds – mostly until a beer arrived – and then proceed

to have a whale of a time. My tastes, confidence and therefore choice of restaurant have matured over the years but the pleasure remains. Getting a bit boozy by yourself, ordering what you want and not having to share – what's not to like?

Solo diners obviously have a lot to answer for: bland chain restaurants, for starters. I'm sure their profit margins are based solely on people eating alone on a Tuesday night in a venue they find unintimidating, quick and pleasingly ordinary. Solo diners can themselves be intimidating: it's natural to feel ill at ease nattering to your mate across the table while sat next to someone eating alone. You'll be worried they are eavesdropping and of course they are – on every single word. They're probably picturing what your house looks like too, and why you're still single. Snooping is undoubtedly the finest thing about eating out alone.

Eenmaal is a restaurant in Amsterdam kitted out exclusively with tables for one. It obtusely brands itself as a place for "temporary disconnection" and discourages the use of smartphones or tablets (this is admirable: overuse of an iPhone is the rookie error of the uninitiated and nervous). Eenmaal does, however, overlook this most fundamental pleasure of being in a restaurant by yourself: the eavesdropping. If hell is other people, heaven is listening in to them at arm's length. No one wants to sit in a silent restaurant with lots of other loners; the point is to be the only one. Ideally close to at least one couple on a first date.

I have an elderly neighbour who I see night after night sitting in front of her television with a tray on her lap and a glass of wine by her side. She is of a generation that would probably feel uncomfortable having coffee by themselves on a Wednesday morning, much less a Thursday night supper in our local trattoria. Seeing someone eat by him or herself in a restaurant – especially at dinnertime – is absolutely acceptable.

It takes some balls and I admire it. Seeing someone with a TV dinner night after night is simply heartbreaking. She is probably perfectly content but imagine if we lived in a world where there was no stigma about eating out alone: I think we'd all be much happier and far more connected. Everything from meals-on-wheels to dating apps would certainly cease to exist.

So get out there. Forget about what the waiter might think and order that second glass of wine. Remind yourself you may actually look rather debonair and beguiling to those that happen to be paying you any attention. Remember that the spotlight is not on you, as much as you might feel it is. And besides, with good food you're never really alone. — (M)

Tom Morris

Tom is a London-based writer, editor and content consultant, and a contributing editor at MONOCLE. He's a whizz in the kitchen, so long as it's one of the four dishes he expertly prepares in rotation. He's useless at puddings, however – who's sober enough at the end of dinner to fuss around with a soufflé? Have a wine and an apple.

How to dine on your own like a pro

1.
Don't be fobbed off with a seat at the bar.

2.
Remember, food critics often eat alone so act the part.

3.
Avoid tapas restaurants: all those tiny dishes will quickly cover the table and you'll simply look greedy.

Covered in glory
by Sophie Grove

The humble tablecloth is an essential element of any good meal. Why? Because it's a laudable tradition that allows for audible conversation.

6.

Picture the scene: it's a Friday evening and the mood in this particular dinner spot is raucous. The vaulted concrete walls of the converted factory space hum with bonhomie. My group settles around a long trestle to peruse the menu over some suitably stiff negronis. But there's a catch: not one of us can hear a word. The clatter of cutlery, clinking glasses and chattering patrons against the hard floor, scrubbed oak tables and large windows creates a perfect din. We cup our ears, lurch across the table and leave the meal hoarse – we've been shouting all evening.

"It's called the Lombard effect," says Cambridge-based acoustician Raf Orlowski, who admits he has a "bee in his bonnet" about chic restaurants that banish all soft surfaces at the expense of conversation. "The sound bounces around and then of course people just keep raising their voices to be heard, adding to the problem."

Along with some cleverly placed acoustic panels care of Orlowski, one item can help deliver restaurateurs

(and diners) from this clattery fate: the tablecloth.

This classic starched-cotton cover is a dying species in restaurant dining rooms even though its soft, draping qualities help to catch some of those bouncing sound waves. And it's not just its sound-muting virtues that are much missed: the tablecloth is a major cultural fixture worthy of preservation.

Whether it's Basque toile, a Swiss tablecloth or Irish linen, I have a stash – boiled, steamed and pressed – ready in waiting for every culinary occasion that could possibly merit one. Because, let's face it, what drinks party is complete without a starched cocktail napkin? What light garden lunch isn't enhanced by a thick herringbone flax yarn runner from the Finnish Lapuan Kankurit? And what dinner party isn't just that little bit more elegant when swathes of crisp white antique Tuscan linen are involved?

Tablecloths are a swatch of history and tradition. I always snap up linen on my travels – it offers no better (and no more useful) memento of a trip, whether

it's to Addis Ababa or Portugal's Vale de Sousa. One recent find on a Cretan hilltop was crafted by an order of nuns and has been the centrepiece of chic tea services for generations.

The hand-embroidered *tischdecken* of Ebneter & Biel – found on St Moritz's Plazza dal Mulin – give any table arrangement a warm, intriguing tactility. Brother and sister Christian and Andrea Biel have kept this venerable business going with playful and glorious designs – think snow scenes at Christmas and grouse in autumn – guaranteed to give your guests something to talk about.

Thick cotton tablecloths that still adorn classic institutions (and kitchen tables) are a labour of love. They're a sign of a caring, restorative approach to meals – a signal that adumbrates a well-considered cuisine. They muffle clashing and clanking at the table and aid audible debate – one of the most important components of any meal – as they swaddle us in a sense of pure, white, cleanliness.

A well-set tablecloth is like a merry fire or a luxurious bath: one of life's joys, so easily marginalised by central heating, showers and wipe-down wood. Let's not let them go quietly into the good night of brittle convenience. Shake out those tablecloths at home and abroad – and let's hear ourselves talk around the table again. — (M)

Sophie Grove

Sophie is MONOCLE's senior correspondent and has travelled widely in the Middle East, Africa and central Asia, reporting on everything from foreign affairs to design. She never misses a trip to a market to stock up on ingredients for dinner parties back on home soil.

Tricks of the tablecloth trade

1.
Keep it crisp and clean, with lashings of starch.

2.
Avoid over doing it; a cloth should add character, not a Michelin formality.

3.
Draw the line at napkin art. Aim for simplicity and high-quality threads.

Fad, glorious fad
by David Sax

Coffee crafted from cat poo had a limited shelf life but the ubiquity of flat whites is enduring;
find out how the novelty of food trends invariably has a more long-lasting effect on our culinary culture.

7.

One of the main consequences of writing a book about food trends is that people will constantly ask for your thoughts on the latest new edible (and quaffable) taste sensation bubbling up at the time. We are, after all, living in the midst of a frenetic global food-and-drink obsession, accelerated by digital (and traditional) media, where every bite or sip that might grace someone's lips in this great big world must first be photographed, captioned, labelled and sent out for evaluation.

Over the past few years I have been called on to examine the meaning of trends ranging from gluten-free diets and cold-pressed juicing to edible insects, bone broths and, of course, the upscaling of every possible dessert (gourmet éclairs, bespoke ice-cream sandwiches, artisan jelly moulds and so on). Most of the time I haven't even tasted these things when I speak about their worth because when it comes to deciphering whether food trends will last, the food itself is often the least important part.

While we might associate food trends with the taste of a particular moment, or the culinary zeitgeist, often we are really just talking about short-term fads. The individual ingredient, cuisine, diet or drink in question is merely an indicator of the larger, long-term shift at play. A fashionable new sandwich (say, the hamburger served between flash-fried buns made from ramen noodles) may be visible and tangible and sold at New York's coolest farmers' market but it has a limited shelf life. It will last a season, or perhaps a bit longer, like a particular shade of denim, and then it must be consumed by the next cool sandwich to take its place.

The bigger food trend behind a fad is a manifestation of something larger. It represents a change in our collective appetite that gradually works to move us forward in the way we eat. If the latest taste is the sapling in front of our face, the larger progression of food culture that it feeds is the forest that surrounds it.

Look no further than your morning cup of coffee to see this play out. Each year someone, somewhere, figures out the next best way to extract a caffeinated drink from the coffee bean and this method spreads across the world. Over the past few years we have witnessed the rise of butter-soaked "bulletproof" coffee, coffee brewed in fragile Japanese vacuum contraptions and the addition of new qualifiers such as shade-grown, single-origin and farm-to-bean. Some of these, like the coffee harvested from the faeces of civet cats, are clearly gimmicks while others, such as the cold-brew process, have a much broader appeal.

Each new method of coffee consumption feeds the larger coffee-drinking trend, which has been evolving for some six centuries since Yemeni traders first brought coffee beans back from the highlands of Ethiopia (and our bleary eyes finally found salvation). As the coffee trend travelled it acquired new tastes and storylines, from the steam-pressed innovations of Italy's espresso to the social hub of Vienna's coffee houses, the instant grounds from the US and the more recent Starbuckification of the world, which gave us drinks such as the Frappuccino – a coffee milkshake that could not be further from those early Ethiopian brews.

The end result of all this (and perhaps the only part that really matters) is that it has led to us drinking more coffee, in many more different ways, than ever before. Coffee today is a global economic force, generating billions of dollars for everyone involved in the journey from bean to cup: farmers in Colombia and Vietnam, export brokers in Singapore, roasters in San Francisco, machine makers in Milan and baristas in Kyoto. That economic power translates into political capital, which in turn influences everything from regional trade agreements to the negotiations of Swedish labour contracts for a mandatory *fika* via the national coffee break (enjoyed, one assumes, with a fresh cinnamon bun).

Food is often our first and most welcoming port of entry for ideas and influences from elsewhere. We are more likely to sip a cappuccino, *mate*, or masala-scented chai before we even consider visiting Italy, Argentina or India. But familiarity with those flavours, brought to us by the food-and-drink trends that popularised and normalised them, opens the door to a greater curiosity about the cultures where those foods first emerged.

Food trends are ultimately ideas about how we can eat better – and this truth determines which fads eventually turn into larger trends. Even if we shake our heads at the latest, seemingly ridiculous food of the moment, we need to keep in mind that this experimentation ultimately lifts all tastes. Today you can get a decent espresso in pretty much any airport in the world and the average cup of coffee at a 7-Eleven is vastly superior to what most high-end restaurants were serving just 30 years ago. That's due, in no small part, to the stops, starts and wild ideas that coffee entrepreneurs have tried along the way (yes, even that poop coffee).

It's easy to get a consumer to try a food due to novelty, curiosity or even social pressure but the ideas that endure – and become the trends that shape the way the world eats – do so because they make us want to return to that taste. There's nothing particularly sexy or fashionable about that. It's just good eating. — (M)

David Sax
Toronto-based David is the author of two food books: *Save the Deli: In Search of Perfect Pastrami, Crusty Rye, and the Heart of the Jewish Delicatessen*; and *The Tastemakers: A Celebrity Rice Farmer, a Food Truck Lobbyist, and Other Innovators Putting Food Trends on Your Plate.*

The trends that stuck around

1.
Colourful desserts: pudding should never be serious.

2.
Farm-to-table: better ingredients always equals better food.

3.
Charcoal grilling: meat plus a fire is the original trend.

Add a pinch of the past
by Andrew Tuck

No matter how incompetent we are in the kitchen, a healthy collection of recipe books will never go amiss;
after all, they have all the right ingredients to conjure up your fondest memories.

8.

I am perhaps 10 years old and it's the summer holidays; it's raining and I am bored. I'm not naturally one to find relief in kicking a ball around the garden so my mum pulls down one of her well-used recipe books from her neatly lined-up collection. There, on page 277, is what we are after. The ingredients needed for coconut ice, next to a photograph of what we should be aiming for: layers of coconut, white-and-pink sugary glee. And, if there's time we will move on to the milk fudge too. This has turned out to be a very good day.

When my parents died some years ago one of the few things I kept was that recipe book – *The Dairy Book of Home Cookery* – which, now that I look inside, I see was published in 1968 "for the dairy industry". Going by my favourite pages, it was perhaps for the sugar industry too. I held on to the book because just turning its pages cascades me through a culinary scrapbook (and occasionally a horror show) of every childhood Christmas and every tea with relatives. Not to mention every Sunday afternoon when the washing-up from the Sunday roast gave way to the baking of cakes and biscuits for the week ahead, as the sounds of whisks and buzzing oven-timers purred and chimed with promise from the kitchen. (And yes, you can steal a shortbread as it cools its heels on the baking tray, even before it's been snowed on by glistening sugar.)

Today the buttery fingerprints left on the pages attach me to a woman who loved to cook and feed, not for show but for family; who made meals where we would all be at the table until the last drop of custard had been drained from the jug. However, those pages are also a reminder of how much the world of food has changed for the better: you really should be grateful that you are not being served a stuffed-cucumber appetiser that involves a peeled prawn being balanced precariously on a dollop of cream cheese, or settling in for a gloopy sweetcorn-and-chicken salad that has been poured over chicory leaves arranged in a circle to resemble a sunflower. Even the roast turkey looks like war rations and you just know that those Brussels sprouts are stinky and overcooked.

Yet when it comes to the cake section, all sneer is suspended. From fairy cakes to chocolate-layer cakes, Swiss rolls to cream horns, it's everything that a sweet-toothed kid could have wanted. And I was that child. There's so much icing – and so much food dye. I want it all.

Today I am about as useful in the kitchen as a melted spatula. I have rather a lot of recipe books for someone who rarely owns any of the ingredients listed in them, let alone has a bain-marie tucked away just in case a salmon lands on the counter.

But there have been moments. There's the cookbook I was given when I went to university (so many uses for a kidney bean); the TV chef's Christmas special from the year I discovered, on the big day, that I didn't even own a potato peeler; the Dean & DeLuca cookbook I was given by friends after a trip to New York and which, because it is low on pictures, has never been used at all; and the Bill Granger cookbook I got after my first stay in Sydney.

Apart from the Granger, these books have not been cracked open for years but they are not going to be parted with. Recipe books are just too good at linking us to the past; at connecting us to who we are through memories of meals both good and utterly awful, fun nights, dropped spaghetti and mistimed blunders (well, they are for me). Their memory-jolting capacity is surely why there are similar line-ups in kitchens all around the world. But excuse me, the coconut ice is calling from its tray with all its petal-pink winking allure to be eaten. I cannot wait. — (M)

Andrew Tuck

Andrew has been MONOCLE's editor since launch and while he may be a terrible cook, he makes a slightly better guest. He is skilled at opening just one more bottle of wine and will even do the washing up without being asked.

Three cookbooks worth leafing through

1.

Esquire Party Book: For Entertaining Around the Clock by *Esquire* magazine, Scotty Welch and Ronnie Welch (1965).

2.

Easy by Bill Granger (2012).

3.

The River Café Cook Book by Rose Gray and Ruth Rogers (1996).

Shake it up
by *Alice Lascelles*

If you're unnerved by the prospect of serving a homemade gin fizz to anyone other than yourself, you need to start with the basics – and it doesn't get much more basic than a glass of water.

9.

If you want to learn how to mix drinks like a pro then start by learning how to present a really appealing glass of water. Because most of the details that separate an average drink from an exceptional one are very simple.

The first thing to consider is the vessel. Much scientific energy has been expended on identifying the "correct" shape for different drinks based on their aromatic profiles but unless you're conducting a lab-standard tasting, this shouldn't concern you too much. What you really need is a glass that gives you pleasure – to look at, to hold and to touch to your lips. This will influence your experience far more than anything else.

Certainly the "right" glass isn't necessarily the most expensive one. My sprawling collection includes everything from vintage punch cups to pricey, state-of-the-art stemware. But the four models I use the most – a curvaceous 115ml coupe, a chunky rocks glass, a tall Collins and a big wine glass for ice-laden spritzes and G&Ts – are all very affordable.

It is worth giving a bit of thought to size. Most of the time people use a glass that is far too big, meaning the contents are invariably flat, warm or watery before you're even halfway down. This is particularly important when it comes to cocktails such as the martini, which should be an icy little thimble, but it goes for water too. Far better to keep it small and replenish often than slog through one big, tepid fishbowl.

Whatever the size and shape of your glass, the one thing it must be is pristine; nothing takes the shine off a drink quite like the mark of someone else's old lipstick. I'm also completely neurotic about the bilge-y smell you get from dishwashers, to the extent that I wash and polish all my glassware by hand (a process that can actually be remarkably soothing for a stinking hangover). You don't have to go that far but try to ensure every vessel is at least odour-free.

Another step that will dramatically improve almost any drink is freezing the glassware first. Just a couple of minutes in the freezer compartment will turn even the most workaday tumbler into an ice-laden chalice that looks utterly mouthwatering. If you can leave it in there for longer, even better – I always try to keep a permanent stock of glasses on cryogenic standby.

Ice is also a crucial tool in your armoury. It heightens acidity, sharpens fizz and makes flavours more crisp and vivid, so use enough to sink the *Titanic* whenever it's called for. Apply the same standards to your ice that you would to any other ingredient; it's going to infuse your drink, after all. Make it with purified water and shun anything that's spent the past few months languishing beside the lasagne at the back of the freezer. The more ice you use the slower it will melt, so pile it high. Or experiment with ice in different sizes and shapes: a giant block doesn't just melt at a slower rate than little cubes, it looks beautiful too.

Finally, don't forget the garnish; it's amazing how even a simple trim can make a glass of water (never mind a cocktail) infinitely more interesting. Instead of the usual slice of lemon try a long peel of orange zest, a spear of cucumber, a few jasmine flowers or a stick of crushed lemongrass. Mint is also wonderful in water; just give the sprig a smack between your palms to release the aromatic oils before tucking it into the glass.

If you can do all this you'll find that you've made a glass of water that doesn't just slake your thirst but appeals to all your senses. A clinking, scented, gorgeous drink that's more than the sum of its parts. Which is exactly what a cocktail should be. — (M)

Alice Lascelles

Alice writes about drinks for the *Financial Times* and is the author of *Ten Cocktails: The Art of Convivial Drinking* (published by Saltyard). She has no dietary requirements – except plenty of ice in her G&T.

Three crisp aperitifs made with soda

1.

50ml Hibiki Japanese Harmony blended whisky, 100ml soda, ice and lemon twist.

2.

50ml Campari, 100ml soda, ice and a wedge of lime.

3.

75ml Cynar, 75ml soda, ice and an orange wheel.

Getting fresh
by Dan Poole

Renounce fancy restaurants and disown your dining room: the best place to enjoy a delicious meal is out in the open air. Just steer clear of the amorous bovines.

10.

Imagine, if you will, sitting in a windowless room with bare walls to consume a slice of dry toast for breakfast. Crunch, crunch, crunch. Swallow. Silence. Crunch, crunch, crunch. Swallow. Silence.

And so on. It would be awful, wouldn't it? Senseless in every sense; deprived of the bountiful pleasures that should be derived from eating. So now, a bit like that scene in *The Matrix* where Morpheus and Neo are in an infinite white space and Morpheus makes a couple of chairs and a telly appear from nowhere, let's introduce some scenery. Those bare walls are the first to go, spinning off into the ether to be replaced by rolling verdant fields that are speckled with feral horses and crowned by misty, snow-capped mountains. And look: beneath you now are the slate tiles of a cool terrace; behind you, French windows leading into the elegant dining room of a peerless hotel.

That half-eaten piece of toast goes next, whipped out of your hand by a smiling and immaculately dressed waiter (rather handsome too, a twinkle in his eye). With the other hand he delicately places a plate of food in front of you, resplendent against the pressed white tablecloth. Two hunks of toasted granary bread are joined by avocado, a few rashers of smoked streaky bacon, cherry tomatoes and a poached egg. Coffee with that, sir? Fresh orange juice, perhaps?

A much-improved scenario. And if you close your eyes and picture yourself within it, what's the most appealing element? No, not that twinkly eyed waiter: the alfresco aspect. Granted, the contrast employed above was a pointedly stark one but you can't deny that dining outside adds a certain *je ne sais quoi* that not even the most refined restaurant interior can begin to match.

But what is it about sipping a sauvignon while a gentle breeze ruffles your hair? Why does a ploughman's lunch taste so much better when there is grass between your toes? To some extent it's psychological, of course: a sense of

freedom prevails, not least because to find yourself in such circumstances you are invariably on holiday. And perhaps there is a biological element: looking at beautiful scenery while listening to, say, a warbling bird in full voice is rewarding at the best of times, so simultaneously indulging your senses of taste, touch and smell must light up the brain like a Sydney Harbour fireworks display.

Freshness must also play a part here. For example, you have to think Guinness goes down all the sweeter in Dublin because the barrel feeding the tap that your pint is pouring out of will have spent far less time in transit between exiting the brewery and entering your gullet. Local knowledge helps too: those behind the bar have to be well versed in the ideal temperature, serving technique and head depth or they'll be found out pretty quickly and fired. There's even science to back all of this up: in 2011, boffins at the Institute of Food Technologists established, thanks to exhaustive research, that the black stuff really does taste better on the Emerald Isle. They did quantitative tests and everything. Tough gig.

While we're on the subject of consumption at source, there's also something to be said for provenance. Affluent parts of the world have become saturated by the availability of any food item from anywhere at any time of year. As such there has been a marked shift towards paying attention to where a meal has come from and, in the process, favouring producers within a reasonable radius. Allied to this social revision is the inherent sense of wellbeing that we humans must get from being close to the land (and sea) when eating; we are hunter-gatherers, after all.

So, fish and chips – featuring the catch of the day, of course – scarfed down while swinging your legs over a harbour wall: blissful. Biting into the juiciest of apples just plucked from an overgrown country-house orchard: idyllic. Eating a bloody fillet steak in

the middle of a field while surrounded by randy bulls in mating season... OK, so a controlled environment is recommended but you get the idea.

As I write, my wife and I are in the process of buying a house with a garden. Once we get past the first few years of being financially crippled, one of the things I am most looking forward to is popping down to the garden centre and buying the seeds and sundries to grow our own herbs and vegetables. Because if everything we've talked about here is essentially about re-establishing a relationship with Mother Earth, cultivating and consuming your own produce must be tantamount to crawling back into the womb and hooking up to the umbilical cord.

In the meantime, mine's a Guinness. And while we're at it, a Melton Mowbray pork pie, a Yorkshire pudding, a Cumberland sausage, a round of cheddar, an Eccles cake and a Bakewell tart. Hold the toast. — (M)

Dan Poole

Dan is MONOCLE's chief sub editor. He lives in the English county of Surrey, which doesn't have a notable regional dish. However, it does have a number of local microbreweries, which he's more than happy to support.

Words of advice for the novice alfresco diner

1.

Beware eating meringue outdoors: it could easily blow away.

2.

Tablecloth clips help if it's windy (your nan will have some).

3.

If it's raining, multiple G&Ts make you waterproof. Fact.

Mind your manners
by Lisa Markwell

Who knows better than a restaurant critic about the potential pitfalls of dining out? Read on for some insider tips for navigating the experience with class – and how to win over the waitstaff.

II.

First, a confession: I've been a restaurant critic for the better part of a decade and I've stolen the menu from almost everywhere I've eaten. My kitchen is quite literally wallpapered with them.

They are not only an *aide-mémoire* to some wonderful meals but also of the settings and the service I've experienced. It was only when I worked in a professional kitchen that I discovered that many restaurants keep notes on their customers too, the better to remember their preferences and foibles; who to make a fuss of and who is a *nightmare*.

It seems that everyone is taking notes these days. I always book anonymously and jot things down surreptitiously, while "texting the babysitter" or in the bathroom. But my life has been made easier in the past couple of years by social media joining the table.

Who's to tell who is a professional critic and who an enthusiastic blogger? Moreover, who can tell who has the greater influence? That's a thorny problem for restaurateurs but this much I've learned from eating out a lot: like any relationship, it takes work.

Let's talk about photography. It's fun to take a picture of great food and share it but when it becomes an act of "art directing" the table and standing on a chair for the correct perspective? Please. Think of the poor server trying to place the dishes and the kitchen watching their work go cold as you decide between filters. Move it along, people. Marina O'Loughlin, critic for UK newspaper *The Guardian*, posts her photographs of meals hours, often days, after she's visited (in her case, to protect her anonymity). Be more like Marina.

One thing all restaurant-goers must do immediately is complain. Only if something's wrong, obviously (nobody likes a whiner) – if the dish is not what you expected or the wine doesn't taste right. The staff would much rather fix it than suffer an online rant later, believe me. Don't be like those (OK me, once) who tell the hairdresser they love their

new style, only to go home and cry for days. However, do your research. Restaurateurs share howls of angst when asked, for instance, for vegetarian options at their steak restaurant or when people complain that there are children in establishments that have kids' menus.

They really, really want you to leave happy. I once spent 24 hours at a top restaurant to experience the reality of dealing with customers around the clock. The staff worked tirelessly to make sure no one had cause to complain, even handing out goodie bags of breakfast treats when a fire alarm interrupted service.

But at the same restaurant I saw jaw-droppingly bad behaviour. I would never have believed that anyone was ghastly enough to order cocktails, a good bottle of wine, three courses and then say they couldn't pay the bill. This particular diner was caught out by the quick-thinking maître d', who asked him to turn out his pockets (which he might have refused to do if he hadn't had that last glass). This revealed his passport, which was held by the manager until the diner returned with the cash the following day.

Be nice to the folk serving you. Clicking your fingers to attract attention is, they tell me (and I believe them), the worst. In any decent place – from the Michelin-starry in Paris to the simplest grills in San Sebastián – engagement is everything. For reasons of strategy and economy I always ask the sommelier to recommend something south of €45 to see what they come up with. They (mostly) enjoy the challenge, and the conversation. Then again I still cringe, years later, about sidling up to the front of house at New York's fabled Spotted Pig and asking for the person I thought could help me jump the queue. "He's not here," came the crisp reply. "But if you want a table, just ask."

Over the years I've got to know many restaurateurs and no-shows are one of their biggest challenges; don't book multiple places with the idea of deciding where you fancy at the last minute and

failing to alert the unlucky rejects. Ever had empty seats at a dinner party or a wedding? It stings, doesn't it?

Two of the best meals I've ever had were at The Sportsman in Kent and L'Enclume in Cumbria. Expensive, yes, but worth the journey and the bill. Tasting menus done well are things of beauty; commit fully to the experience and it's like great theatre – utterly absorbing for the hours that it lasts.

Finally, I'm forever blowing my cover by going into the kitchen to offer congratulations if the meal is terrific – and I'd strongly recommend you do the same. Not just for the chef, who probably knows, but for the unseen team making the sauces, doing the prep and washing up the dishes – it makes such a difference to them.

Next time you do, you might find a treat from the kitchen comes your way – because there's a discreet mark next to your booking, noting you as a good customer. How to be a good diner? The short answer: don't be a dick. — (M)

Turning the table; a diner's suggestions for top service

1.
Never interrupt to ask, "How's your meal?" We'll tell you.

2.
Never assume the male diner is paying the bill; this is the 21st century.

3.
Don't disappear after dessert; our last memory is the one that sticks.

Lisa Markwell
Journalist and broadcaster Lisa is the former editor of *The Independent on Sunday* in the UK. She is a restaurant critic, food writer and keen cook, whose ravioli was recently praised by the doyenne of British critics Fay Maschler, no less.

Raise a glass
by *Amy Richardson*

Most people know how to drink responsibly (or should be given the benefit of the doubt, at least) so why are cities around the world increasingly cracking down on this most sociable of pastimes? They should look to the Mediterranean for a lesson in Dionysian pleasures.

12.

One night, I was among a crowd of thousands pressed shoulder to shoulder watching the public screening of a football match in Lisbon's harbourside Praça do Comércio. After Portugal netted the winning goal and the streets erupted, we were swept out of the main square in a cacophonous wave of flag-caped, cavorting Portuguese towards the Marquês de Pombal, where the party was to kick on well into the night.

We passed kiosk bars along Avenida da Liberdade and restaurants overflowing with merrymakers; police officers benignly watched the festivities unfolding as makeshift sound systems boomed and impromptu dance parties broke out across the city's boulevards and *praças*. Young and old alike contributed to an infectious, joyful outpouring of national pride and Lisbon's public spaces were – exhilaratingly, jubilantly – just that: communal areas overtaken by folks of all ages and backgrounds as they danced, drank, belted out the national anthem and came together.

As I was jostled along, plastic cup sloshing in my hand, I realised I was caught up in the kind of atmosphere that, back home in Australia, would likely be considered one small step away from civil disobedience. It was a sobering thought.

As a former Sydneysider, I've watched as that once-great city has had all the fun stomped out of it by draconian licensing laws. Anyone wanting to open a small bar, art gallery or any other type of business that might choose to ply a glass of bubbly or two now has to jump through a mind-boggling array of hoops in order to do so. Bar-hopping late at night is now a no-no as is purchasing a bottle of wine after 22.00 because, naturally, you might be overcome with the urge to beat someone over the head with it on the way home.

The result is, of course, that many Australians – both in Sydney and elsewhere – simply stay at home. Aside for some rare exceptions, events that should be celebrated out on the streets with fellow revellers are celebrated indoors, either in private residences or in vast drinking barns where the atmosphere can be less than family-friendly.

Imagine that happening in France. How much would Paris be diminished if, in summer, you couldn't enjoy a drop of red wine with your roquefort as you picnicked along the banks of the Seine? Or picture London if you weren't allowed to venture out onto the pavement to soak up some rare rays of sun in front of a pub, pint glass in hand?

There, as in Italy, Spain and numerous other European countries, public places are enjoyed both with or without a drink (or two). And somehow, people who think that the occasion calls for a bit of a tipple manage to do it without burning down shopping malls or participating in orgies of indiscriminate violence.

Along Copenhagen's most touristic yet irrefutably gorgeous harbourside stretch, Nyhavn, a glass of beer in one of the outdoor bars will part you with more than twice the kroner that it would in other areas, and finding a table among the hordes of tourists is thirsty work. Happily, anyone who wants to can walk into a nearby shop, pick up a bottle of wine or a few Mikkellers, and settle down along the waterfront to enjoy it. The Danes' enlightened approach to public drinking has an egalitarian upshot. Areas such as these don't become purely the stomping ground of holidaymakers or those with money: they're for everyone to enjoy.

In Japan people are able to avail themselves of streetside vending machines full of Sapporo and Kirin. The Chinese are even more footloose and fancy-free: alcohol can be bought in supermarkets and corner shops at all times and consumed in most situations (including on public transport). People are trusted to behave themselves with alcohol and, by and large, they do.

It's true that some countries simply view the role of alcohol differently from others. In the US and Australia, drinking is seen as something you do to delineate a change in your day; it's a point of demarcation between your nine-to-five responsible self and your after-hours, kick-back-and-get-loose persona. In more Mediterranean climes, however, alcohol is just another part of the working day, not something to avoid until you clock off.

Europe also leads the field when it comes to recognising that a vibrant nightlife offering is a boon to both the economy and culture of a city: Amsterdam, Paris and Zürich are among those who have appointed "night mayors" to protect the interests of those individuals and businesses who don't believe a city should shut down at 22.00.

Of course, accessibility and acceptance comes with its own prickly set of problems and countries need to put in place policies to deal with issues that arise from the abuse of alcohol.

What I'm suggesting is that when a city allows its citizens to use public spaces for their intended purpose – socialising, relaxing and community-building activities – then they become truly global cities offering a high quality of life. And if those scenarios happen to include trusting people with the odd glass of wine, well then I'll drink to that. — (M)

Amy Richardson

Amy is the associate editor for MONOCLE's book series. Being Australian, she has consumed many beverages around the world but dancing in Medellín's Parque Lleras with a glass of *aguardiente* in hand remains a highlight.

Some of the most bizarre drinking laws around the world

1.

In La Paz, Bolivia it's illegal for married women to drink more than one glass of wine in a bar.

2.

Scotsmen who are found to be wearing underwear beneath their kilt may be fined two cans of beer.

3.

In Lefors, Texas, if you consume more than three sips of a beer while standing you're technically a criminal.

5.
Local
Flavours

Where best to enjoy a regional treat

Food is a universal obsession and we're privileged to be able to enjoy Turkish in Tokyo and Basque in New York. But what about the foods that are best enjoyed on home soil? National dishes (and adopted ones) betray much about a country's culture and history. Take the entrepreneurial, postwar origins of Berlin's beloved currywurst or gin's less-than-genteel reputation in 18th-century London. How did far-flung New Zealand perfect the flat white and what does pad Thai tell us about the Southeast Asian nation's sense of identity? Here's a light-hearted look at a few storied foodstuffs that speak volumes about the places that pioneered them. Many were honed by immigrants, taken up by taste leaders, bickered over by neighbours or banned by governments. So join us on a culinary world tour of the best regional dishes and where to buy them.

Bagel
New York

Brought over by migrants, it's become the
breakfast bun of the Big Apple

The "roll with a hole" has managed to become not just a
New York staple but the de facto breakfast bun of the US.
It wasn't always this way: the bagel originated in Eastern
Europe and was brought over to the city by Jewish
migrants in the late 19th and early 20th centuries. Their
establishments in the Lower East Side promoted the food;
nowadays a *schmear* of cream cheese on an everything-
bagel is about as New York as a hot dog (another import,
by the way). The fact that the kettle-boiled bread is so
good in the Big Apple is down to the water, apparently.

Three of the best

1.
Russ & Daughters
Multiple venues; russanddaughters.com

2.
Black Seed
Multiple venues; blackseedbagels.com

3.
Barney Greengrass
541 Amsterdam Avenue, Upper West Side; barneygreengrass.com

Pastel de nata
Lisbon

First created by monks, these
custardy treats are divine

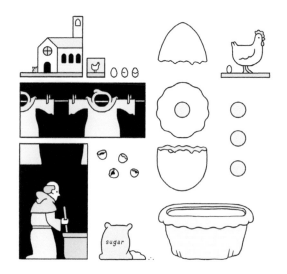

Like many treats and sweets found across Portugal, the
pastel de nata (a custard tart dusted with icing sugar
and aromatic cinnamon) was originally created by
monks. Religious orders were so prolific when it came
to inventing new confectionery that the Portuguese even
have a catch-all name for these sweets: *doces conventuais*.
The reason that monks got into the business in the first
place is down to the fact that they were using thousands
of egg whites in the starching of their habits and
found themselves with yolks aplenty to spare. With the
Portuguese colonisation of Madeira, a ready supply of
cane sugar became available, too, meaning that the best
thing to do with egg yolks was to turn them into pastries
and sweets. There is no greater pleasure than sitting
outside a café in a cobbled square in the Portuguese
capital, surrounded by the faded grandeur of the
city's old imperial edifices, sipping a strong
black *bica* (espresso) and scoffing a *pastel de nata*.

Three of the best

1.
Pastéis de Belém
84-92 Rua de Belém, Santa Maria de Belém; pasteisdebelem.pt

2.
Fábrica da Nata
62-68 Praça dos Restauradores, Bairro Alto; fabricadanata.com

3.
Pastelaria Aloma
*67 Rua Francisco Metrass, Campo de Ourique;
omelhorpasteldenatadelisboa.com*

Soba noodles
Tokyo
Rich or poor, this age-old Japanese staple is a joy to consume

Japanese farmers have been growing buckwheat, otherwise known as soba, for more than 1,500 years but it wasn't until the 16th century that the crop was used for noodles. By 1860 there were already about 4,000 *sobaya* (soba restaurants) in old Edo (Tokyo). The humble and healthy foodstuff can be eaten in many ways: in hot broth with tempura on top; with a raw egg (*tsukimi*); or with grated yam (*tororo*). Many favour the simplest style of cold noodles served with dipping sauce (*zaru*). It's also a classless delight: commuters shovel down a bowl while standing, while others prefer to eat in more refined surroundings. Soba has worked its way into the national consciousness; people traditionally hand it out to their neighbours when they move to a new house and *toshikoshi* is eaten on New Year's Eve as a culinary metaphor for longevity and long-lasting fortune. And in a cuisine with multiple noodle varieties only soba has earned the epithet as being exclusively *nihon* (Japanese).

Three of the best

1.
Kyourakutei
3-6 Shinjuku-ku, Kagurazaka; kyourakutei.com

2.
Teuchisoba Narutomi
8-18-6 Chuo-ku, Ginza; narutomi-soba.net

3.
Hosokawa
1-6-5 Sumida-ku, Kamezawa; edosoba-hosokawa.jp

Beer
Munich
The heartland of brewing, Bavaria's beers date back to the Bronze Age

The earliest evidence of beer in Bavaria can be traced back to the Bronze Age; an earthenware jug, dating from 800BC, found in a northern village suggests that Germans have long known how to make a decent brew. Today, as then, Bavaria is the heartland of beer-making. Of Germany's 1,349 breweries, almost half are based in the southeastern state. Every year in Munich the city's original institutions – including Augustiner, which was founded back in 1328 – set up tents at the legendary Oktoberfest. Some six million litres are consumed at the world's most popular folk festival, including Helles (a light lager), Weissbier (a pale wheat beer) and Radler (beer with lemonade). Over the course of more than 200 years the event has only been cancelled 24 times – primarily during wartime. It takes a lot to keep the Bavarians from their beer.

Three of the best

1.
Augustiner
Multiple venues; augustiner-braeu.de

2.
Hofbräuhaus
9 Platzl Altstadt-Lehel; hofbraeu-muenchen.de

3.
Hacker-Pschorr
Multiple venues; hacker-pschorr.com

Petiscos
Rio de Janeiro
A deep-fried delight harking back
to Rio's Portuguese past

It's fair to say a city's most ubiquitous style of drinking
venue speaks volumes about its residents' collective
personality and attitude to life. Rio has *botecos*.
You'll know a *boteco* or *botequim* (the names are
interchangeable) by several pointers: the crowds spilling
out from the open fronts onto the street outside on any
given evening; the rounds of *chope* (ice-cold frothy lager)
being handed around; and, of course, the circulating trays
laden with golden fried snacks or *petiscos*. The food is
simple and the selection is roughly the same everywhere:
small pies filled with either prawn or crab; *bolinhos de
bacalhau* (cod balls); and *pasteis* (pastry parcels filled with
either cheese or meat). The delightful finger food is a
distant cousin of tapas that accompanied the Portuguese
across to Brazil between the 16th and 19th century. The
empire may have subsided but these preprandial snacks
are tasty relics well suited to their adopted home.

Three of the best

I.
Jobi
1166B Avenue Ataulfo de Paiva, Leblon; jobibar.com.br

2.
Astor
110 Avenue Vieira Souto, Ipanema; barastor.com.br

3.
Pavão Azul
71 Rua Hilário de Gouveia, Copacabana; +55 (21) 2236 2381

Dim sum
Hong Kong
Bite-sized blue-collar buns that have
lasted the test of time

When it comes to food, China is a nation of regional
specialities. People from the north, for instance, are noodle
experts, while southerners – especially in Guangdong
province and Hong Kong – pride themselves on seafood
and dim sum. Dim sum itself is a catch-all phrase for
bite-sized hors d'oeuvres, invariably paired with *yum
cha* (literally "drinking tea"), popularised among pier
workers on Hong Kong's docks in the early 19th century.
Its popularity hasn't waned since then. Dim sum, which
means "touch the heart", is too simple a term to convey
the variety of dishes it covers; there are as many as 150
items on any given menu and about 1,000 options in total.
Dumplings, buns, wraps, noodles, puffs, tarts and puddings
can be stewed, steamed, cooked, pan-fried, deep-fried and
stir-fried. Consistency of quality, skin-to-filling ratio and
freshness are the variables that separate one dim sum spread
from another. *Har gow* (shrimp dumplings), *siu mai* (pork
filling wrapped in dough and topped with caviar), and *lau
sha bao* (buns filled with runny custard) are must tries.

Three of the best

I.
Social Place
139 Queen's Road, Central; +852 3568 9666

2.
Duen Kee
57-58 Chuen Lung Village, Route Twisk, Tsuen Wan; +852 2490 5246

3.
Sun Hing
8 Smithfield Road, Kennedy Town; +852 2816 0616

Flat white
Auckland
An Antipodean take on coffee finds perfection in the Pacific

Coffee can be contentious. Take, for instance, the much-disputed invention of the flat white – the espresso shot with steamed milk (less milk than a latte and less frothy than a cappuccino). For decades a feud has raged across the Tasman Sea about whether New Zealand or Australia can claim this popular brew. Immigrants from Europe brought espresso coffee down under following the Second World War. New Zealanders maintain that around 1986 (the date is also debated), Derek Townsend began offering cappuccinos with stretched milk (served through the drink rather than as froth on top) at DKF Café in Auckland. Although we can't vouch for the fact that the city was the birthplace of the flat white, it's certainly done more than most to perfect it. By so doing, it's added a distinctly Antipodean stamp to an Italian way of serving a delicacy that originated in Ethiopia – a cosmopolitan tale served by the cupful.

Three of the best

1.
Kokako Café (*see page 231*)
537 Great North Road, Grey Lynn; kokako.co.nz

2.
The Return of Rad
397 Mount Eden Road, Mount Eden; thereturnofrad.co.nz

3.
Eighthirty
Multiple venues; eighthirty.com

Meze
Istanbul
Plates fit for Persian princes have become a Turkish tradition

There is no consensus on the origins of meze but some say it began with Persian kings who, fearful of potential poisoners but mindful of the courtly purse, would have their food tasters dine on a multitude of minute plates – tiny samples of the meals they were planning to eat. This habit of food tasting, so the story goes, was one of many spoils of war carried back to Anatolia by the Ottoman sultans from the conflicts with the Safavids in the 16th century. This royal routine caught on among the elites of the imperial capital, Constantinople, many of whom liked a little local tipple of *raki* (anise-flavoured alcohol) with their small plates. Since Muslim law forbids alcohol, *raki*-fuelled mezes were largely the business of Istanbul's minorities, especially the Christian Greeks and Armenians; they doled out plates to the tune of accordion players in the city's lively *meyhanes* (bars). It's a tradition we're happy to say has held firm.

Three of the best

1.
Agora Meyhanesi 1890
185 Mürselpasa Caddesi, Fatih; agorameyhanesi.com

2.
Meze by Lemon Tree
83B Mesruitiyet Caddesi, Beyoglu; mezze.com.tr

3.
Jash
9 Pürtelas Hasan Efendi, Cihangir Caddesi, Beyoglu; jashistanbul.com

Pad Thai
Bangkok
The rice-noodle rallying cry for Thai nationhood

Bangkok's street-food scene is particularly vibrant and crowds gather at all manner of vendors. While the *kway teow pad Thai* – to give it its full name – is ubiquitous, the dish's etymology hints at Chinese origin. The stir-fried, rice-noodle delicacy is made with egg, fish sauce, prawns, garlic and chilli, and often served with roasted and finely chopped peanuts and a sliver of lime. Former prime minister Plaek Phibunsongkhram promoted the dish in the 1940s as an emblem of Thai nationhood in his attempts to westernise the country and distinguish its culture from that of the Chinese. While the presentation is often modest – food is usually served on plastic plates and eaten with cheap cutlery – the flavours can be exquisitely complex.

Three of the best

1.
Pad Thai Loong Pha
315 Maha Chai Road, Phra Nakhon

2.
Pad Thai Thip Samai
313 Maha Chai Road, Phra Nakhon; +66 (0)2 226 6666

3.
Blue Elephant
233 South Sathorn Road, Sathon; blueelephant.com

Ceviche
Lima
Pioneered in Peru, this citrus-cured fish dish was refined by immigrants

Nothing defines Peruvian cuisine quite like ceviche. Although variations exist throughout Latin America's coastal regions – from Chile to Ecuador – nowhere is it more celebrated than in the Peruvian capital. There is fierce debate over its origins, with suggestions that the Mochica people from northern Peru were the first to pioneer the dish, marinating raw fish in sour tropical fruits. The Spanish brought with them new ingredients like lemon and salt, while the Japanese influenced both the fine cutting of the fish and a shorter marinade time. The etymology of the word (also spelled *cebiche*) is also disputed: some suggest it comes from the Quechua word *siwichi*, meaning fresh fish, or from the Spanish *escabeche*, a marinade of vinegar – common before the advent of lemon or lime. Whatever the case, the fresh zing of fish and seafood that "cooks" in the acidity of citrus fruit, combined with a decent amount of chilli, is the de facto lunchtime dish of *limeños* and has won over the hearts of diners the world over.

Three of the best

1.
La Picantería
388 Francisco Moreno, Surquillo; picanteriasdelperu.com

2.
Al Toke Pez
886 Avenida Angamos Este, Surquillo; +51 (1)96 124 9702

3.
El Mercado
203 Hipólito Unanue, Miraflores; rafaelosterling.pe

Gelato
Rome

Italy's iconic frozen treat dates back
to ancient Rome

Calling it ice cream won't do: sure, the ingredients are similar but a slower churn and less cream distinguish Italian gelato from its sweeter cousin. Made from water, sugar and fruit pulp (or milk, eggs and sugar for all non-fruity flavours), some say the frosty treat was presaged by the ancient Romans who would store snow collected from the mountain tops and enjoy it lathered with hive-fresh honey. The recipe was refined in the 9th century when the Arabs invaded Sicily and brought *sherbeth* with them (a precursor to sorbet). Today the phenomenon feels uniquely Italian and there are about 37,000 gelaterie throughout the Bel Paese (more than half the number found throughout Europe). It may be a surprise to hear, then, that the very first such shop was set up in Paris by a Sicilian in 1686.

Three of the best

1.
Fatamorgana
Multiple venues; gelateriafatamorgana.com

2.
Otaleg
594 Viale dei Colli Portuensi; otaleg.com

3.
Gelateria Carapina
37 Via dei Chiavari; carapina.it

Currywurst
Berlin

Once popular with labourers, this postwar
fare now resonates with revellers

Currywurst has become an emblem of Berlin. It all began with Berliner Herta Heuwer, who invented the speciality in her hometown in 1949 after being given ketchup (some say Worcestershire sauce) and curry powder by British soldiers stationed there. In a fit of inspiration she mixed the ingredients together and drizzled the concoction over grilled sausages. Delighted with her creation, Heuwer began selling the so-called currywurst at a street stand on Stuttgarter Platz in occupied West Berlin, where it became a protein-heavy snack particularly popular with construction workers busy rebuilding the city. By 1959 she had patented her sauce as "Chillup" and stands started to spring up across town. According to the Nation German Meat Association, some 800 million *currywürste* are devoured in Germany every year and 63 million in Berlin alone, which is as many as 15 sausages per Berliner. If you were inclined to tie them together end to end you'd be left with a currywurst chain long enough to link Berlin to San Francisco.

Three of the best

1.
Curry 36
36 Mehringdamm, Kreuzberg; curry36.de

2.
Witty's
5 Wittenbergplatz, Schöneberg; wittys-berlin.de

3.
Konnopke's Imbiss
44 Schönhauser Allee, Prenzlauer Berg; konnopke-imbiss.de

Pho
Hanoi

Heartening broth that's best for breakfast
or as a welcome winter warmer

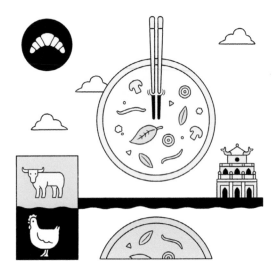

Pho first came to the boil in Hanoi during French
rule around the early 20th century. Colonial flavours
still linger in the Vietnamese capital but few leftovers
can compete with the popularity of this slow-cooked
broth served with flat rice noodles and beef or chicken.
Influences from Vietnam's south have sweetened the
taste somewhat and added extra topping ingredients but
northern purists swear by the simpler traditional recipe:
a sprinkling of herbs, a squeeze of lime juice and some
chopped chilli. The all-important broth brings out queues
of hungry pho fans, particularly at breakfast time and
during Hanoi's cold winter months. Follow the locals'
lead and leave a little soup in the bowl.

Three of the best

1.
Pho Cuong
23 Hàng Muoi, Hoàn Kiem

2.
Pho Thin
13 Lò Dúc, Hai Bà Trung

3.
Pho Suong
24B Ngõ Trung Yen, Hoàn Kiem; +84 916 197 686

Ouzo
Athens

The centuries-old spirit raised
in celebration of Greek independence

Produced across the Hellenic world, ouzo, an anise-
flavoured distilled spirit, is Greece's aperitif of choice.
It's habitually enjoyed with a splash of water and ice,
which gives the transparent liquid a milky hue. The origin
of ouzo – like its diluted form – is unclear, but some
argue it can be traced back to the 14th century and the
all-male monastic sanctuary of Mount Athos. Monks
were known to distil marc (the morass left over from the
wine-making process) and flavour it with anise. The drink
gained favour in the early 19th century during Greece's
struggles for independence from the Ottomans. Due to
its high alcohol content, ouzo is best ingested alongside
some ballast in the form of meze, and, when possible,
while sat in a warm Greek breeze by the Aegean Sea.

Three of the best

1.
Yiasemi
23 Mnisikleous Street, Plaka; yiasemi.gr

2.
Aperanto Galazio
Eastern beach, Varkiza; +30 21 0965 5951

3.
C-Lounge
27th km Athinon-Sounio Avenue; islandclubrestaurant.gr

Kimchi
Seoul
The Korean capital's best-preserved recipe is a cultural phenomenon

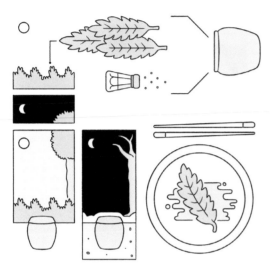

The world may be crazy for K-pop but there's another dishy, diminutive and slightly unlikely South Korean export on the rise: kimchi. The tangy, crunchy and spicy fermented-vegetable concoction is now a side dish for all settings and seasons, despite its origins as a winter substitute for fresh produce. Every autumn, many South Korean families come together to make it, pounding, mashing and rubbing cabbage, radish or cucumber in accordance with closely guarded recipes that have been passed down through the generations for centuries. Unesco added kimchi-making to its list of intangible cultural heritage in 2015. It may have a long history but residents of South Korea's beauty-conscious capital are as likely to pick up a second helping for its reputed anti-ageing properties as its place in the country's culture.

Three of the best

1.
Jungsik
11 Seolleung-ro 158-gil, Gangnamgu; jungsik.kr

2.
Poom
3F Daewon-jeongsa, Huam-dong; poomseoul.com

3.
Coreanos Kitchen
Multiple venues; coreanoskitchen.com

Schnitzel
Vienna
Born and breaded in the Austrian capital, the Vienna cutlet is the veal thing

The humble wiener schnitzel has travelled well but it's most at home in Vienna. Many myths surround the background of this golden-breaded, ideally 4mm-thick cutlet of veal. In the 1960s, amid political tensions between Austria and Italy over the disputed region of South Tyrol, claims emerged that the schnitzel was in fact stolen by the Viennese from the Italians. The story went that an Austrian field marshall called Radetzky had co-opted the recipe of the Milanese, a breaded cutlet popular in the Lombardy capital where his army was stationed during the Italian revolution. Fortunately for the Viennese, this tall tale has since been convincingly debunked. Here's where you can find true wiener schnitzel that should always be served with a wedge of lemon for an acidic kick.

Three of the best

1.
Zum Schwarzen Kameel
5 Bognergasse, Innere Stadt; kameel.at

2.
Kussmaul
12 Spittelberggasse, Laimgrube; kussmaul.at

3.
Pfarrwirt
5 Pfarrplatz, Döbling; pfarrwirt.com

Meatballs
Stockholm

Meaty mouthfuls with Ottoman roots
have been round for centuries

Knowledge of Sweden's culinary soft-power emblem – the mighty meatball – is due in part to the world's largest furniture company Ikea and the moustachioed Swedish chef from long-running US television show *The Muppets*. But Sweden can't lay complete claim to *köttbullar*, as these saucy, spherical delights are colloquially known. After spending years in exile in Turkey with the Ottomans, King Charles XII returned to his homeland in the early 18th century with insurmountable debt and a minced-meat recipe that has held strong to this day. Ask a Stockholmer for their favourite place to enjoy meatballs and they'll likely give you their mother's home address, quickly followed by a hotly debated list of open-to-the-public alternatives.

Three of the best

1.
Pelikan
40 Blekingegatan, Södermalm; pelikan.se

2.
Bakfickan
12 Jakobs Torg, Norrmalm; operakallaren.se

3.
Husmans Deli
31 Nybrogatan, Östermalm; husmansdeli.se

Paella
Valencia

Seafood speciality named for its pan
is a Mediterranean marvel

From language to landscape, Spain is diverse. Yet one ubiquitous image unites the country from the coast to the Canary Islands: paella *valenciana*. The saffron-coloured rice dish is an ancient amalgamation influenced by two occupying cultures: the Moors, who began rice cultivation in the 10th century; and the Romans, who are said to have introduced the wide, shallow pan. In fact, the word "paella" doesn't refer to the succulent mix of seafood, vegetables, rice, chicken, rabbit and, occasionally, snails swimming inside but the iron or stainless-steel pan itself. An array of different regional recipes for "pa-e-ya" (pronouncing the "L" is a no-no) reflects a patchwork of gastronomic heritage but paella *valenciana* is undoubtedly the most iconic; symbolising family, fraternity and the merry Mediterranean spirit.

Three of the best

1.
La Pepica
6 Avenida Neptuno, Poblados Maritimos; lapepica.com

2.
La Sirena
8 Carrer del Literat Azorin; +34 661 532 059

3.
Riff
18 Calle del Conde de Altea, Eixample; restaurante-riff.com

Smørrebrød
Copenhagen
Piled high on rye, this Viking fare has
invaded modern menus

The tale of Denmark's open sandwich can be traced back
to those hungry Vikings who, while seeking sustenance
for sailing and pillaging, filled their bellies with slices of
rye loaf topped with onions (using the stocky bread as a
kind of edible plate in the absence of crockery). During
the Middle Ages the humble onion topping was upgraded
to include meats and by the late 1800s smørrebrød
was a lunchtime staple for the working classes. But the
piled-high modern take, which is now copied the world
over, can be traced to Copenhagen's enterprising tavern
owners, who began enticing blue-collar workers to spend
their hard-earned kroner on more opulent takes on this
lunch on the go. A handful of these traditional taverns –
usually found in basements – are still in operation in
the capital today.

Three of the best

1.
Restaurant Schønnemann
16 Hauser Plads, København K; restaurantschonnemann.dk

2.
Aamanns Deli & Take Away *(see page 236)*
10 Oster Farimagsgade, København Ø; aamanns.dk

3.
Orangeriet
13 Kronprinsessegade, København K; restaurant-orangeriet.dk

Gin
London
Once a headache for the UK capital, this
spirit has gained its refreshing reputation

Gin arrived in London in the late 17th century from
the Netherlands (they don't call it "Dutch Courage"
for nothing) but within a matter of decades its wanton
consumption lead to serious concerns regarding its link
to criminality and destitution. Come 1751 a Gin Act was
passed in the UK to curb the sale of unlicensed liquor –
and with it an endearing duo of proselytising prints by
English artist William Hogarth. The first, called "Beer
Street", is a convivial slap-on-the-back affair depicting
happy people enjoying an English ale. The second print,
"Gin Lane", is another picture entirely. Think depictions
of madness, infanticide, depression and death. Luckily
the drink's refreshing merits have outlasted the panic
about its pitfalls and today a gin with tonic water is more
popular than ever – brewed in small batches in London
and beyond. Make ours a London Dry.

Three of the best

1.
The London Gin Club
22 Great Chapel Street, Soho; thelondonginclub.com

2.
Dukes Mayfair
Dukes Hotel, 35 St James's Place, St James's; dukeshotel.com

3.
Chiltern Firehouse
1 Chiltern Street, Marylebone; chilternfirehouse.com

PART 2.

Stocking Up

6.
Food Markets

Where to meet the freshest sellers

Markets are having a moment. For millennia they've been evocative, noisy, messy meeting points for deal-making and socialising but today these age-old institutions have taken on a more powerful social significance. They're an antidote to the impersonality of point-and-click delivery services and offer a lesson in the value of promoting provenance and sustainability (something that large chilly supermarkets should heed). Markets remind us that luxury isn't necessarily about having access to whatever you want, whenever you want it. Instead it's about the importance of what's fresh and abundant. What's more, traders and stallholders need to be authorities on the goods they tout. Today, from Madrid to Oslo, Vancouver to Sydney, markets are finding favour by sidestepping short-sighted threats from developers to become community hubs once again. For a really fresh approach to shopping it's well worth trading a backlit screen or a big-chain supermarket for something a little more meaningful.

Carriageworks Farmers Market, *Sydney*
Right side of the tracks

A colourful cornucopia of vegetables, cheese, Asian delicacies and sweet treats, Carriageworks is Sydney's finest farmers' market. It was launched in 2009 in the airy, light-flooded former Carriage and Blacksmith Workshops at the inner-city Eveleigh Rail Yards site. The rail yards closed in 1988 and sat in a state of disrepair until 2002, when the New South Wales Ministry for the Arts bought and hatched a plan for the derelict buildings. The two-hectare premises now encompass the Saturday food market (which was formerly known as Eveleigh but switched its name in 2015), a performing-arts centre, and office and gallery spaces in railway garages used in the 19th century for the construction of carriages.

As the market's creative director, Sydney chef Mike McEnearney (of No 1 Bent Street) oversees the roster of stallholders, about 70 of whom have grown or made what they are selling. At Block 11 Organics' stall, heirloom crookneck squash are sitting beside fuchsia-red breakfast radishes and ruffled bunches of *cavolo nero*. The Sorbello family from Dural, a suburb 36km northwest of the city centre, is here with colourful tomatoes in all sorts of shapes and sizes. Jordan Wimbourne from Country Valley Dairy at Picton brings tubs of award-winning yoghurt and bottles of milk; at a nearby stall, Pepe Saya sells bright-yellow butter and tangy buttermilk. And there are local chefs aplenty, including Kylie Kwong of the Billy Kwong restaurant in Potts Point who preps her signature pillowy Chinese pork buns drizzled with chilli sauce.

The hangar-like space is filled with passionate sorts. Nick Anthony of La Tartine, a bakery from Somersby on the NSW Central Coast, lives and breathes sourdough. Along with his wife Lottie and brother Mark, Anthony started selling fresh loaves of wholemeal wheat, white wheat, whole rye and spelt at the market soon after it opened. Part of their reason for having a stall is "an education thing: to teach people about how bread is made, where the flour comes from and the meaning of 'sourdough' and 'organic'", according to Anthony. The other part is about having face-to-face contact. "We use our market customers as guinea pigs when testing a new product; [we] get their feedback before we offer it to the wholesale

shops. It's nice to have that one-on-one with the consumer. We have customers asking about our little daughters who used to get up to come with us to the market [to help set up] at 03.00. They have now finished university but it's nice to have those same people still coming to buy our bread."

Just down from La Tartine you'll find another family operation: the Farmer George stand, where George Hamilton and his daughters sell fresh grass-fed lamb that they have reared at their farm in Mudgee, a town 265km northwest of Sydney. Like Anthony, for Hamilton, mingling with customers is key. "One of the main benefits of having a stall here is [being able to] earn a living using old-fashion selling methods: direct to the buyer," he says. "People get to know us, we get to know them and they come to visit the farm and to see our operation." Hamilton set up shop in the market in 2015 and the stall is now his main selling platform, although he also supplies restaurants such as Gowings Bar & Grill at the QT Sydney hotel.

Given that Australia is so vast, distances between major cities and the regions where produce is grown can be sizeable. This can make it difficult to remain faithful to the "locavore rule", which states that you should only buy produce grown within 180km, so Carriageworks has established its own way of determining a grower's sustainability practices and eco credentials. A Farmers' Market charter ensures that all stallholders safeguard a checklist of requirements. Market vendors must grow the bulk of their produce and make up the difference with goodies from a similarly sustainable farm.

The market is dedicated to upholding this standard: the management conducts unannounced farm audits in order to ensure the traceability and authenticity of what's on sale. With Carriageworks a leading light on Sydney's dynamic food scene, such measures are essential to make sure that the high level of quality expected continues to be met or exceeded. — (M)

Founded
2009

Architect
Tonkin Zulaikha Greer adapted the historic site

Why visit?
For the variety of vendors – from vegetable farmers to chefs cooking Asian delicacies – and the airy, character-filled space

When to visit
Saturday, 08.00 to 13.00

Shopping list
Hot pork buns from Kylie Kwong; oversized tomatoes from Sorbello; bread from La Tartine, which you can smother in butter from Pepe Saya; Farmer George's lamb

1, 2, 3.

As well as selling fresh produce, the markets offer ready-to-eat options for hungry shoppers

4.

Outside the Carriageworks market

5, 6, 7.

High standards are maintained regarding the vegetables and meats on sale, adhering to strict sustainability guidelines

8, 9.

The markets are as much about community as they are shopping

Granville Island Public Market, *Vancouver*
Industrial revolution

A diminutive multicoloured water taxi chugs its way from the Hornby Street jetty in Vancouver across the rippling blue expanse of False Creek. The first stop on its route is Granville Island, home to one of the most remarkable market settings in Canada. Occupying land that once serviced Vancouver's metalwork industry, the market today is bringing renewed life to the area by selling the finest produce British Columbia has to offer in its bustling halls of meat, vegetables and sweet treats.

"We meet so many interesting people throughout the day," says Natalie Zanko, store manager at Granville Island Tea Company, which was founded at the market in 1999 by husband-and-wife team Mark and Deborah Mercier. The stall is lined with handsome dark-wooden shelves, each housing a glossy black tin of tea, their contents sourced from Japan, China, India, South Africa or Brazil.

It's just one of the 50 or so permanent market stalls at Granville Island Public Market, selling everything from glistening jars of British Columbia honey and Québécois cheese to fresh loaves of bread, house-roasted coffee beans and trays of sugar-topped doughnuts. "It's always busy here," says Michael Francis, a butcher and manager at the Tenderland meat stand, which opened at the market in 1981. Nearby, colleagues are preparing some speciality sausages, made with meat including Alberta-raised beef and veal farmed outside Montréal.

Commissioned in 1915, the man-made "island" was constructed as a response to demand for more space by the city's industrialists, flush with orders for wood alongside chains, wire and metal ropes from within Vancouver's growing metalwork sector at the turn of the 20th century. By the 1960s most of Granville Island's heavy industry had moved to Vancouver's outskirts and the island became something of a "junkyard, a bit of a wreck", according to Scott Fraser, marketing and communications officer at Granville Island. "Then this strange idea of an 'urban park' came up for the island."

The plan was that dilapidated industrial buildings would be revamped as workshop spaces, art galleries, a small community theatre and a public market. "In 1979, when the market opened, the idea of going to the butcher or the fishmonger and talking to the small-business owners or even farmers had eroded," says Fraser, noting the boom of big-box supermarkets across North America at the time. "But the public market has grown and for almost 40 years it has become this heart of Vancouver's community."

Demand for space at the market is high: a stand might only become available for new sellers once every two years. And when a space does emerge, the market managers deliberate deeply about the kind of business that should fill it. "We don't want to end up with 50 bakeries or 20 florists," says Fraser. "We always want to make sure we have a vibrancy and variety."

Many of Vancouver's most recognisable food retailers got their start here and gaining a spot clearly means a lot to sellers. "We opened a second location at the University of British Columbia campus in Vancouver in early 2016," says Ashley Jongsma, owner of The Stock Market, a soup, stock and condiment maker. "But the market is a wonderful place to be."

And there's potential good news for sellers who have long coveted a stand. The departure of the Emily Carr University for Art and Design, which has inhabited former industrial buildings on Granville Island since the 1990s, means plans to expand are underway.

"The market has been in this continuous love affair with the people of Vancouver since the day it opened," says Fraser. "There's an amazing sense of ownership and they protect it. They love this place." — (M)

Founded
1979

Why visit?
It's set on a man-made island with wonderful views of Vancouver

When to visit
Every day, 09.00 to 19.00

Shopping list
Doughnuts from Lee's Donuts; Alberta prime beef from Tenderland; oil from the Vancouver Olive Oil Company; Oyama Sausage Company; Benton Brothers Fine Cheese; Granville Island Tea Company

1, 2.
Fruit and vegetables
account for a fraction
of the produce on sale

3, 4.
The market is comprised of
about 50 permanent stalls

5.
Snacks are on offer
for shoppers battered
by hunger

6.
Granville Island was
originally built to
provide more space for
Vancouver's industrialists

Mathallen, *Oslo*
Neighbourhood revival

A vast former ironworks in the Vulkan district on the banks of the Aker River hosts Oslo's Mathallen Food Hall. Opened in 2012, the steel-and-brick building stands between the affluent neighbourhoods of St Hanshaugen and Grünerløkka in what was, until recently, a forgotten stretch of the Norwegian capital. Since the turn of the millennium, property developer Aspelin Ramm has been investing in the area's revival and working on the dormant industrial site. For the Mathallen project the company turned to homegrown architecture firm LPO Arkitekter.

Taking cues from food markets in other European cities, Mathallen sports a pared-down industrial look, replete with exposed steel beams. The airy interior is sheltered by a pitched roof that features a skylight spanning the length of the building, bathing the nearly 30 businesses inside with natural light. After purchasing groceries or a cooked meal, customers can dine at one of the long bench tables.

"Our goal was to breathe life into this part of the city," says Sverre Landmark of Aspelin Ramm, while touring the building that is now home to a comprehensive selection of independent restaurateurs and producers who share a focus on quality and a sustainable approach to agriculture. There are businesses selling fresh seafood, red and white meat, cheese, fresh bread, beer, fruit and vegetables, as well as coffee.

"It's also very important to meet the shop manager, who is almost more important than the concept," says Frode Rønne Malmo, the market's manager, emphasising the importance of human relationships to the success of such businesses. "We rely on well-educated, sales-oriented staff who can inspire our customers."

Among the sellers is Annis Pølsemakeri, who sells Norwegian sausages and cured meat – all hand-prepared in the Gudbrand Valley. Elsewhere, Den Blinde Ku offers a selection of cheese while the poultry and chicken sandwiches sold by Stangeriet have been well received. Tenants have been offered low rents in return for committing to the venture for a minimum of three years.

In fact Mathallen has become one of the most attractive places in Oslo to get lunch or cocktails. "It is certainly a fantastic place to tell people about our coffee," says Gabriel Waters of independent roaster Solberg & Hansen.

Another reason that Mathallen has been drawing in the crowds is the wide array of international cuisines available. Vulkanfisk, the market's largest seafood stall, sells some of the best sushi in the city, while Hitchhiker's springy bao buns have developed a committed following.

Throughout the year, Mathallen hosts more than 100 festivals and workshops for food fans, the majority of them held on the mezzanine level. "We believe that we should be a place that inspires people to care more about food," says Malmo. Butcher Annis Pølsemakeri conducts classes on how to prepare cuts of meat from the whole animal, while chefs from Kulinarisk Akademi instruct on the finer points of making your own pasta. The Wednesday pub quiz at Smelteverket is also not to be missed. Sverre Landmark credits the market's success and survival to this mix of retail, service, events and education.

"We also often see that the most interesting stalls at Mathallen are from new generations who inherited a farm or a monger tradition from their family," he says. "They often have a desire to delve deeper into the original methods and to take part in an even larger part of the value chain than the previous generation. Luckily the customers here appreciate this way of thinking." — (M)

1

2

Founded
2012

Architect
LPO Arkitekter

Why visit?
For the freshest food from Norway's finest small producers

When to visit
Tuesday and Wednesday, 10.00 to 19.00; Thursday and Friday, 10.00 to 20.00; Saturday, 10.00 to 18.00; Sunday, 11.00 to 17.00

Shopping list
Cheese from Den Blinde Ku; salmon from Vulkanfisk; farm produce from Bondens Butikk; beef from butcher Annis Pølsemakeri

1.
Staff at Solberg & Hansen

2.
Husets is a new
interpretation of the
corner shop

3.
Mathias Steinbru,
part-owner of Von
Porat restaurant

4.
The busy floor of
Mathallen food hall

5.
Platter at Von Porat

6.
Taking a break
from shopping with
a pour-over coffee

7.
The steel-and-brick
market

8.
Friends shelter from the
cold outside

Mercado Central de Pescados, *Madrid*
Net worth

It's 03.00 on a Tuesday morning and quite possibly the quietest time of the week in the ever-busy Spanish capital. Over at MercaMadrid, the busy multi-lane tollgates tell a very different story. Perched on the city's southern edge, the sprawling complex is the final stop for hundreds of trucks, ready to offload fresh catches plucked from the Mediterranean and the Atlantic waters off the coasts of Galicia and Morocco. The nearest shoreline may be hundreds of kilometres away but this sprawling complex is one of the world's biggest seafood markets, making the landlocked Spanish capital the unlikely location for some of the finest ocean fodder in Spain.

The acrid smell inside is soon accompanied by the sight of hundreds of frenetic men, jostling on the cold, glistening concrete floor for their own prized catch of crustaceans. Stretching into the distance, the central corridor is staffed by an equally energetic army of merchants, eager to sell the pick of the net to schools of discerning fishmongers, chefs and supermarket sales reps. At 33,000 sq m, the Mercado Central de Pescados is just one of 50 buildings and warehouses that make up MercaMadrid. Built back in 1981, today it serves as the hub of fresh food in a 500km radius of more than 12 million consumers and is responsible for more than €1.3bn of trade annually.

"You have to eat fish because it's good for your health," calls out Ángel Onaindia, who is never one to miss a potential sale. Situated at the start of the central corridor, his Casa Somorrostro stall is awash with fresh fish and has a rather conspicuous (and patriotic) collection of Spanish flags suspended above them.

There are about 200 different suppliers to choose from but stalls don't shy away from their respective specialities. A sturdy man in an apron makes a show of slicing succulent tuna fillets to one side, while on the other are large crates filled with hard-shelled Spanish delicacies including razor clams, goose barnacles and periwinkles. Several small pools squirm with the multi-hued lobsters of the Atlantic, while on another corner, 59-year-old Manuel Diáz Bilbao is quietly purveying a slimy selection of octopuses. "I am very fond of the octopus," he says. "And I never eat them."

A typical workday here starts at 02.45 and ends at around 10.30. A short walk away, a separate building hosts the Interactive Fish Centre, an amusingly named educational facility catering to visiting groups of children to school them on the benefits of a healthy seafood diet. Unsurprisingly it is sponsored by the high-rolling merchants here, keen to nurture a new generation of consumers. It also gives the fish market's team of nine veterinarians (whose role as inspectors means they are often referred to as the "market police") a chance to speak to a friendlier, more receptive audience.

Back on the market floor it's 07.00 and all surfaces of metal and concrete are being hosed down. Chief ice man Agustín Sebastian has offloaded the last of his 10,000kg of ice sacks, while stall managers are on the phone putting in orders to ports around the country for the next day of trade. Meanwhile, over at the adjoining café, men and women tuck into a well-deserved lunch. "People eat paella here before the sun even comes up," says the chirpy man behind the kitchen counter. Between the customers swilling beers is 74-year-old Ángel Mozos Ramírez, who owns the Serpeska stall. It's been a good day for the veteran fish merchant but it's not over yet. As the owner of Madrid restaurant La Lonja, he understands the importance of eating fresh fish fillets and gives us a tip before continuing on his way. "Don't order fish at a restaurant on a Monday," he says with a coy smile. "This market is closed on Sundays, which means you're most likely going to get the catch from the week before." After 35 years, the message on the MercaMadrid market floor seems to be as fresh as ever. — (M)

Founded
1982

Why visit?
This landlocked seafood market is one of the world's largest and slickest such operations

When to visit
The market floor is open from 03.00 to 09.00 but you'll need permission to visit (wholesale only)

Shopping list
Squid (to make Madrid's staple crispy squid sandwich); *navajas* (razor clams); Mauritanian lobster; seafood from Mare Nostrum, one of the original stallholders

1.
Workers at the Mercado Central de Pescados

2.
The market as the sun rises

3.
Illuminated signage hangs from above

4.
Pick of the mix

5.
Ángel Mozos Ramírez with Serpeska's prize catch

6.
In a big market it helps to have a big sign

7.
Cockles and baby clams

Naschmarkt, *Vienna*
Viennese whirl

"The Belly of Vienna" stretches the length of five blocks, from central Karlsplatz to Kettenbrückengasse in the inner-city district of Mariahilf. A dashing mix of delicatessens, butchers, fishmongers and greengrocers, here you can find exotic eats such as dried Sudanese hibiscus flowers, tiny jars of glossy Ossetra caviar and fresh green papaya, as well as local offerings including quince vinegar and wild boar sourced from the forests surrounding the city.

Dating from 1790, the market was originally known as the Aschenmarkt after the ash-wood barrels in which milk was sold. But in the early 19th century the name evolved into something even more fitting: *naschen* means "to snack". In 1910, it was relocated from a spot 300 metres away in the now-trendy Freihausviertel by order of emperor Franz Josef, who wanted a rail line built to the imperial family's summer residence, Schönbrunn Palace. The monarch sent a delegation of architects to draw inspiration from markets around the world and the design for the gently curved roofs of the current buildings were modelled on an inverted ship's hull.

"Almost all the people of Vienna come to visit the Naschmarkt – it doesn't matter whether you are an artist or a lawyer," says Ronen Benaim. He has been keeping sweet teeth happy since 2009, when he established the Schoko Company hut (as the stalls are known) with a view to selling the finest Austrian chocolate. Schoko Company offers almost 300 flavours of fair-trade chocolate from Styria-based manufacturer Zotter. The most popular is the handmade range, which comes in dark, milk and white chocolate and in conventional flavours such as nougat, as well as more adventurous combinations including tequila and salt or bird's eye chilli. "The chocolates range from bizarre to classic but all of them are tasty," says Benaim.

Schoko Company sits alongside family-run businesses that have been plying their trade for generations. Fisch-Gruber, a fishmonger, is one of Naschmarkt's oldest and most venerated berths. For more than 135 years it has been selling seafood from all over the world, whether salmon from Scotland, sea bass from France or trout from Italy. Meanwhile, Martina Himmelsbach has been offering a bevy of colourful fruit and vegetables for two decades; her grandmother set up the stand 65 years ago before handing it to her mother. Several decades ago it used to stock about 80 types of fruit and vegetables but now there are more than 200 varieties.

"The best thing about Naschmarkt is the people I get to work with," says Himmelsbach. "About 90 per cent of the people who buy from me I have known for 15 or 20 years – they are somewhere in between a client and a friend. You really know them and you know what they like." And what they like is quality produce that, whenever possible, is locally sourced. In summer months Himmelsbach's goods are almost exclusively Austrian and include sweet, plump strawberries as well as white and green asparagus. In 2015 her husband opened a shop-inside-a-shop butcher that sells pork from lower Austria alongside lamb from Salzburg.

Between the huts you'll find restaurants that rank among the best in Vienna: seafood joint Nautilus is known for its lobster; Middle Eastern spot Neni for its hummus and ginger-and-pumpkin soup; and Palatschinkenkuchl for its spread of more than 40 sweet and savoury pancakes. In the evenings, friends gather in these cafés and bars to feast on the international fare and gulp down summery Aperol Spritzes to the alternating melodies of buskers and DJs.

These days about 64,000 customers a week visit the 125 permanent and 25 mobile stalls according to Marktamt, the government office that administers the city's markets. Visitor numbers peak on Saturdays when a flea market springs up on an adjoining block and bargain-hunters rummage through the eclectic assortment of old crockery, clothing, appliances and furniture before waltzing past for a feed.

In recent years the heritage-listed market has undergone an upgrade to its century-old infrastructure. The €15m project, which was completed in 2015, saw on-site facilities improved and parking spots added, though thankfully the market's old-world charm and vibrant energy have remained untouched. — (M)

1

2

Founded
1790

Architect
The architecture was commissioned by emperor Franz Josef

Why visit?
You get tasty food, vintage furniture and a glimpse of Otto Wagner's famous Majolikahaus apartment block opposite the market

When to visit
Weekdays, 06.00 to 19.30; Saturday, 06.00 to 17.00

Shopping list
Chocolates from Schoko; sea bass from Fisch-Gruber; beef from Urbanek; fruit and vegetables from Himmelsbach

3

5

4

6

8

10

7

9

1.
Radishes to relish

2.
One of Naschmarkt's greengrocers

3.
Tempting cheese and wine

4, 7, 9.
Alfresco dining options add to the market's appeal

5.
There are hundreds of varieties of fruit and vegetables to choose from

6.
'Mohnzelten': traditional filled pastries

8.
Gegenbauer vinegar shop

10.
Naschmarkt's name derives from the German word 'to snack'

Vanha Kauppahalli, *Helsinki*
Harbour bites

As Baltic-bound ferries chug through Helsinki's South Harbour, the doors of the city's portside food market open as they have most days since 1889. Plump gulls circle overhead eyeing scraps of food as traders unload vans and lug boxes of fish, bread and coffee beans from the dockside towards the filigree-framed doors of the low-slung market hall. The Vanha Kauppahalli building's long history has mirrored Finland's own. Through Russian rule, war, independence and upheaval – scarcity and prosperity – the traders here have furnished Finnish tables with produce for more than 120 years.

In February 2013, however, the doors of the old hall closed as the city reinstated the then shabby shell to its former glory. A €15m revamp later and the neo-renaissance pile in Helsinki's administrative heart is once more the focal point of a community, as well as becoming an embassy for Finland's increasingly exciting culinary offerings. Inside, intricate pinewood stalls house some 25 independent businesses. Many traders have occupied pitches here for decades but, because of the hiatus prompted by renovations, others have left. It's a turnover that's made room for new entrepreneurs to fill these shared stalls.

Anna Härö is a poster girl for this new generation. Having worked in a nearby stall for six years, the then 26-year-old took a loan from her father to secure a vacant shop in time for the market's reopening in June 2014. Here a steady stream of locals queue for seasonal game, eyeing tender cuts of moose or cold-smoked reindeer as well as the free-range poultry, beef and tender lamb on show. The market's narrow walkways meet in a high-ceilinged central atrium, which opens to reveal rafters, a corrugated roof and large windows that frame the passing ferries outside. Through a hatch behind the service counter of Story restaurant, busy chefs in neat aprons can be seen adding the finishing touches to dishes that range from traditional *kermainen lohikeitto* (creamy salmon soup) to tasty clams.

Co-founded by restaurateur Anders Westerholm – the owner of a nearby wine bar and three local sushi spots, among other ventures – Story's space adds an airy modern touch to otherwise traditional interiors. Here friends clink wine glasses at sturdy wooden tables beneath up-cycled *katiska* (fish trap) lampshades and polished pendant lamps. For many visitors the market is the first taste of the Nordic nation's storied cuisine. A few hundred metres from its door is the jetty, where holidaymakers come ashore in search of Finland's famously unusual dishes; bear pâté and smoked herring are demanded in accents from across the globe.

Long-time stallholder fishmonger E Eriksson has added a small 12-seat bistro and raw bar to its existing pitch thanks to the market's popularity. Under the glass-fronted fish counter are the mouthwatering reasons for the fifth-generation company's longevity. Delectable tranches of salt-and-sugar-cured gravlax sit next to smoked herring and peppercorn-strewn whitefish. On Mondays and Thursdays oysters arrive from France, along with prawns from Sweden and condiments such as flaky Swedish rock salt.

Although the new and resettled stallholders are taking the headlines, the facelift wouldn't have been possible without funds from city administrators. And Vanha Kauppahalli's rebirth isn't an isolated project: another market site, the 1914-built Hakaniemen Halli, is also being painstakingly renovated. "[Markets] are the heart of the city. We have sellers who have kept their stalls for generations," says Ritva Viljanen, Helsinki's deputy mayor, from the city's town hall opposite the market. "It's important to keep them while encouraging new ones." It sounds straightforward enough but it's the careful touch with which the city is honouring its culinary past that is whetting our appetite for its future. — (M)

Founded
1889

Architect
Gustaf Nyström

Why visit?
For the perfectly preserved pinewood stalls

When to visit
Monday to Saturday, 08.00 to 18.00. Also open on Sunday during summer, 10.00 to 16.00.

Shopping list
Salmon soup from Story; *vendace* (breaded fish) from E Eriksson; meat from Anna Härö's butcher's shop

1.
Barista at Robert's coffee

2.
Neo-renaissance Vanha Kauppahalli building

3.
Pinewood market stalls

4.
Kaarina Petäjä at the Vegetaari smoothie stall

5.
One of Vanha Kauppahalli's choice dining options

6.
Olli Andström showing off a box of Baltic herring

7.
Enjoying a drink at Story

8.
Sharing a coffee and a view of the harbour

Maltby Street Market, *London*
Word of mouth

Compared to London's more seasoned food markets, including Borough and Broadway, Maltby Street is a fledgling. But since opening in 2011, this unique pint-sized strip of vendors has acquired a reputation as one of the city's more interesting and appetising street-food offerings.

It all started with a handful of renegade traders who splintered away from south London's Borough Market in an attempt to escape restoration works. They began selling their fresh produce on Saturdays from within storage spaces under Bermondsey's tumbledown railway arches, just south of the Thames. Far from a transport hub and hidden from the main thoroughfare, this breakaway faction gradually won a devoted following of neighbouring residents.

As word spread, the market gained traction and in 2013 local businessman Adrian Amos stepped in to manage the market alongside his antique-furniture company Lassco. Amos enlisted the help of food writer Rachel McCormack to establish Maltby Street as London's clandestine darling of street food. Now, every weekend 30 traders pitch their stands among the lumberyard salvage and vintage furniture of Amos's antiques warehouse Lassco Ropewalk. "Adrian was and is the master of strategy," says Eddie Ruffett, a long-time trader and owner of food stand Waffle On. "He's an old fox, very clever, but he's an elusive character; sometimes you think he's merely a mirage."

But as many stallholders like Ruffett attest, it's Amos's elusiveness and reliance on word-of-mouth marketing that have helped solidify the distinctive character of Maltby Street Market. The quality of the food and furtive branding approach are key to its high standing among food-and-drink enthusiasts. Business owners such as Ruffett now serve more than 300 portions every Saturday and about 250 on Sundays. But management refuses to let even the most veteran of vendors rest on their laurels.

"It's all about the product," says market manager Theo-Lee Houston. "I want to mix the new and the old because there's a lot the new ones can learn from old-timers, but at the same time, the newcomers keep everyone on their toes."

Along a 100-metre strip some of the UK's best produce is on offer, from Dorset-caught crab, lobster and scallops at Keith Bagley's Market Gourmet champagne-and-shellfish bar to London-distilled tipples by Little Bird. Customer-turned-trader Alexander Pashby is also on hand serving hand-cut triple-cooked chips with grass-fed British beef from Islington-based butcher Turner and George. "The reason I love this market is the atmosphere," says Pashby as he watches over his staff tending the charcoal barbecue at The Beefsteaks stand. "It's partly to do with the space, the fact that it's long and thin with these high sides," he says, sweeping a hand skyward as a train rattles along the rail arches overhead. "And it's partly to do with the traders: you don't get this collection of traders anywhere else."

Manager Houston says most of the familiar faces all live within a 2km radius. "The following in the area is amazing; our customers all feel part of the Maltby Street Market community," he says. This fortified sense of community is palpable when walking the narrow laneway.

Illustrating this distinctive atmosphere is a scene involving a tussle with money beneath the arch where chef Grant Hawthorne has pitched his African Volcano stand. Longstanding customers are making futile attempts to pay for their grilled prawns and towering pile of pulled pork, both topped with Hawthorne's signature Mozambique-inspired peri-peri sauce. But Hawthorne refuses their money, insisting the couple's continuing support is remuneration enough.

"We do get quite a few tourists but we have a lot of regulars," says Hawthorne as he waves goodbye to the couple, who have left with a few extra chicken wings in hand. "These are people who have been coming here for years and what's really great is seeing our regular customers bring their partners to us. Then their parents, then their grandparents." In a previous life Hawthorne was head chef at multiple acclaimed restaurants but went out on his own to trade beneath the awning of flags flying above the market. "People are now taking their parents for lunch in a market," he says. "It's heartwarming." — (M)

1

Founded
2011

Why visit?
To eat top-notch street food while surrounded by vintage furniture

When to visit
Saturday, 09.00 to 16.00; Sunday, 11.00 to 16.00

Shopping list
Peri-peri-seasoning rub from African Volcano; butter-poached lobster in a brioche bun from Market Gourmet; Eddie Ruffett's Waffle On stand; The Beefsteaks for melt-in-your-mouth British beef

2

3

4

5

6

8

1.

There's a 'healthy' mix of sweet and savoury here

2.

The Sub Cult, offering sandwiches and sides

3.

Little Bird's gin

4.

Street food at its finest

5.

Maltby Street Market

6.

The Cheese Truck is a market regular

7.

Underneath the arches

8.

Ice-cream seller

9, 10.

Well-deserved drinks

7

9

10

Grand Central Market, *Los Angeles*
Stepping up

Los Angeles has always been a city of divergent neighbourhoods. From the Hollywood Hills set peering down on the city to the beach bums at sea level milling about Venice, it wasn't long ago that Angelenos were deemed to only mingle within a close-knit work and social circle. As for the notion of heading Downtown? That was simply out of the question.

Today's LA is proving that those preconceptions no longer ring true. And Downtown – which for decades fought underinvestment and disinterest from the rest of the city – is being reborn. Perhaps no other business best marks how far the area has come than Grand Central Market, a vast open-plan covered food hall featuring some 40 vendors that dates back to 1917. "We think of this as the heart of Downtown," says Christophe Farber, the market's director of business development, as he sips a brew from G&B Coffee, one of the newer establishments to have joined Grand Central's ranks.

Walking into the open-sided building means being hit by multiple sensory stimuli. First there is the audible buzz of people swarming down the market's flanks, sitting down at tables to eat or taking a pew on a bar stool. Then there are the vendors themselves, the majority of them little bars and restaurants; mini empires of international cuisine. Alongside the unique smells wafting from each place, stalls also have their own neon signs, one of the rules established by the market. "Every tenant has to have one," explains Farber. "Luckily in LA we have such an incredible group of talented artists." On show is everything from the towering mermaid outline of Mexican ceviche and seafood joint La Tostadería to the simple but effective white-glow sign of Sticky Rice, written in English and Thai.

The picture didn't always look this good. Skipping back to the financial crisis of 2008, Farber says Grand Central was "a skeleton of itself" that was at risk of going out of business. A managerial decision was made to overhaul the tenant list from the then Latino-dominated fodder to "super high-quality, locally sourced, artisanal" offerings. Farber is keen to point out that this didn't signal the evil clutches of gentrification pushing out long-established vendors – and the best "legacy" vendors have survived.

Indeed, wandering around the market today there not only seems to be a refreshing co-existence between old and new but also a genuine sense of community.

"I think the heritage vendors actually stepped up their game so we could play along," says Reed Herrick, executive chef and owner at DTLA Cheese and Kitchen, famed for its grilled sandwiches. "I think everyone is kind of pushing forward [together]." Sarah Hymanson, who recently moved from New York where she was sous-chef at Brooklyn's Glasserie restaurant, echoes the feeling. She now co-owns Madcapra, a stall serving the tastiest falafel sandwiches you're likely to find in LA, alongside salads and other Middle Eastern-inspired fare. "I love the history of the market, I love the diversity of the market, I love the camaraderie," she says, adding that it helped to give her a built-in network of food contacts, which she would have been hard-pressed to find elsewhere.

However, recently arrived tenants don't dominate Grand Central Market. Over at one end of the hall, China Café is struggling to keep up with its lunchtime covers; there isn't an empty chair at the restaurant's bar. It's the second oldest establishment in the market, dating from 1959, and has changed little over the years. The menu signage – like the food – is unashamedly old school and "only the prices are a little bit different" to the early days, according to grinning owner Rinco Cheung as he serves a steaming bowl of wonton soup.

Grand Central has plenty of stories, from Fernando Villagomez, who took a punt and opened sophisticated seafood joint La Tostadería alongside his original *carnitas* stall, to the slightly unsavoury-sounding Eggslut, a breakfast seller that is causing queues snaking around the block. "The city is really becoming a wonderful place to live in," says Reed Herrick, slicing into a large chunk of one of his cheeses. And with Grand Central Market continuing to produce everything from traditional Salvadoran *pupusa* (tortillas stuffed with meat and cheese) to cold-brew coffee, only a fool would disagree. — (M)

Founded
1917

Architect
John B Parkinson
(designed in 1896)

Why visit?
For a snapshot of Los Angeles at its diverse best and a place where gentrification can work, co-existing with the past

When to visit
Every day, 08.00 to 22.00

Shopping list
Four Pillars rare dry gin from Courage & Craft; *beurre de baratte* from DTLA Cheese; a choice of Mexican *moles* from Chiles Secos; La Tostaderia for its fresh and spicy ceviche; Madcapra for its green falafel sandwich

1.

Mexican food at Tacos Tumbras a Tomas

2.

Belcampo Meat Co sign

3.

Avocado toast at DTLA Cheese and Kitchen

4.

Spoilt for choice in LA

5.

Happy staff at Mexican-food vendor Villa Moreliana

6.

Thai lunch at Sticky Rice

7.

Cheese wheels at DTLA

8.

Berlin Currywurst has a few stools but is meant for on-the-go eating

Fukuoka Fish Market, *Fukuoka*
Race against time

Hours before most residents in Fukuoka in southwestern Japan sit down to breakfast, the Fukuoka Central Wholesale Market's fish auctions and wholesale brokers will sort and sell 275,600kg of sea specimen, from mackerel and pike conger to bigfin reef squid, sea urchin and much more.

The early start for the market, at a downtown wharf facing Hakata Bay, ensures that fish brought by boats, lorries and late-night flights from around the country can be served and sold hours later at sushi counters and supermarkets in Fukuoka and nearby cities. Diners would accept no less. "Traditionally in Fukuoka if the fish wasn't served raw it wasn't considered fish," says Masahiro Nishiyori, director of the fish market in the Nagahama district. "The sashimi culture here is the reason everything has to be so fresh."

It also explains the market's frenetic pace. For 283 days a year, it's a race against the clock: as the fish begin trickling in around 21.00, they are sorted by type and size, divided into wooden crates and Styrofoam boxes, covered with ice and lined up on the concrete floor for the 03.00 start of the wholesale auctions. About two hours later the floor has cleared and the 43 brokers who have bid for their share of the day's catch are doing a brisk business with hundreds of buyers from supermarkets and chefs from traditional *ryotei* restaurants, sushi bars and *izakaya* gastropubs.

Fukuoka had Japan's first centralised fish market back in the late 19th century. Today the market – built by the city at its current site in 1955 and upgraded between the 1990s and 2000s – is spread across 120,000 sq m of docks, warehouses, freezers and refrigerators. In a year, Fukuoka's 82,000 tonnes of fresh, farmed, frozen, dried and processed seafood translates to ¥48bn (€400m) of trade.

More than 300 types of sea creatures pass through the market but Fukuoka's speciality is what Japanese call *aomono*: amberjack, mackerel, sardines, Pacific saury and other fish with oily, blue-tinted skin. They account for half of the market's fresh fish (and even more during the year-end holidays); most is netted within a few hundred kilometres of the southwestern island of Kyushu and brought directly by fishing boats or by lorries from 30 other ports across the prefecture.

The *serinin* (auctioneers) are the market's resident fish experts and Hidenori Tominaga, who wears the white cap of his post, ranks among the most seasoned. During a career spanning three decades, he has learned to identify any fish at a glance. Knowing a sea bream from a sea bass is as important as being able to tell when the fish is at its plumpest. "The more fat a fish has, the higher the price," says Tominaga of Fukuoka Chuo Uoichiba, one of the market's two auction houses. He spends a moment inspecting the fatty section near a dorsal fin before he's calling out prices to 30 brokers surrounding him, while an assistant with a clipboard jots down who is buying and for how much.

Lately, as fish consumption in Japan has declined, market brokers have looked overseas to make up for shrinking sales at home. Yasuo Ogiwara, who heads broker Matsumo, is now sending amberjack and bluefin tuna directly to customers in Hong Kong, while others are exporting to Jakarta, Dubai and Atlanta. "Location is our biggest advantage," says Ogiwara. "We can put fish on the early flights out of Fukuoka airport and it will reach other regional cities in time for dinner."

Fukuoka officials have been exploring ways to encourage Japanese consumers to eat more fish. Since 2008, the market has opened its doors to the public one Saturday a month, with cooking demonstrations and workshops on proper filleting techniques. "The brokers prepare boxes of fish that you would rarely see on supermarket shelves and usually more than 10,000 people turn up," says market director Nishiyori. After decades of conducting their business behind closed doors, the market's opening up appears to be paying off. — (M)

Founded
1955

Why visit?
It's a chance to see one of Japan's sushi capitals

When to visit
Tours are available for the 03.00 auctions or for the entire market from 09.00 to 15.00. The market opens to the public on 'Residents Day' once a month

Shopping list
Aomono fish caught in nearby waters (mackerel, Pacific saury, Japanese anchovy, herring and sardines); rosy sea bass, also known as blackthroat seaperch

1.
Freshness is guaranteed

2.
The boats arrive with the day's catch

3.
Workers must race to move the seafood quickly

4.
Hundreds of thousands of kilos of fish are sold here

5.
Keeping things on ice

6.
Boats unload their catch

7.
One of the market's veteran auctioneers

8.
Motorised flatbed carts

9.
Wholesale brokers claim their fish with paper slips

10.
Boats must offload and sort their catch in the small hours

7.
Food Retailers

Where to shop

Food shops are a pleasure to peruse but we don't always grasp
their importance. The best ones help small-scale producers
reach sellers, sustain age-old brands and offer visitors a vital
opportunity to enjoy, savour and select goods they may not
have otherwise encountered. They also anchor communities.
A thoughtful independent – of any size – can be a remedy to
the big-brand supermarket drudgery of ever-fresh ingredients
and perfect-looking (but often tasteless) produce that's travelled
halfway around the world before hitting your plate. By contrast,
our selection – from butchers and vintners to a knife shop and
cheesemonger – are toothsome touchstones for all that retail can
offer. They're businesses that thrive on human interaction, the
care taken by their proprietors and the quality of their products.
A decent food shop is a simple sell so here are some favourites.

General Store, *London*
Community service

"We decided to position our lives around food," says Merlin Jones, who co-founded General Store with his wife Genevieve Schiffenhaus (*both pictured*) in 2012. After quitting their jobs, the pair spent a year learning to make cheese and bake bread before starting the independent shop in Peckham, a now-thriving pocket of southeast London. "We opened the shop to bring our appreciation and experience of food production into a retail environment," says Jones.

The seasonal offerings lining the shelves are mostly sourced from the UK and Europe and are chosen with accessibility in mind. "We want people to be able to cook a meal with what they buy," says Schiffenhaus. Some products – such as smoked fish from north London's Hansen & Lydersen – have a short journey to the shop; others, including the hazelnut chocolate spread from Piedmont, have further to travel. And with each passing year, Jones and Schiffenhaus put more time into finding standout items. "This process really takes patience," says Jones.

Yet the best thing about running the shop, according to Jones, is getting to know people in the neighbourhood. "The vast majority of our customers reside locally and are repeat weekly customers; they are our lifeblood." — (M)

Open
Wednesday to Sunday

Contact
174 Bellenden Road
+44 (0)20 7642 2129
generalsto.re

Go for
La Grotta ice cream
Rollright cheese from Oxfordshire
Bray's Cottage pork pie
Piedmontese hazelnut chocolate spread

Loblaws, *Toronto*
Big player

Maple Leafs Garden (MLG) is a Toronto landmark. Built in 1931, it was the home of the Toronto Maple Leafs ice-hockey team until 1999. The Loblaws chain bought the building in 2004 and launched a supermarket in it seven years later.

The reopened MLG hints at its past life: a blue maple-leaf-shaped installation assembled from old spectator seats adorns the entrance and if you head down aisle 25, you'll notice a red circle on the floor marking the centre of the former ice rink.

Billing itself – in somewhat grandiose terms – as "food's greatest stage", the vast shop presents its produce with dramatic flair. There's a wall of cheese more than five metres high and an open prep-kitchen. Employees frenetically slice prosciutto and rush to serve lattes, fresh juice and sushi.

But much of Loblaws' success is down to its personal touch. Smiling staff are always on hand to help and instead of fluorescent overheads, warm lighting feels as if it reduces the cavernous shop to a more human scale.

The sunny hues of the brand's colours – orange and red – are everywhere: on the floors, the striped uniforms and the trolleys. They are an emblem of executive chairman Galen G Weston's optimistic forecast: "The world is headed to small stores and we recognise the trend. But there's a place, if done the right way, for a large market-like urban store." — (M)

Open
Every day

Contact
60 Carlton Street
+1 416 593 6154
loblaws.ca

Go for
Bleu Bénédictin
cheese from Quebec
President's Choice
chocolate chip cookies
(the Loblaws' house brand)
Freshly baked bread
from Ace Bakery

Épicerie Générale, *Paris*
Banana-free zone

Following the success of its first shop and café in Paris's 7th arrondissement, Épicerie Générale opened a second outpost in South Pigalle in 2014. For founders and Marseille natives Maud Zilnyk and Lucio Hornero it was important to sell organic and ethically sourced food. So, before opening, they toured France to find the best.

"We like Italian and Spanish food but wanted to support small French producers because they are slowly disappearing," says Zilnyk. "You'll never find a banana at Épicerie Générale." Instead you'll find some of the best organic produce from across the country, sourced primarily from farmers who use environmentally sustainable practices.

The team continues to travel the countryside, visiting makers and searching for new or forgotten flavours and unusual larders. "Meeting farmers and producers is an essential component of the Épicerie Générale DNA," says Zilnyk. "It allows us to genuinely know our products and serve our customers better."

The farmers and producers are also regularly invited to Paris to present their products in store and meet customers. Aside from the loyal following of nearby residents, Épicerie Générale also counts fashion heavyweights such as Hermès, Maison Michel and APC as regular customers. — (M)

Open
Monday to Saturday

Contact
43 Rue de Verneuil
+33 (0)1 4260 5178
epiceriegenerale.fr

Go for
Ham from Cahors
La Ferme de Gratte Semelle
olive oil from Tarascon

Victor Churchill, *Sydney*
Rare find

Father-and-son team Victor and Anthony Puharich say they drew on the designs and atmosphere of traditional European butchers shops when creating this institution on Sydney's tree-lined Queen Street. In fact their shop – which dates back to 1876 – is more like a Champs-Élysées high-fashion emporium in its sense of theatre and panache.

The fit-out by Michael McCann from interiors studio Dreamtime Australia does more than showcase the meat on offer: it employs humour and more than a few dramatic flourishes. Inside, shoppers will find a full Himalayan rock-salt wall, speciality cuts parading on an installation of cog gears and a flock of wall-mounted CCTV cameras pointed at a juicy joint.

None of this flair distracts from the meat itself, which is the first and last act. High-grade Wagyu, dry-aged premium Black Angus and rare-breed Kurobuta Berkshire pork are just some of the fine cuts available. The attentive staff take time to talk customers through a purchase, helping them pick the perfect pork chop for their dish.

Like any good butchers, Victor Churchill also offers freshly made meals; French chef Romeo Baudouin looks after the array of sauces, condiments, terrines and charcuterie on sale. When a picnic in nearby Centennial Park is in order, Sydneysiders grab some of his gastronomic delights, including braised beef cheeks, rabbit casserole and coq au vin. — (M)

Open
Every day

Contact
132 Queen Street,
Woollahra
+61 2 9328 0402
victorchurchill.com

Go for
Rangers Valley Black
Angus sirloin
Kurobuta rare-breed
pork cutlets
Pasture-fed beef sausages

Kama Asa Shoten, *Tokyo*
Sharp trade

Based in Tokyo's restaurant-supply district Kappabashi, Kama Asa Shoten has been designing kitchen tools for and supplying them to the catering industry since 1908. When Daisuke Kumazawa succeeded his father in 2004, the focus of the shop was still business-to-business. But with Japan's economy stagnating and the dining sector in a rut, Kumazawa worried that the business wasn't sustainable.

In 2011 he hired Eight Branding Design's Akihiro Nishizawa to help with a makeover. He got rid of the cluttered shelves, retrained his staff and created displays featuring the Japanese artisans who handcraft pots and pans and many of the shop's collection of 1,000 knives. The product line-up didn't change but Kumazawa made boxes for items that had never had any use for them and included pamphlets with recipes and tips on maintenance.

The changes broadened Kama Asa's appeal beyond chefs and restaurateurs who know what they want and buy in bulk. It also coincided with a surge of interest in "Made in Japan" products and Japanese cuisine that has brought the shop double-digit revenue gains annually and a stream of commissions for kitchen-tool exhibitions around the country and in Paris. It's a promising turn of fortune for a business that only a few years ago was struggling to stay cutting-edge. — (M)

Open
Every day except the
New Year holiday

Contact
2-24-1 Matsugaya
+81 (0)3 3841 9355
kama-asa.co.jp

Go for
Nambu cast-iron
sukiyaki pot
Hinoki cypress
cutting board
Mi-oroshi single-edged
filleting knife

Bi-Rite, *San Francisco*
Cook's choice

It's the chef's perspective that makes Bi-Rite Market in San Francisco a staple in the community. Owner Sam Mogannam ran his own restaurant for years before taking over the food shop from his father and uncle in 1998. The family has owned the business since 1964 and Mogannam grew up stocking the shelves with his brother and co-owner Raph.

The two maintained the shop's retro design but the new formula combines hospitality with sincere attention to detail in sourcing pantry staples and produce from northern California. "It's a small selection that is cherry-picked," says Mogannam. Simon Richard, the produce buyer, often buys just one crop from a specific farmer because he knows it will be good that season.

Provenance is everything to Mogannam; the pride of Bi-Rite Market is the staff's ability to recite the story behind anything on the shelf. "We've started educating people on where their food comes from," he says. Farm-direct produce is part of the foundation of the company, which works with more than 50 farms in California to ensure that seasonal pickings are available at peak ripeness. In 2008, Bi-Rite began growing its own fruit and vegetables in Sonoma County, about an hour away. Mogannam even sells jams made by his mother from the fruit grown at her own Placerville orchard. — (M)

Open
Every day

Contact
3639 18th Street
+1 415 241 9760
biritemarket.com

Go for
Sëka Hills California wildflower honey
Firebrand sourdough loaves

Okomeya, *Tokyo*
Street life

Togoshi is a residential neighbourhood with a tight-knit community on the south side of Tokyo. Atsuo Otsuka knew the area well as his grandparents lived there. When he set up his web design and branding company, Owan, he found himself thinking about Togoshi. "There were a lot of empty properties – I wanted to do something," he says.

His first move was to open a café. It was a small step but it sparked a change in perception: creative young people started moving in. Otsuka then took over a coffee roastery. "The place we were buying our coffee from looked like it might be shuttered when the owner retired. So we took over the business." Otsuka's wife, art director Yoko Shiraishi, renovated the space as Mr Coffee.

He next opened a rice shop, Okomeya, on the same street. The site was an old vegetable shop with plenty of atmosphere. Jo Nagasaka of Tokyo-based Schemata Architects came up with the fresh look while keeping the bones of the old building and Shiraishi created simple and crisp packaging. The rice on sale here is pure *koshihikari*, grown without pesticides in Niigata; it's twice the price of the normal variety and exceptionally tasty. If you want to buy the daily *onigiri* rice balls you have to be quick, they sell out fast. *Shotengai* (local shopping streets) are under threat in Japan but Okomeya shows that, if done right, they still have a place in the modern world. — (M)

Open
Closed Monday and every other Tuesday

Contact
4-8-6, Togoshi
Shinagawa-ku

Go for
Ume (plum)
Onigiri (rice ball)
Donburi bento lunch
Bag of *koshihikari*
rice from Niigata

Barthélémy, *Paris*
Ageing beauty

No fridges, branding or use-by dates can be found in fromagerie Barthélémy in Saint-Germain-des-Prés – just wall-to-wall cheese. Owner Nicole Barthélémy has been in business for more than 40 years and believes that it's better to have a small shop overflowing than a big one that's bare.

There's often a queue for the famed light-as-clouds fontainebleau that's made daily by the madame of cheese herself. So revered is her passion and knowledge of fromage that she has been the key supplier to the Élysée Palace and the prime minister's residence since the 1970s. On any given day more than 200 varieties are available after having been matured in the underground cellar. Nicole sources her cheese from some of the most esteemed dairies in France that still honour age-old techniques, including – of course – the use of raw milk.

Depending on the season, mounds of the best semi-soft reblochon from the Alps, cow's milk neufchâtel from Normandy and crumbly laguiole from Aveyron are on display. Nicole is also mindful of the rising price of artisanal products and stocks her shelves to ensure customers can access quality goods. Rumour has it that she sells a literal tonne of mont d'or every few months, requiring a full-time staffer solely to care for this soft cheese and tenderly turn it by hand. — (M)

Open
Tuesday to Saturday

Contact
51 Rue de Grenelle
+33 (0)1 4222 8224

Go for
Mont d'Or in the winter
Reblochon in the summer
Fontainebleau year round

Vila Viniteca, *Barcelona*
Class by the glass

Long before Barcelona's Born district got its groove back, the family behind the counter of this food and wine shop had been steadfastly feeding and pleasing their patrons for decades. The shop first opened back in 1932 when this former textile district was teeming with tradesmen eager for a well-earned snack. More than eight decades later, Vila Viniteca is overseen by Joaquim Vila, the third generation of his family to take the reins. One of his toughest decisions was a move to carefully update the popular venue. It worked: loyal residents weren't frightened off and were joined by a number of reputable wine-makers and food-lovers from around the world.

Today wine tastings are hosted in a space across the narrow street, while the family's clever eye for produce and carefully nurtured relationships with local producers has made their shop more than just an unassuming delicatessen. Vila Viniteca is as much a social enterprise – flaunting the values of sharing and conviviality – as a place to savour the finest Spanish drop.

A testament to Vila's gravitas is the community of food-minded businesses that have sprung up in its wake. Vila is regarded as one of Spain's most important wine dealers and along the narrow stretch of Carrer del Agullers the entire neighbourhood appears to revolve around his vibrant shop. — (M)

Open
Monday to Saturday

Contact
7 Carrer dels Agullers
+34 937 777 017
vilaviniteca.es

Go for
La Mujer Cañón, one of Madrid's best reds
Soft but rich Baridà goat's cheese

Globus Delicatessa, *Zürich*
Sourcing the superlative

Josef Weber founded Zürich's premier department store – known today as Globus – in 1892. The first shop of its kind was modelled after the Parisian *marché*, a central tenant of which was the delicatessen. Globus's food hall rose to prominence in the 1960s and has since expanded into eight of its Switzerland-based branches. Natural materials in the design, such as stone and oak, mirror the timber shelves and glass cabinets in which the extensive selection of fresh produce is showcased.

"We procure the majority of our goods directly from the source," says Thomas Herbert, CEO of Globus. More than 25,000 products from all over the world include 40 varieties of smoked ham, as well as regional fruit and meat from the woolly Mangalitza pig. "Much is sourced straight from our neighbourhood; the rest comes from the other end of the world, such as the best crawfish, caught just off the tiny South Atlantic island of Tristan da Cunha."

For Herbert and his team it's important for the produce to tell a story, and his Delicatessa staff are always on hand to talk about the origin and journey of each product. "That way they taste even better," he says.

Everything is built around the experience, and every so often the food hall is transformed into a restaurant where local and international cooks are invited to rustle up a festive dinner for the delicatessen's patrons. — (M)

Open
Monday to Saturday

Contact
11 Schweizergasse
+41 58 578 1111
globus.ch

Go for
Organic extra virgin olive oil
Porcini mushroom and truffle paste
Rooibus vanilla tea

El Bocon del Prete, *Bassano del Grappa*
Down to earth

In a small city such as Bassano del Grappa in Italy's Veneto region, residents are used to shops where personal contact is just as important as quality food. As such the closure of Andrea dalla Rosa's (*pictured, on right*) much-loved 50-year-old family grocer was a terrible loss but when he teamed up with food technologist Alberto Fantinato (*pictured, on left*) in 2013, the town earned a worthy replacement.

El Bocon del Prete sells anything from small Veneto-cellar wines to Bassanese charcuterie and its own pasta sauces. "We look for producers that put their heart into their work," says Fantinato. "Be they rearers of pigs from Jabugo or cattle breeders from the nearby Grappa massif, what matters is they represent their own territory and their traditions in the best way."

The pair are always on hand to tell the story of a product and even drop off groceries for their elderly customers. "In a world where everyone is in a rush and supermarkets flatten life and taste, shopkeepers have an important role," says Fantinato.

Much of the fresh produce is made in the surrounding towns (a baker walks his loaves to the shop every morning), proof that a commitment to Bassano is top of the shopping list here. "We love our city and want to make it better," says Fantinato. "Without history and roots we are nothing." — (M)

Open
Tuesday to Sunday

Contact
29 Via Gamba
+39 (0)4 2421 9055
elbocondelprete.it

Go for
Capo di Stato red wine
Aged Bastardo cheese
Khorasan-flour pasta

Tierenteyn-Verlent, *Ghent*
Hot stuff

The Belgian institution Tierenteyn-Verlent, in St Jacobs neighbourhood, makes and sells the original Ghent mustard, something likely to be found in the cupboard of every proud Belgian.

It began with Peter Tierenteyn who, serving in the French military in Dijon, overheard Napoleon and another soldier discussing the art of grinding mustard seeds with stones rather than the usual pestle and mortar. Tierenteyn brought the "Dijon technique" home on his return, and opened Tierenteyn-Verlent.

The family recipe was passed down until 1947, when the historic business was sold. Today the shop and its carefully guarded recipe are in the hands of Catherine Caesens, whose father bought the business in 1958.

Each week Caesens prepares 400kg of the preservative-free mustard, which is generously served to customers – who often bring in pots for refills – from a large serving jug. The landmark shop has been housed at 3 Groentenmarkt since the mid-19th century. Its entrance is marked by a bronze crescent moon – now a symbol of the brand – and, inside, the old-fashioned wooden shelves are lined with stoneware jugs by La Roche Pottery Works and Austrian rococo-style labelled jars filled with handcrafted mustard, pickles and herb mayonnaise. — (M)

Open
Monday to Saturday

Contact
3 Groentenmarkt
+32 (0)9 225 8336
tierenteyn-verlent.be

Go for
Original Tierenteyn-Verlent mustard
Herb mayonnaise
Mango chutney

Delicatessen, *Istanbul*
Eclectic dreams

A restaurant, bakery and deli counter in one, Delicatessen has large bay windows that look out onto Mim Kemal Oke Caddesi in Nisantasi, the heart of the European side's fashion district. Here locals peruse the carefully selected produce and pause for back-to-basics brunch, prepared with ingredients that are available for individual sale. It was launched by restaurateur and chef Elif Yalin in 2010; her discerning eye for hearty produce from Turkey and abroad attracts a steady flow of regulars.

Delicatessen has a refreshingly international spread, with a selection of meat that includes spicy local cold-cuts and Mediterranean specialities, which are hard to come by in Istanbul. Homemade marmalades and Anatolian honey catch the light on the marble countertops, alongside freshly baked bread and pasta by Rummo. Yalin has also sought out some of the finest small-scale producers in the country, from Aegean olive oils to Kars-made gruyère cheese and cornflour milled on the Black Sea coast.

Delicatessen's team is ready with tips on how to make the most of Turkey's breadbasket bounty, while downstairs an open kitchen serves diners who sit next to the extensive wine cellar. "We want our clientele to feel encouraged to share their thoughts on good food and their lives," says Yalin. "The space is about more than shopping and sharing food." — (M)

Open
Every day

Contact
19 Mim Kemal Oke Caddesi
+90 212 225 0604
delicatessenistanbul.com

Go for
Mussels from Balikesir
Sucuk (Turkish sausage)
Walnut jam from Antakya

St John Bakery, *London*
Rising star

"We like to think that our baking is an exaggerated form of home baking, without any of the compromises of commercial production," says Laszlo Kovacs, head baker at St John Bakery. The business belongs to chef Fergus Henderson's St John stable, which includes the Bread & Wine restaurant in Spitalfields. Initially part of the Spitalfields outfit, Henderson moved the bakery to South London in 2012 as demand ballooned.

"Most of the products we offer stem from traditional English recipes," says Kovacs of his breads, cakes, tarts and doughnuts (all made with UK-sourced ingredients). The bakery has achieved near-legendary status for excelling at the classics. Rows of white and brown sourdough loaves – proved for a marathon-like 72 hours – sit alongside the popular raisin loaf and Henderson's signature Eccles cake. Yet few items can compete with the famed doughnuts: pillows of slightly chewy dough filled with custard or seasonal jams.

Nestled under an old railway arch, the bakery is a big presence in the community. "When our arch opens to the public every weekend, locals come to collect their weekly bread," says Kovacs. Many cafés and restaurants also purchase Kovacs' loaves and sweet treats, and the bakery does a good trade at the St John stall at the nearby Maltby Street Market (*see page 136*). — (M)

Open
Saturday and Sunday

Contact
72 Druid Street
+44 (0)20 7237 5999
stjohngroup.uk.com

Go for
A custard-filled doughnut
Henderson's signature
Eccles cake
A brown sourdough loaf

Julius Meinl, *Vienna*
Elegant emporium

The boy with the fez on a can of Julius Meinl coffee might well be one of Austria's most recognisable logos. The history of this famed emporium dates back to 1862 when the eponymous founder began selling pre-roasted coffee, as well as catering for the ruling Habsburg family.

Meinl is still family-owned (it's now in the hands of the fifth generation, in fact) and its sprawling flagship on Vienna's Graben – the retailer's most famous location in the city centre for the past 40 years – stocks more than 17,000 delicacies from around the world. These are generously displayed and sold on three floors: there's a wide-ranging coffee department, a tea department (its impressive assortment comes in part thanks to Julius Meinl II's Japanese wife), a bakery and a patisserie – and sections for luscious speciality meats, cheese and fish.

As well as the grocery there is a café, a basement wine bar lined with floor-to-ceiling bottles and an acclaimed restaurant. Meinl still caters as well but you no longer have to be blue-blooded to book. In all departments, service is extremely knowledgeable but always friendly and easygoing; this isn't somewhere that you'll ever feel intimidated. And despite its vast inventory, the shop painstakingly sources small specialist producers and rare delicacies from Vienna and further afield in Austria. — (M)

Open
Monday to Saturday

Contact
19 Graben
+43 (0)1 532 3334
meinlamgraben.at

Go for
Poppy-seed cake
Carp from Waldviertel
Venison sausage

Gourmet Market, *Bangkok*
Hit refresh

"There is so much colour in the produce we have access to year round," says Luckana Naviroj, senior executive vice-president of The Mall Group as she splits open a bright-green lotus-fruit root. Walking through Gourmet Market, a fresh concept that's part of the Mall Group at Bangkok's bustling EmQuartier development, she discusses rosy-red rambutans and ripening mangoes with the passion of a seasoned farmer. Because she is.

At the heart of Gourmet Market's success are the relationships it has with local producers: it connects with farms in many of Thailand's 76 provinces, most of which are small-scale and can rely on The Mall Group's logistics networks and merchandising know-how.

Naviroj says her greatest achievement has been enabling producers to scale up alongside Gourmet Market, which opened its first establishment in 2001. She pays farmers more than the going rate to provide a better-quality product for her shoppers. The Mall Group also dispenses business-development advice to help producers carve out their point of difference.

Naviroj flies in farmers to gain an understanding of Gourmet Market and its customers. "When I bring them here it's the same experience as when I go to their farms; there is so much to see and so much to learn," she says. "Thailand is not a developed market so we have to create the supply chain ourselves." — (M)

Open
Every day

Contact
622 Sukhumvit Road
+66 2 269 1000 (ext: 2055)
gourmetmarketthailand.com

Go for
Rambutan, a fuzzy red fruit with a sweet centre
The market's own Gourmet soups
Bespoke gift hampers brimming with lavish produce

Isetan department store, *Tokyo*
Rich pickings

Imagine finding the takeaway counters of a nation's acclaimed restaurants, butchers, condiment producers, patisseries, chocolatiers and bakeries all in one place – and attempting to resist as they urge you to try their plentiful samples. That's what many Japanese department-store food halls are like; known as *depachika*, they're typically in the basement and usually make it impossible for you to leave empty-handed.

Mitsukoshi, Japan's oldest department store, was the first to devote basement space to food in the late 1970s. Copied by almost all of the industry, the *depachika* make up about a third of Japan's department-store revenues. You could grab lunch, take home dinner and send a thank-you or condolence gift – and easily part with a sizeable chunk of your paycheque.

No shop has a finer selection than Isetan in Tokyo's Shinjuku district. There are counters devoted to speciality stalls that sell only seaweed, green tea, pickles or traditional sweets; refrigerated cases packed with grilled freshwater eel and raw Wagyu beef slices; racks of bento box lunches; glass displays of shortcakes, parfaits and delicate butter cookies.

Nearly every region in Japan is represented but there are also imports, including *baumkuchen* from Holländische Kakao-Stube of Lower Saxony and Pierre Hermé macarons from Paris. There's even a wine cellar with more than 2,000 bottles. — (M)

Open
Every day

Contact
3-14-1 Shinjuku
+81 (0)3 3352 1111
isetan.mistore.jp

Go for
Itowashigoro Shoten
yakitori (chicken)
Patisserie Sadaharu
Aoki Paris macarons
Uogashi Meicha "Shan"
sencha green tea

Conserveira de Lisboa, *Lisbon*
Preserved in time

Since 1930, Conserveira de Lisboa has stocked a cornucopia of tinned fish amid the faded grandeur of Lisbon's Baixa neighbourhood. More than 100 varieties of hand-wrapped cans on its shelves contain everything from tuna and sardines to squid and eel, all caught in Portuguese waters. Skinless; boneless; in vegetable or olive oil; plain or with tomato sauce: the range is staggering.

The family-run firm underwent a subtle rebrand in 2010 to update its traditional image, courtesy of Lisbon-based studio We are Boq, but a glance will tell you that very little has really altered. Part of the shop's enduring charm is the fact that everything inside – the wooden shelving, cash register and countertops – reflects more than eight decades of history. "We never let the quality go down and that's the reason we are still here," says Tiago Cabral Ferreira, speaking across the counter over which his grandfather once traded.

A few things have had to change, namely the packaging and expiration dates: although the tins' contents will actually keep for decades, an update was required in order to comply with the European five-year limit for canned fish. No such limits on this old-school institution however, which has survived and surpassed its own expected sell-by date many times over. — (M)

Open
Monday to Saturday

Contact
34 Rua dos Bacalhoeiros
+351 218 864 009
conserveiradelisboa.pt

Go for
Tricana mackerel fillets
Cat logo-clad Minor
Prata do Mar sardines

Stockmann Herkku, *Helsinki*
Finishing touch

"Many of our customers tell us they have memories of the food here from their childhood," says Susanna Ottila, director of Stockmann's delicatessen chain Herkku. The shop's food hall first opened in 1949 and, she says, "It is important for us that children learn to appreciate food with great taste, to make new memories while visiting Herkku with their parents or grandparents."

The food hall at Stockmann's Helsinki flagship reopened in 2010 after a 10-year overhaul to make room for its wide selection of products – and its exceptional cheese counter that stocks almost 500 cheeses, and dairy products from independent regional farms. The interiors are a mixture of wooden shelves, careful lighting and benches. It's a far cry from the usual dazzle of over-lit spaces and the 30,000 mostly seasonal and Finnish goods for sale are immaculately presented and restocked frequently.

Customer service is where Stockmann's (founded in 1862) excels, with daily food demonstrations and a service desk to provide advice. "The Herkku chain employs hundreds," says Ottila. In place of the hum of refrigeration units there's the chatter of shoppers and staff, and this simple recipe translates into results. Some 10 million customers visit the Helsinki flagship every year. — (M)

Open
Every day

Contact
52 Aleksanterinkatu
+ 358 9 1211
stockmann.com/herkku

Go for
Cloudberry jam
Swiss Tête de Moine
Sans Rival cake

Petra Mora, *Madrid*
Land of plenty

This oversized Spanish pantry in Madrid's upmarket Salamanca district is modelled on the idea of a well-stocked delicatessen. Basque gourmand Mikel Zeberio roamed the Spanish countryside gathering his pick of the finest produce and iconic recipes. "Spanish cooking can vary but what unites tables across the country is the spirit of sharing," he says. A meal in a northern Spanish village might typically begin with *jamón* and cheese, transition into heavier staples such as tortilla and then step up to an *arroz con sepia* (rice with cuttlefish) – but a spread in the west might look entirely different. Petra Mora aims to show off the culinary diversity across the Iberian peninsula.

The idea of preparing a homelier spread is present throughout, from the finely cut *jamón* to a selection of traditional staples including *conservas* (canned delicacies from the sea) and a range of rices and desserts. The 600-strong selection boasts bright and playful packaging; a team of smartly aproned attendants offer tips on how to best fill your basket. If you're more inclined to give the truffled eggs or *navajas* (razor clams) a miss, head straight over to safer territory in the cured meats and cheese section. While you're there, ask for the cheese sourced from the rare Serrana goats of the Villuercas highlands – it alone is worth the trip. — (M)

Open
Monday to Saturday

Contact
21 Calle de Ayala
+34 980 635 390
petramora.com

Go for
Filetes de anchoa en aceite
(anchovies)
Habitas Baby jar of split beans
Villuercas goat's cheese

8.
Smart Packaging

Where to find tasty design

Packaging may seem like whimsical window-dressing but there's plenty to be said for the power of a well-designed jar, wrapper, tin or bottle to get your brand out there. From plastic lemons and pinky-hued Viennese wafers to tinned fish and tea, we've scoured the shops and supermarkets for 12 time-tested and truly sumptuous examples of iconic packaging (and it betrays our predilection for precise Japanese design). Our round-up shows how typography can typify the experience of quenching your thirst and how the shape of a container can itself contain meaning.

I.
Zuiyo plum wine, *Japan*

Founded in 1867, Zuiyo was the first brewer in
Kumamoto, southern Japan, to produce clear saké. The
brewery's 180ml glass "one cup" *umeshu* (plum wine)
bears a beaming image of Kumamoto prefecture's
popular mascot, Kumamon, a mischievous black bear
with red cheeks and a surprised expression.

2.
Pocari Sweat sports drink, *Japan*

Otsuka Pharmaceutical has sold more than 30 billion
cans and bottles of its sports drink since it was launched
in 1980. The salty-sweet flavour with a hint of grapefruit is
an acquired taste but as this South Korean can shows, the
brand image can cross borders with clarity. Its reputation
is cemented by its bold typography and tasteful swish.

3.
Manner wafers, *Austria*

This hazelnut confectionery, clad in pink and stamped
with Manner's iconic trademark image of St Stephen's
Cathedral, Vienna, saw the light of day in 1898, eight years
after Josef Manner I founded the business. The wafers
became synonymous with Austria's capital and by the
1960s the foil-fresh treats had hit big overseas.

4.
Mehmet Efendi coffee, *Turkey*

Turkey's oldest coffee brand has its origins in the 19th
century but its captivating branding dates from 1933.
The handiwork of Ihap Hulusi Bey, a design hotshot of the
day, the art deco-influenced logo forms both a face and a
streetscape of minarets in front of a setting sun. The Arabica
beans inside this comely coffee tin are roasted in Turkey.

5.
Yamasu Sugimoto Shoten tea, *Japan*

For tea brands in Shizuoka, Japan's largest
tea-producing region, it's not easy to stand out. Not so
for family-run Yamasu Sugimoto Shoten, whose green tea
and roasted hojicha come elegantly wrapped in paper with
willow tree and wave motifs designed by third-generation
president Kazuyoshi Sugimoto's wife, Midori.

6.
Martelli pasta, *Italy*

The Martelli family continues to make their delectable pasta in the Tuscan village of Lari. The maccheroni is hand-kneaded from Italian durum wheat and shaped with bronze cutters, giving it a rough texture ideal for absorbing a meaty sauce, before being dried for 50 hours as custom dictates; once served, its life span is significantly shorter.

7.
Asahi Shuzo saké, *Japan*

This brewer from Niigata prefecture has been going
for more than 180 years and teamed up with the East Japan
Railway for superb saké *Otona no Kyujitsu* (Holiday for
Adults). It's made from fermented rice, koji yeast and spring
water during the winter in northern Japan. The label
features an illustration of a winged suitcase on washi paper.

8.
Jif lemon juice, *UK*

Keeping your lemon juice fresh for six months is
the least of this playful creation's achievements. It was
launched in the UK in the mid-1950s and although some
contend a similar product in Italy predated Jif's model,
it is Unilever that has enjoyed the success thanks to
staying sweet on this time-tested design.

9.
Kirin shochu, *Japan*

Drinking shochu, a Japanese-distilled liquor, from a
box doesn't sound all that gracious but Kirin's Tarucho,
a name that suggests a barrel in miniature, manages to
make the prospect appealing. The compact Tetra Pak
cube has earned Kirin a place in the hearts (and liquor
cabinets) of Japanese consumers.

10.
Kewpie mayonnaise, *Japan*

Toichiro Nakashima launched Japan's first bottled
mayonnaise in 1925. Production halted as ingredients
dwindled during the Second World War but Kewpie
recovered to become a favourite. Made with rice vinegar
and egg yolk, it has a distinctively rich taste. The cute logo –
designed in 1909 by artist Rose O'Neill – doesn't hurt either.

11.
Fisherman's Friend lozenges, *UK*

Pharmacist James Lofthouse developed this medicinal
lozenge – for fishermen as the name suggests – in 1865.
Although the formula has been honed, the packaging has
changed little since they were first launched in Lancashire.
The austere look and menthol flavour have found surprise
success in Southeast Asia.

12.
Miss Can tuna, *Portugal*

Vintage-looking fish tins are two a penny in Portugal
but Miss Can's bright hues are a breath of fresh air. The
Soares Ribeiro sisters resurrected a canning tradition that
has been in their family for more than 100 years when they
launched Miss Can in 2013. Sardine, mackerel and tuna are
steamed in Portugal and come in spiced or plain olive oil.

PART 3.

Roll Up Your Sleeves

Kitchen essentials

We set the table for success with a line-up of plates, pans, cutters and colanders. From sharpening up your knife selection to scales, brushes and sponges, we've assembled what you'll need to cater to any crowd.

The small things

Plenty of attention is paid to the provenance of our produce but precious little to the tactile pleasures of a cast-iron pan or a winsome whisk. With a range of plates, bowls, glasses and graters (plus the odd bird-shaped sugar bowl and cat-like ceramic shaker for a little levity and charm), our selection will see you through almost any recipe and offer solutions to everything from weighing out ingredients to getting the washing-up done. Expect Irish-linen tea towels, US-made pans, German potato-ricers and smart Japanese eggcups.
Dinner is served.

1. **Cutlery** by Kay Bojesen, *kaybojesen.com*
2. **Tea towel** by 31 Chapel Lane, *31chapellane.com*

1. Knife by Kama Asa Shotem, *kama-asa.co.jp* 2. Knife by Sabatier K, *sabatier-shop.com*
3. Chopping boards by Formlady, *formlady.co.jp* 4. Knife by Kai Corporation, *kai-europe.com*
5. Whetstone by Kiya, *kiya-hamono.co.jp* 6. Coffee grinder by Milco, *milco.co.jp*
7. Knife by Kai Corporation, *kai-europe.com* 8. Grater by Muji, *muji.com*

④

A cut above
Knives are a worthy
investment and as you'll
notice from our pointedly
Japan-leaning line-up,
we think the nation leads
the pack when it comes
to the craft. Kai Shun's
stately blades are created
by repeatedly heating and
cooling the Damascus
steel they are made
from, leading to superior
sharpness and durability.

⑤

木屋特選
砥石

⑥

⑦

⑧

Pasta craftsman
Marcato has rolled out its
pasta machines from the
same factory near Padua,
northeastern Italy since
1938. The Atlas 150's
aluminium mechanism can
be set to cut three shapes
(lasagne, fettuccine or
tagliolini) and make
the fuss of pasta-making
a more manageable affair.

⑤

⑥

Small but strong
A canny kitchen
investment that's space-
saving and sturdy
(its blade is made from
carbon-steel). It's also
thrifty at less than €15;
good products needn't
cost the earth.

⑦

⑧

Do the twist
Yes, there are counter-
filling collections of
blenders, which make
whisking a breeze but
this rotary version offers
a tactile take on getting
some air into your
batter. German retailer
Manufactum stocks
a robust, handsome
selection.

1. Pasta machine by Marcato from Divertimenti, *divertimenti.co.uk* 2. Pastry brush
by Patissier France from Labour and Wait, *labourandwait.co.uk* 3. Small whisk by Muji, *muji.com*
4. Grater by Muji, *muji.com* 5. Measuring jug by Pyrex from Divertimenti,
divertimenti.co.uk 6. Tin opener by Labour and Wait, *labourandwait.co.uk*
7. Rotary whisk by Manufactum, *manufactum.com* 8. Electric scale by Hario, *hario.jp*

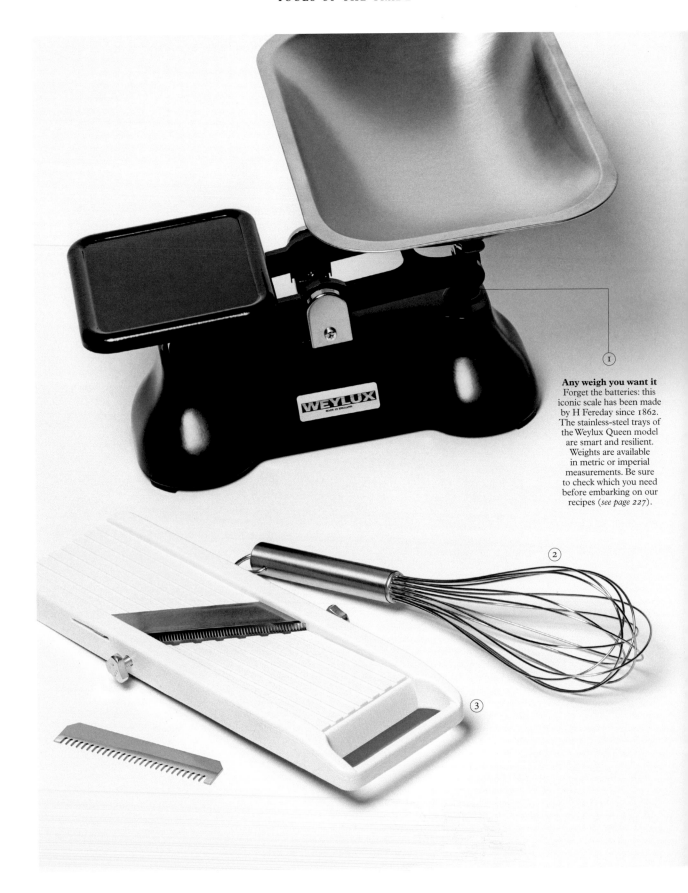

Any weigh you want it
Forget the batteries: this
iconic scale has been made
by H Fereday since 1862.
The stainless-steel trays of
the Weylux Queen model
are smart and resilient.
Weights are available
in metric or imperial
measurements. Be sure
to check which you need
before embarking on our
recipes (*see page 227*).

1. Scales by Weylux from Objects of Use, *objectsofuse.com* 2. Balloon whisk by Muji, *muji.com*
3. Mandoline slicer by Benriner from Japanese Knife Company, *japaneseknifecompany.com*
4. Stainless steel colander by Divertimenti, *divertimenti.co.uk* 5. Orange peeler by Abbey Horn, *abbeyhorn.co.uk*
6. Tofu server by Kanaami-Tsuji, *kanaamitsuji.net* 7. Jam spreader by Muji, *muji.com*
8. Metal strainer by Kanaami-Tsuji, *kanaamitsuji.net*

Not-so-heavy metal
Started in Kyoto in 1984, Kanaami-Tsuji specialises in metal-weaving, a notoriously tough-to-master art that is said to have been practised in the region for more than 1,000 years. Founded by Kenichi Tsuji, the firm – now run with his son Toru – employs six craftsmen and makes delicate utensils that include classic tofu servers, filigree tea strainers and baskets.

Built to last
It's inconceivable that many acts of domestic cookery are beyond Crane's tough (and exceedingly heavy-duty) range of cookware. Each piece is sand-cast and topped with matte-black enamel, then fired at temperatures of 840c. Each cast-iron piece is chip and scratch-resistant – in fact, dropping one is more likely to damage your kitchen floor than your new pan.

1. Saucepan by Mauviel from Borough Kitchen, *boroughkitchen.com* 2. Ladle by Muji, *muji.com*
3. Ladle by Another Country, *anothercountry.com* 4. Griddle pan by Crane, *cranecookware.com*
5. Wooden spoon by Muji, *muji.eu* 6. Casserole dish by Crane, *cranecookware.com*
7. Tongs by Divertimenti, *divertimenti.co.uk*

Wooden spoon prize
Japanese homeware giant
Muji's utilitarian range
of utensils will make even
the most parsimonious
shopper happy. Items
including this spatula are
liable to last longer than
other more outlandish
purchases.

Whisk trade
The Turmix company
began in the early 1930s
in Switzerland but became
globally recognised a
decade later when inventor
Traugott Oertli developed
his first domestic blender.
Today the range includes
a blender, hand mixer,
stick mixer and juicer,
each produced with
characteristic Swiss
precision.

1. Electric hand mixer by Turmix, *turmix.com*
2. Bamboo steamer by Dexam, *dexam.co.uk*
3. Baking dishes by Falcon Enamelware,
falconenamelware.com 4. Roasting pan
by Mauviel from Borough Kitchen,
boroughkitchen.com 5. Stainless steel measuring
cup by Muji, *muji.com* 6. Skillet pan by
Borough Furnace, *boroughfurnace.com*

Scrappy contender
John Truex and Liz Seru
founded Borough Furnace
in Syracuse in 2011. Their
skillets are made to order,
created from scrap iron,
and pick up an endearing
patina with age.

Tea time
Designed by Yu-Fen Lo of
Taiwanese brand Cuckoo,
this dainty teapot is made
of stone and has a wooden
heat-resistant handle
to ensure a steady grip.
Although a useful kitchen
staple, it's also portable
enough to take outdoors.

Bowled over
Sandra Haischberger opened her shop and atelier Feinedinge in Vienna in 2008 after she was discovered at Blickfang, an annual event in Zürich promoting the work of young designers. The Alice tea set is available in seven different colours and made from French Limoges porcelain. The literal translation of the brand name is "fine things". A fair description, we'd say.

1. Fruit bowl by Bird & Branch, *birdandbranch.london* 2. Teapot by Cuckoo, *pinyen-creative.com.tw*
3. Sugar bowl and toothpick holder by Playmountain, *playmountain-tokyo.com* 4. Chopstick holder by Kihara with Monocle from The Monocle Shop, *monocle.com* 5. Glass tumblers by Toyo-Sasaki, *toyo.sasaki.co.jp* 6. Pudding bowl by Feinedinge, *feinedinge.at* 7. Coffee cup by Hasami Porcelain, *hasami-porcelain.com* 8. Soy sauce pot by Hasami Porcelain, *hasami-porcelain.com*
9. Salt shakers by Hakusan, *hakusan-porcelain.co.jp* 10. Matches by Hay, *hayminimarket.com*
11. Plate by Kihara with MONOCLE from The Monocle Shop, *monocle.com*

Glassy affair
Founded in 2009 by
Irish siblings Mark and
Jonathan Legge, Makers &
Brothers stocks charming
homeware from hand-
picked Irish craftfolk. "We
are taking a quiet, human
approach to this project,
founded in simple things:
the handmade, objects of
integrity," says Jonathan.
This carafe and glass by
Kilkenny's Jerpoint Glass
Studio was the brothers'
first collaboration.

Setting the bar
Since starting in 2014, Common's mission has been a humble one: to create homely pieces that can be used regardless of their setting or what's on the menu. The firm behind this tempting tableware – Niigata-based Tsubame Shinko – has been at the sharp end of the cutlery trade since 1919.

1. Wine glasses by Iittala, *iittala.com* 2. Decanter by Makers & Brothers, *makersandbrothers.com*
3. Teapot by Marimekko, *marimekko.com* 4. Steak knife by Laguiole, *laguiole.com*
5. Corkscrew by Alessi, *alessi.com* 6. Champagne glasses by Lobmeyr, *lobmeyr.com*
7. Wooden bowls by Seto Susumu from Objects of Use, *objectsofuse.com* 8. Chilli shaker by J, *j-period.com*
9. Plates by Iittala, *iittala.com* 10. Salt and pepper shakers by Lisa Larson, *lisalarsonsweden.com*
11. Fork by Kay Bojesen, *kaybojesen.com* 12. Cutlery by Common, *commontableware.com*

1. Bottle brushes by Labour and Wait, *labourandwait.co.uk*
2. Dish sponge by Muji, *muji.com*
3. Sponges by Kamenoko Tawashi, *kamenoko-tawashi.co.jp*

Soak it up
Kamenoko's brand name
means "baby turtle" in
Japanese. And while the
Atsuki Kikuchi-designed
reptile logo that adorns
the plastic outer packaging
is cute, these sponges
are also as hardy as their
namesake. Each contains
ions of silver that help kill
germs, making purging
your plates a pleasing
activity.

Host with the most
Having these understated – yet absolutely essential – party tricks up your sleeve will see you pull off the perfect soirée

I.

Keep it simple
Avoid overcomplicating your menu

Cook something easy that everyone likes (it sounds obvious but is often not adhered to). A decent selection of cold cuts as a starter, served with bread and oil, is a handy time-saver. Often a cheeseboard will suffice for desserts – but be generous and treat your guests to the best produce that you can find. For the mains, prepare dishes that you're familiar with and that you're excited to eat too. Make an effort but don't show off; this is a surefire way to fall at the first hospitality hurdle.

2.
Best-laid plans
Don't be too rigid about seating

Name cards are deeply naff at small gatherings; splitting couples not always as exciting as you think; and boy-girl is a bit old hat (not every boy likes girls and vice versa). Form a seating plan in your head if your table is large enough to demand it but, on the night itself, be sure to direct guests as if it's a spur-of-the-moment proposal.

3.
Time it well
Resist getting cooped up in the kitchen

The way you cook is worth considering as closely as what you cook. Pick a dish that's made in the oven and can be taken out as people arrive. This gives guests something to look at – and look forward to – and avoids the stress of cooking in front of people and sweatily flash-frying last-minute greens that have gone cold. Plus, do as much prep as you can in advance. You don't want to be tinkering away in the kitchen for so long that your guests wonder whether you've been locked in the cellar.

4.

Friends united

Carefully consider your guestlist

Only invite people you like and who will get along. Again it seems obvious but too many people bring together friends who are likely to butt heads, new neighbours they barely know or couples who can't stand each other. Strive for a mix that forges connections. If saucy and newly single Sarah has a penchant for publishing then be sure to invite your unattached editor friend. And spare a thought for clashing demeanours: don't sit rowdy Robert next to delicate David unless you're sure they'll hit it off.

5.

Keep things breezy

Regulate the temperature

People obsess over getting their plates out hot but neglect to keep their dining rooms at an agreeable temperature. Take your guests' coats when they arrive but make sure the room is warm enough to justify it. Slow-braising a lamb for five hours will make the house muggy so allow for a breeze to keep proceedings feeling fresh. Be wary of smells too; fish tastes good but the soft furnishings shouldn't smell of sea bass when people arrive.

6.

Top table
Provide proper seating

Kitchens may be the heart of the home but no one remembers meals spent standing or crammed around a too-small table. A decent dining-room table, such as the soft-edged oak Ercol Teramo, can anchor a room. This model can also be extended to cater for bigger crowds and a couple of high-backed bentwood Thonet No18 chairs will have you and your guests sitting pretty too.

7.

Neat and tidy
Declutter your tableware

In terms of table setting, be correct but not a prig: everything should be in the right place and facing the right way but people having to wash a glass to enjoy, say, some dessert wine isn't the end of the world. Having five glasses for each person is showy. Likewise, fish knives and salad forks have their places but use them as little as possible to get the job done.

8.

Gift aid

Don't expect invitees to bring anything

From the starters to the desserts, be sure to have all bases covered; don't rely on your guests to stock your fridge and cupboards. But if anyone asks if there's anything they can bring say, "Something to drink, please." Don't get into the poisonous realm of everybody turning up with a different pudding; everyone will love one person's and hate someone else's – and that's sad to watch.

9.

Scrub up

Dial back the dress code

Getting all trussed up in a suit is hopelessly formal, not to mention uncomfortable. Don't set a prescriptive dress code but if they ask do invite people to attend in something smart and comfortable. You know your crowd: you can wear shorts or a dress in summer if you like. While any chef worth their salt should own an apron, it shouldn't be seen at the dinner table.

10.

Chin-chin
Keep the drinks flowing

It's not the end of the world to be not quite ready when guests arrive – but it is essential to make them an aperitif immediately. As you get changed they will be at least one drink ahead (important) and have the opportunity to nose through your bookshelves and records in an unguarded way (vital). Be generous. People shouldn't need to jangle the ice in their empty glass and interrupt your repartee to request a refill. Or simply make them the first drink and then let them know where you keep the spirits and mixers.

II.

Team building
Cater to the crowd

Don't stand on ceremony. People mucking in by carrying certain bits and bobs to the table is an icebreaker and a good leveller. You don't want people hovering nervously behind their chairs as if waiting for someone to sing the national anthem or say grace. Asking someone (especially someone you fancy) to chop some mint, for example, is good. Asking them to chop an onion, less so. In general, though, it's good to get people involved.

12.

Table service

Plates, cutlery and glassware

Crockery-wise we favour something simple and stackable such as Iittala's unpretentious Teema collection (*see page 209*) or Figgjo's smart Relieff set. Slates belong on roofs and chopping boards are best suited to bread, cheese and cold cuts so have decent serving crockery with a lip to avoid spillage and spattering. Cutlery should match and glassware should gleam. These are small efforts but form a crucial part of a comfortable experience in which guests will feel cared for.

13.

Perfect setting

Laying the table

A few soft touches in the form of linen and napkins from Fog Linen Work or Chapel Lane (*see page 195*) will create a comfortable dining environment, while a carafe from Makers and Brothers (*see page 208*) and a few ceramic bowls and cups from Feinedinge (*see page 207*) or Mud Australia will add texture and tactility to your place settings. A white tablecloth is all good but a worn wooden dining table or gingham cloth are fine by us too.

14.

Keep it snappy

Avoid overdoing the number of courses

Assume that your guests will arrive a little hungry and thus don't keep them waiting long to eat: half an hour after everyone arrives is a good rule of thumb. Likewise, keep the spaces between courses short enough for guests to anticipate the next round without passing out before it arrives. A nibble, starter, main and choice of pudding is easy enough. Try not to drag things out with protracted courses and extras.

15.

Serving suggestions

Hands-on approach

Plating up for your guests is a pain and your dishes are likely to cool as you're doing it. Let people serve themselves from large bowls and platters to avoid doling out portions that people won't finish. And don't skimp on the sauces and sundries: little things, such as condiments to complement your dishes, can add profoundly to proceedings.

16.

Spirited away
Cocktails should be simple but strong

Cocktail-making can be a time-consuming distraction so we'd recommend sticking to a handful of time-tested options (and making them strong). An Aperol Spritz or pokey negroni are excellent summer sippers, while an old fashioned, martini or French 75 are year-round staples (*see page 225*). Don't get drawn into the world of egg whites, sweet-and-creamy liqueurs or imported and unheard-of spirits. Chubo's heavy-duty Master bartender set will make light work of the preparation.

17.

Light meal

Set the tone with leading lights

It's an abused term but the room's ambience should be
considered closely. Natural light and a few understated
flowers show care and attention, while a flattering
evening light that dims (but not so much as to obscure
your starters) is also worth perfecting. Skultuna's brass
candle-holders throw an agreeable light. An ashtray on
the terrace table will also put the smokers at ease.

18.

Put a cork in it
Don't let the wine do the talking

The pleasure of a crisp glass of white or punchy red can
be diminished by excessive analysis or tedious highfalutin
discussion (the people who know the least about wine
often talk the most about it). Take your wine shop's advice
on pairings and know what you're serving but don't bore
people to death with the minutiae of its terroir or tasting
notes. As before, we'd suggest being generous without
being showy. One decent red, a white and maybe a rosé
(if the sun's shining) will be more than enough.

19.

Supper soundtrack

Music makes people come together

Parlour games are usually a poor choice so instead select some music and let that buoy the mood. Start with something that's relaxing and unobtrusive but quickens as the evening passes. Don't be too formal in introducing it but a post-dinner boogie can be a fun way to work off supper. We've assembled some of our favourites overleaf.

20.

Fitting farewell

Bring things to a graceful conclusion

So you've drained the bottles, licked clean the plates and shown your guests to the door. Now get them out of it. Don't allow people to drag out the goodbyes, be assertive with the stragglers and direct with the dawdlers. Do pop away the perishables, but leave the washing up until the morning. Don't be ashamed to take tomorrow night off and tuck-in to a takeaway.

Five tips for attendees

I.
No thank you to thank-you cards

They're mumsy, outdated and will ultimately end up being ungracefully binned. Why not bring a small gift instead? How about a nice loaf of bread?

2.
Hold your tongue

You may think you know best on a subject but be mindful not to venture opinions that will rankle and ruin your host's evening. Likewise don't start conversations that might grate. Newly divorced Diane probably doesn't want to get into it.

3.
Help, don't hinder

Do offer to chop the limes, set the table or bring through the bread. Don't explain how long you usually marinade the pork for or how everyone *swoons* over your soufflés.

4.
Don't be early

15 to 20 minutes late is fine and will give your host ample time to correct the inevitable cooking miscalculations. Any later and you should let them know and apologise profusely.

5.
Bring a bottle

Then shut up about it. Even if you've forked out for an expensive one and brought it with you, accept that it's not the main event. Let the host know that your offering is for their enjoyment and quietly stow it out of sight so they can open it if and when they want to.

10 albums for when you want things to happen

I.
Gene Ammons
Boss Tenor (1960)

2.
Camille Saint-Saëns
The Carnival of the Animals (1886)

3.
LL Cool J
Mama Said Knock You Out (1990)

4.
Genesis
Foxtrot (1972)

5.
Alice Coltrane
Journey in Satchidananda (1971)

6.
Ella Fitzgerald and Duke Ellington
Ella & Duke at the Côte d'Azur (1967)

7.
Françoise Hardy
Ma Jeunesse Fout L'Camp (1967)

8.
Kamasi Washington
The Epic (2015)

9.
Harry Nilsson
A Little Touch of Schmilsson in the Night (1973)

10.
Various artists
Come Together: Black America sings Lennon & McCartney (2011)

Five fuss-free fail-safes worth committing to memory

I.
Martini
50ml gin, 10ml dry vermouth, 10ml olive brine, large green olive

Mix ingredients over ice. Stir well, strain into a cocktail glass and pop in an olive.

2.
Old fashioned
10ml sugar syrup, 6 dashes Angostura bitters, 50ml single malt whisky, lemon

Combine the syrup and bitters over ice in a lowball glass; slowly add whisky then stir to dilute. Garnish with a twist of lemon.

3.
Negroni
25ml Campari, 25ml gin, 25ml vermouth, slice of orange

Fill a tumbler with ice and layer up the spirits in equal measure. Slip in a fresh slice of orange just before serving.

4.
Aperol Spritz
50ml Aperol, 75ml prosecco, 25ml gin, splash of soda water, slice of orange

Fill a large tumbler or wine glass with ice cubes, Aperol, prosecco and gin (in that order). Stir once and finish off with a splash of soda water and a slice of orange.

5.
Sidecar
60ml cognac, 30ml triple sec, 1 tbsp lemon juice, 1 tbsp orange juice, sugar

Mix cognac, triple sec, lemon and orange juice over ice and strain into a sugar-laced martini glass.

9.
The Recipes

From our favourite chefs and our own repertoire

.

Restaurant recipes

Pea-and-pancetta croquetas (228) Mussels with new potatoes
and garlic (229) Ceviche (230) Sweetcorn-and-courgette fritters with
beetroot salad and summer salsa (231) Salmon soup (232) Stuffed
artichokes (233) Roasted-tomato soup (234) Spaghetti with clams (235)
Chicken smørrebrød (236) Steak tartare (237) Sea urchin spaghetti (238)
Roast Wagyu short ribs (239) Roast chicken (240) Pork tenderloin, wild
mushrooms with crème fraiche and tarragon (241) Wiener schnitzel (242)
California burger (243) Solomillo pork with pobre potatoes (244) Steak with
Café Lisboa sauce (245) Bloody Maria (246) Chocolate pots (247) Custard
rice pudding (248) Kadaif with milky syrup (249)

Monocle recipes

Yoghurt flatbread with braised leek and burrata (252) Gruyère and speck
toasties (254) Warm potato-and-pancetta salad with hazelnuts (256)
Asian-style omelette with crab and miso butter (258) Sesame soba-noodle
salad with prawns and pickled cucumbers (260) Pearl barley with maple-
roasted carrots, shallots and feta (262) Roasted celeriac soup with cheesy toast
and rocket pesto (264) Orecchiette pasta with courgette, sausage and chilli
(266) Rack of lamb with chilli-roasted fennel and butternut squash (268)
Sea bass en papillote (270) Baked meatballs with cherry-tomato sauce (272)
Butterflied sumac chicken with warm aubergine and chickpea salad (274)
Asian fish burger (276) Lemon and ricotta cake with limoncello syrup (278)
Rice pudding with poached rhubarb and gingersnap crumb (280)

Oldroyd, *London*
Pea-and-pancetta croquetas

Recipe

Serves 8

Ingredients
550ml (2⅓ cups) milk
1 bay leaf
¼ of a nutmeg, grated
3 black peppercorns
1 shallot, sliced
1 small garlic clove, sliced
75g (5 tbsps) butter
200g (1⅔ cups) peas
1 tbsp olive oil
100g (4oz) pancetta, chopped
75g (⅔ cup) flour
Small bunch of parsley, chopped
3 eggs
100g (⅔ cup) polenta
150g (3 cups) panko breadcrumbs
6 tbsps vegetable oil
Salt and pepper
Mayonnaise, to serve

The method
Heat 450ml (1¾ cups) milk with the bay leaf, nutmeg and peppercorns over low heat for 15 minutes. Remove from heat, strain and set aside the milk mixture.

Sweat the shallot, garlic and 50g (3 tbsps) butter in a pan until soft. Add 50ml (3 tbsps) milk and 150g (1¼ cups) peas. Bring to boil then reduce heat and simmer for 1 minute. Remove from heat, cool for a few minutes and blitz in a food processor. Roughly chop the remaining peas and set aside.

Heat olive oil in a large frying pan over medium-high heat and cook the pancetta. Melt remaining butter in the pan and add flour, stirring quickly until the mixture is golden and begins to thicken. Slowly add milk mixture and whisk until smooth. Set aside to cool slightly, then stir in parsley, pea purée and reserved chopped peas. Pour mixture onto a large tray and place in the fridge to chill for at least 2 hours.

Whisk eggs with remaining milk in a large bowl. Place the polenta and the breadcrumbs in separate bowls. Shape one tablespoon of the mixture into an 8cm-long croqueta. Dip into the polenta, followed by the egg mixture and then the breadcrumbs to coat evenly. Repeat to make approximately 24 croquetas.

Heat half the cooking oil in a heavy-based frying pan over medium-high heat. Once the oil is hot add croquetas to pan and fry in batches, turning occasionally, until golden. Replace the oil halfway through. Use a slotted spoon to transfer cooked croquetas to a plate lined with kitchen roll and season to taste. Serve with mayonnaise.

"I didn't know I wanted to be a chef," says Surrey-born restaurateur Tom Oldroyd with a grin. "When I was 15 I worked in a pub kitchen, everything was cooked in a microwave and nobody wanted to be there – they'd rather talk about holidays or fishing."

Standing by the window on the sun-dappled first floor of his own restaurant on busy Upper Street in north London, it's clear that Oldroyd (*pictured*) has found a more agreeable setting for his art. Sandwiched between a kebab shop and a nail salon, his teeny venture established itself within no time upon opening in 2015. But don't let the diminutive size throw you: big things are happening in this snug two-storey stop-in.

If you include the outside tables, the restaurant accommodates 38 diners on sunnier days. Inside is a smattering of low wooden tables, plants and a few tall bar seats. A narrow kitchen under a spiral staircase turns out an array of lip-smacking European dishes, from crisp croquetas to mouthwatering *malfatti* (ricotta dumplings).

Upstairs a few brass wall lights by Michael Anastassiades for Flos bounce a warm light back from the Stiffkey blue walls that Oldroyd, his fiancée and a few friends painted by hand. Everything about the place feels personal, deliberate and unfussy. But the young chef has taken a roundabout route through London's hospitality industry.

"I left school quite abruptly," he says, grinning again and refusing to elaborate. "I then went straight to work at a hotel in Guildford." Having moved to London in 2006 he got a taste for professional kitchens at a since-closed establishment called Alastair Little. "Trying to get your foot into the restaurant scene is a good way to lose weight and save money. I just didn't stop cooking or thinking about cooking."

Oldroyd quickly graduated from prepping the ingredients to cooking under the tutelage of head chef Juliet Peston. "She was fantastic. I loved her ethos around food: everything had to go together and it was all about the flavours, which fascinated me." After three years Oldroyd was snapped up by restaurateurs Russell Norman and Richard Beatty and went on to launch nine restaurants across London with the Polpo group. He left in 2015 to try his hand with his own place.

"Opening your own restaurant is more enjoyable but more stressful; you've got no one but yourself to blame," says Oldroyd, as he tosses a creamy ball of pea-and-ham purée with béchamel sauce into a tray of orange polenta – the finishing stage in the making of his signature dish. "We'll always have croquetas on the menu – they are just the best way to start any meal." — (M)
oldroydlondon.com

Franklin, *Hobart*
Mussels with new potatoes and garlic

Recipe

Serves 2

Ingredients

500g (1¼lbs) mussels in shell, scrubbed and debearded
150g (6oz) new potatoes
150ml (⅔ cup) grapeseed oil
3 garlic cloves, crushed
15g (½oz) samphire
15g (½oz) spinach
200ml (¾ cup) chicken stock
½ lemon, juiced
Salt and pepper

The method

Place mussels in a large pot and cook, covered, for 3 to 5 minutes. Carefully remove mussels from shells and retain the meat and juice in separate bowls.

Boil potatoes in lightly salted water for approximately 15 minutes, or until just cooked. Set aside to cool slightly, then peel.

Heat oil in a frying pan over medium-high heat with a pinch of salt. Add garlic and fry until golden brown. Remove from heat and set aside, retaining the oil.

Boil a pot of water. Add samphire and spinach and blanch for 2 minutes. Remove from heat, drain and refresh under cold running water. Drain and set aside.

Add potatoes, chicken stock and mussel juice to a large pot and cook over medium heat until the liquid is reduced by a quarter.

Place garlic, oil and lemon juice in a bowl and season. Mix well.

Heat a griddle pan over medium-high heat and add mussels to sear quickly, turning once with tongs (approximately 1 minute each side). To serve, place mussels, potatoes and greens in a bowl and drizzle over the dressing.

"Hobart felt like it was growing and to find a space like this is extraordinary," says David Moyle (*pictured*), the genial chef and founder of Franklin, which opened here in 2014. From a berth at the brushed-concrete bar during a busy mid-week lunch service you'd be hard-pressed to guess you were sitting in a sleepy city of some 200,000 on a remote island in the Southern Ocean.

The art deco building once housed the presses of *The Mercury* newspaper but today the space is a restaurant bedecked with Danish chairs from Hay in pale beech, Tasmanian-oak tables and a lively open kitchen where five chefs busily pluck, chop and prep the steady stream of afternoon orders. Architecturally there's a hard industrial look that is softened by animal-fur rugs and airy floor-to-ceiling windows that wouldn't look out of place in Los Angeles or Sydney. But there is something irreducibly Tasmanian about proceedings here: the food.

"The beauty of Tasmania is that you get some extraordinarily interesting ingredients," says Moyle, whose previous posts include running kitchens in Melbourne and Byron Bay, plus a stint at Tasmania's Peppermint Bay. He has always had an interest in design but found his footing as a chef after moving to Melbourne from Port Fairy, Victoria, at the age of 17. Since then he has set a ferocious pace in establishing and developing his own

kitchens, working with lauded chefs such as Bill Marchetti and Andrew McConnell (*see page 46*). All that before settling in this unlikely food frontier in 2012.

But moving to Tasmania isn't as simple as the idyllic surroundings and bucolic pace of life suggest. "The curse is that growers or producers don't have a business where they can provide regular delivery," says Moyle. It's a common woe: the produce here is some of Australia's most prized but the remote location means distribution channels can't always be relied upon.

Franklin's menu is a tasteful homage to the island's grown goods: fresh periwinkles and slow-growing angasi oysters from the mudflats of Port Arthur. There's also a culture of backyard businesses here that churn out butter, olive oil, honey and tangy cheese. That's before we put in a word for Tasmania's full-bodied, cool-climate pinot noirs. All of it adds up to make Franklin's fare some of the most distinctive in Australia.

Tasmania has long been lampooned for its isolation (and a perceived hickishness) by mainlanders but those who actually make the journey across the Bass Strait, the choppy 240km that separates the island from Australia proper, rarely regret the trip. As Moyle's sumptuous plates suggest, there's something truly special growing here. — (M)
franklinhobart.com.au

Canta Rana, *Lima*
Ceviche

Recipe
Serves 4

Ingredients
1 large red onion, very finely sliced
Pinch of sugar
Pinch of salt
1kg (2¼lbs) white fish fillets (sole or sea bass), diced into 1cm (½ inch) pieces

Leche de tigre marinade
10 limes, juiced
½ tbsp coriander, chopped
½ tbsp garlic, crushed
½ tbsp ginger, finely grated
½ red chilli, chopped
1½ tbsps of salt
Coriander, to serve

The method
Place the sliced onion in a bowl with a pinch of sugar and salt. Fill with cold water. Stand for 30 minutes, rinse and drain.

In a large bowl combine lime juice, coriander, garlic, ginger, chilli and salt. Add diced fish and set aside for a couple of minutes to marinate.

To serve, add onion and garnish with coriander.

Every food-lover in Lima knows the way to the Canta Rana restaurant in the Barranco neighbourhood. This time-honoured *huarique* (hole-in-the-wall serving Peruvian food) has been an institution in the city for decades, even though the place is nothing more than a simple house with an old tiled floor and basic wooden tables.

As Lima developed into the fine-dining capital of South America, so the yearning increased for restaurants serving home-cooked, uncomplicated food in familiar settings. The affable atmosphere at Canta Rana aptly reflects the personality of jovial owner Vicente Furgiuele (*pictured, second from left*), a committed football fan – evident from the floor-to-ceiling fútbol memorabilia, posters and flags – and an avid cook.

"I started here in 1985 in the same location, a stone's throw from the small El Capullo market of Barranco," says Furgiuele. "Before that I worked in pizzerias, a bakery and in restaurants around Latin America until I decided to open Canta Rana, which was half the size of the current restaurant. We started with six dishes on the menu – now we have over 160."

The menu features Lima's classic ceviche (raw fish with red onion, coriander, lemon and other ingredients, depending on the recipe), *tiraditos* (similar to Japanese sashimi) and *chaufas* (fried rice with meat). In true

Peruvian style the portions are enormous and accompanied by side dishes such as *choclo* (giant corn) and sweet potato. There are a couple of Asian-inspired dishes too, an important part of Peru's cultural inheritance (about 5 per cent of the population has an Asian background). For each of his recipes Furgiuele selects only local species of fish that aren't endangered.

"I like to be with the patrons and take care of their needs – I have a lot of fun here," says the owner, having just instructed his 15-strong team of cooks and waiters as the restaurant fills up (it's near impossible to find an empty seat during the busy lunch hour). "We have clients that have come for 30 years just for the ceviche."

Today ceviche joints are opening the world over and although Furgiuele celebrates this, he is wary of the quality. "The secret of a good ceviche is the freshness of the produce, the speediness with which the fish is processed and especially the *leche de tigre*," he says, pointing to a bowl of the lime-based marinade that is used to cure the seafood in the dish. "When done properly it gives ceviche an authentic Peruvian taste – and if you drink a shot of it after a big night it's also a great cure for hangovers." — (M)
+51 (1) 247 7274

Kokako, *Auckland*
Sweetcorn-and-courgette fritters with beetroot salad and summer salsa

Recipe
Serves 2

Ingredients
1 medium courgette
2 tbsps olive oil
1 medium onion, diced
1 garlic clove, crushed
1 sweetcorn cob
1 egg, lightly whisked
1 tbsp parsley, chopped
50g (⅓ cup) chickpea flour
1 tsp baking powder

Beetroot salad
1 golden beetroot
1 candied or red beetroot
1 lemon, juiced
1 tbsp parsley, chopped
Olive oil, to dress salad

Summer salsa
2 large vine tomatoes, deseeded and diced
50g (4 tbsps) red onion, diced
1 red chilli, finely diced
1 garlic clove, crushed
1 tbsp parsley, chopped
1 tbsp coriander, chopped
20ml (4 tsps) olive oil
Salt and pepper
Fresh goat's curd, to serve

The method
For the fritters, grate the courgette into a bowl. Lightly salt and set aside.

Heat a frying pan over low-medium heat and add 1 tablespoon of oil. Add the onion and garlic and sauté until soft (approximately 6 to 8 minutes). Set aside in a large bowl to cool.

For the beetroot salad, grate the beets into a bowl, add lemon juice and season. Toss through a few parsley leaves and dress with a splash of olive oil.

For the summer salsa, place all of the ingredients together in a large bowl. Combine gently and season.

Squeeze the excess water from the courgette with your hands and add to the onion and garlic. Use a sharp knife to cut down the length of the corn close to the core, to remove the kernels. Add to a bowl with egg, parsley, chickpea flour, baking powder and season. Mix gently to combine.

To cook the fritters, heat 1 tablespoon of oil in a heavy-based frying pan over medium-high heat. Once the oil is hot add large spoonfuls of the fritter mix to the pan and cook in batches. Flip fritters when lightly golden (approximately 5 to 8 minutes).

Serve fritters with spoonfuls of beetroot salad, summer salsa and curd.

You'll find Kokako in a 1940s post office in Auckland's Grey Lynn, a rapidly gentrifying inner-city liberal stronghold. The café has become a welcome addition to a once forlorn retail strip at the corner of two major arterial roads. Since opening it has won a loyal following for its fresh, simple breakfasts and lunches; it's so good in fact that few realise it exclusively serves vegetarian food.

In a city where brunch is a social event, lacking bacon on your menu could be a recipe for disaster. Not here. The café and coffee roaster – the company, which was Auckland's first organic coffee brand when it launched in 2001, runs a wholesale roasting operation out of a space across the road – opened here in 2013 after the site had sat empty for about a year. "I kept driving past and wondering why no one was leasing it," says managing director Mike Murphy.

Kokako let the space from New Zealand Post in 2012. Designer Chris Stevens – now a shareholder in the company – stripped it back to its bones, removing decades of ad-hoc additions that had turned the interior into a warren of small, dark spaces and exposing beautiful concrete beams, classic metal-framed windows and natural light. The fit-out was simple: French industrial lighting, demolition windows and custom-made metal chairs based on a vintage pair that Murphy inherited from his father.

It's an open, functional space. A central glass atrium where staff host coffee tastings is separated from the main café by a glass-paned garage door, giving customers a range of seating pockets in which to enjoy their drinks. The kitchen, too, is open. "We wanted this to be a transparent environment," says Murphy.

At first the post office's closure caused an uproar in the community but it's fair to say that most have become equally attached to its replacement. On any given day there might be a couple of loiterers in one corner nursing hangovers, a business meeting and freelancers tapping away on their laptops, snacking on a plateful of head chef Danny Simpson's sweetcorn-and-courgette fritters.

Simpson changes the menu four times a year in line with the seasons. "We try and keep it simple, easy and accessible," he says. Almost all the produce is organic and most of it can be traced back to the farm that it was grown on: tomatoes come from Curious Croppers just south of the city; beetroot from Canterbury on the South Island; and cheese from cheesemonger Zany Zeus in Wellington. That said, Murphy is happy to concede that many customers are just as often here for a no-nonsense plate of eggs. — (M)
kokako.co.nz

Sea Horse, *Helsinki*
Salmon soup

Recipe

Serves 4

Ingredients

6 large potatoes, peeled and diced into
2cm (¾ inch) pieces
2 onions, peeled and diced into 2cm
(¾ inch) pieces
10 whole allspice berries
1 bay leaf
1 tbsp (or cube) fish stock powder
200ml (¾ cup) cream
400g (14oz) salmon fillet, diced
3 tbsps dill, chopped
Salt and pepper
Rye bread and butter, to serve

The method

Place 800ml (3⅓ cups) of water in a
large stockpot over a high heat and add
the potato, onion, allspice berries, bay
leaf and stock powder. Bring to the boil.
Reduce heat to medium and simmer,
stirring occasionally, until the potato
begins to soften (15-20 minutes).

When the potato and onion have
thickened the water, add the cream and
salmon to the stockpot and continue
simmering for approximately five
minutes. Remove the bay leaf and the
allspice berries and season. Add dill
and serve with rye bread and butter.

In the well-heeled Helsinki neighbourhood of
Eira sits Sea Horse, a stalwart of the capital.
Since opening in 1934 it's been serving the
kind of Finnish comfort food that continues
to make it a popular spot today. However, it
hasn't always been so rosy. In the late 1990s
the restaurant had become a run-down
drinking hole and almost closed for good.
"News spread that the restaurant was in dire
straits and up for sale; we couldn't see such
a landmark die so we had to save it," says
restaurateur Petri Laitinen, who stepped in
and bought it with his childhood friend Ari
Väresmaa in 1999.

Laitinen and Väresmaa set to work
restoring the restaurant to its former glory.
Guided by old photographs of the place
found in the city's Hotel and Restaurant
Museum, a carpenter was hired to recreate
the original furniture. In 2000 artist Kimmo
Kaivanto got involved, harmonising artwork
with Oili Syvälähde and Kai Brandt's 1970s
art deco seahorse mural (a much-loved
trademark) in the main dining room.

The most important thing was to
reinstate the original menu. "We went
through old cookery books and spoke to
Anna Liisa Paukku, who had been the
restaurant chef for 20 years since the 1960s,"
says Laitinen. "We decided to continue the
existing traditional Finnish menu and add
a few new dishes [including a reindeer fillet

with a thick cranberry and red-wine sauce].
If it isn't broken, why fix it?"

As a starter, a popular choice is the hearty
salmon soup served with a hunk of rye bread.
"Although it's also available as a main course,
it's served in such a big bowl that I've never
seen anyone finish it," says chef Eetu Seivo
(*pictured*). "People find it more manageable
as a starter." Although the recipe is simple,
timing is crucial and the potatoes and onion
must thicken the broth before generous cubes
of salmon are added.

A homely atmosphere coupled with
a menu that doesn't change has drawn in
customers from around the world – not
least Tokyo. The restaurant has a menu in
Japanese for the crowds craving cabbage rolls
stuffed with ground meat, onion and rice. It's
a democratic environment: no matter who
you are you have to wait your turn to be
seated. It's common to spot politicians
and well-known Finns waiting for a table.

"Quality food can't be prepared in
a rush," says Seivo. "It's like having an
unhurried dinner at home with friends
and it's this very casual experience that
our customers enjoy." — (M)
seahorse.fi

Balla, *Sydney*
Stuffed artichokes

Recipe

Serves 4

Ingredients

Sauce
2 tbsps extra virgin olive oil
1 garlic clove, thinly sliced
1 small onion, finely chopped
350ml (1½ cups) tomato passata
1 tbsp tomato purée

Stuffed artichokes
4 artichokes
½ lemon
60g (1 cup) breadcrumbs
50g (3 tbsps) sultanas
3 tbsps grated parmesan
115ml (½ cup) extra virgin olive oil
2 eggs
Salt and pepper

The method

For the sauce, heat 2 tablespoons of oil in a frying pan over medium-low heat and add the garlic and onion. Sauté until soft (approximately 6 to 8 minutes). Add passata, tomato purée and salt, then stir. Simmer for 5 to 6 minutes. Remove from heat and set aside.

Remove the outer leaves of artichokes. Cut off top quarter to reveal layers and the heart. Remove stem. Rub the exposed cut leaves with the lemon, squeezing some juice into the heart.

For the artichokes, place breadcrumbs, sultanas, parmesan and 1 tablespoon of oil in a bowl and mix well. The mixture should hold together; if it's falling apart, add more olive oil. Season well.

Fill artichokes with the mixture. Crack two eggs into a bowl and lightly whisk. Dip the tops of each artichoke into egg.

Heat 100ml oil in a large frying pan over medium-high heat. Place artichokes in the pan, egg-dipped top first and sear (for approximately 1 minute, or until sealed). Turn the artichokes on their sides and add sauce to the pan until it almost covers them. Reduce the heat to medium-low and simmer gently for 1 hour.

To serve, slice artichokes in half lengthways and spoon over some sauce from the pan.

"Just two people found us on the first night," says Italian chef Stefano Manfredi of his first restaurant, which opened on Harris Street in Sydney's Ultimo neighbourhood in 1983. "But they were an elegant couple."

Manfredi opened his eponymous venture at the age of 28 and was part of a small group of chefs working to introduce their beloved northern-Italian cuisine to Sydney. With the help of then wife and current business partner Julie Manfredi-Hughes, the venue's reputation has quietly grown, allowing him to build a low-key but respected series of restaurants that currently numbers five.

Manfredi was born in Brescia and moved to Australia at the age of six; he began cooking as a child beside his mother and grandmother. "When we opened our first restaurant I felt as though it was the beginning of a new cuisine: 'modern Australian'. There were new varieties of potatoes, salad leaves and mushrooms suddenly available. Cheesemakers were producing interesting cheeses that weren't cheddar. It was revolutionary for Australia, which until then had pretty much subsisted on British ingredients."

Since the mid-1990s Manfredi has been extending his reach, continuing to open restaurants that are rooted in his love of simple cuisine from the motherland. "Tradition and heritage are important but so is responding to what's around you," he says. "It is essential to be open to new ideas and it helps to give a sense of place to the food and the dining experience."

The low-key Balla joined Manfredi's collection of restaurants in 2011. He can still be seen rushing between his kitchens but he also finds time to write; his recipe column in *The Sydney Morning Herald* was published for some 20 years. He's also published books, including *Stefano Manfredi's Italian Food*, a love letter that explores the country's wine, culinary history and recipes.

"I'm excited by Sicily and Sicilian food at the moment," says Manfredi. "I love Catania, the people, the culture, the markets; it is a city I could live in. The produce is so rich – due to the volcanic soil – and the island's cuisine has evolved as a result of its history. Constant invasion means it's a melting pot of influences."

Manfredi clearly remains as inspired and committed as ever. "I feel like we are at the beginning of a new phase with my restaurants Balla, Pizzaperta and Bells. All are authentic and traditional but from a more modern point of view." — (M)
manfredi.com.au

De Kas, *Amsterdam*
Roasted-tomato soup

Recipe

Serves 4 (as a light meal)

Ingredients
700g (1½lbs) vine-ripened tomatoes
2 garlic cloves, peeled
4 tsps extra virgin olive oil
1 small bunch of thyme
1 small bunch of rosemary
1 small bunch of basil
5-6 splashes of Tabasco
½ lemon, juiced
Salt and pepper
Basil leaves and tomato, to serve

The method
Preheat oven to 200c (400F/GM6). Place the tomatoes and garlic on a tray and roast in the oven for 30 minutes. Remove from oven, cool slightly, then place in a blender with the oil, thyme, rosemary and basil. Blitz for 30 seconds.

To serve, transfer to bowls. Season generously with salt, pepper, Tabasco and lemon juice. Garnish with basil and sliced tomato.

NOTE *Ripe, red tomatoes picked in season are essential to the flavour of this dish.*

"Fresh produce is the heart of the food at De Kas; what we harvest in the morning is served the same day," says chef Bas Wiegel with a nod to the extensive kitchen gardens in Amsterdam's Frankendael Park. When owner Gert Jan Hageman opened the restaurant in 2001 it was the only one in the city using sustainably sourced produce. "At that time we were considered revolutionary – it was not usual to serve menus based on vegetables."

Delft-born Wiegel joined De Kas as a junior sous chef and worked his way up to chef de cuisine after completing culinary school in the Netherlands and working in various kitchens across the country. He and his team of 12 create Mediterranean-influenced food, about 70 per cent of which comes from the restaurant's own nursery. Whatever they can't produce themselves comes from environmentally conscious Dutch suppliers: farms provide organic meat and dairy, while the fish is caught in the Wadden and North Sea.

De Kas occupies a striking eight-metre-high greenhouse that dates back to 1926 and was once part of the city's municipal nursery. Refurbished by Dutch interior designer Piet Boon, it now houses the glass-roofed main dining room that accommodates up to 140 guests. The adjoining private garden room is set among the plump vegetables and herbs of the nursery.

De Kas serves about 50,000 diners a year, offering a set lunch and dinner menu that changes according to what's just been harvested. Rich in vegetables and served with meat or fish (or you can opt for vegetarian), all the dishes are prepared in an unfussy manner to retain the flavour of the ingredients. "It's not a secret but if you cook with love and respect for the produce you use then most of the time it comes naturally," says Wiegel. "Working with fresh ingredients is so motivating for me; the vegetables come first."

Some of Wiegel's culinary hits include fresh strawberries marinated in balsamic vinegar, Bloody Mary sorbet, fig ice cream and tomato crostini. "Simplicity and flavour," the chef insists, while chopping the four different types of tomatoes – ostentatiously named Crimson Carmello, Gold Rush, Green Zebra and Chocolate Cherry – that are needed for his roasted tomato soup. "When you use more than one type you get more depth."

And when you sit back and enjoy a steaming bowl of tomato soup seasoned with basil freshly cut from the herb garden out the back, you'll be left with no choice but to agree. — (M)
restaurantdekas.nl

Puebla 109, *Mexico City*
Spaghetti with clams

Recipe
Serves 4

Ingredients
500g (1lb) packet of spaghetti
4 garlic cloves, crushed
1 small bunch of parsley, chopped
1 tbsp butter
400ml (1⅔ cups) single cream
2 lemons, juiced
400ml (1⅔ cups) white wine
1kg (2¼lbs) small clams, washed and cleaned
Salt and pepper

The method
Cook pasta according to packet instructions, or until al dente. Place a large heavy-based frying pan over medium heat and add garlic, parsley, butter, cream, lemon juice, white wine and clams.

Cook for five minutes until clams open (discard any that don't).

Add the pasta, season and serve.

Bunkered in a thick-walled house on the border between Mexico City's bohemian Roma neighbourhood and its financial district, Puebla 109 offers residents and visitors a place to enjoy simple food and savour fresh Mexican ingredients. "It's the style of La Roma," says executive chef Eduardo García (*pictured*). "People want good food – and simplicity, not pretension."

The restaurant is decked out with worn wooden floors, exposed ceiling beams and rough brick walls. It's adorned with an extensive collection of works by local artists – including the Cuban-Mexican artist Luis Alberu – all of whom are long-time friends of the owners. "We wanted to make it comfortable like a home," says Marcela Lugo, one of the restaurant's five founders. "We've got a library, a dining room with an open kitchen, private meeting rooms and a bar on the first floor with cantina tables for playing chess and backgammon."

La Roma and nearby Condesa are districts busy with creative people who don't work in offices, and Puebla 109 has emerged as a focal point where, before the cocktail and food crowds arrive, members can come to work or hold meetings.

The lunch service starts at 14.00 and the restaurant doesn't close until 02.00. Besides serving a Mediterranean-inspired menu featuring dishes such as charred octopus with a chipotle-goat-cheese sauce and spaghetti with clams, Puebla 109 also hosts special meals with guest chefs from around the country. "There are so many great chefs in Mexico right now and we want people to be able to see them work," says Lugo.

Walking past the hostess's table in the dining room, Lugo points towards the wine cellar. "We're really focused on offering national products; we only have Mexican wine – 71 different labels to be exact," she says. "We've also got coffee from Oaxaca and Chiapas," adds chef García. Originally from Guanajuato, García worked in Atlanta and Manhattan before returning in 2007 to cook with renowned chef Enrique Olvera.

In the kitchen, next to his indoor wood-fire grill, García drops a dozen clams into a frying pan laden with butter, minced parsley and white wine. "Cover that," he tells a sous chef as he steps back to his worktable. "You have to let it cook until the clams open – five minutes, not too long," he adds as the first shells start to pop. Moments later, lunch is served. "Simple food is the best." — (M)
puebla109.com

Aamanns, *Copenhagen*
Chicken smørrebrød

Smørrebrød (literally, buttered bread) dates back to before the industrial revolution, when it is said that agricultural labourers would use slices of rye bread as plates to bear various toppings, primarily pork, herring and potato. Around the late 19th century there was an explosion in smørrebrød restaurants that would compete with ever more elaborate toppings but then there was little subsequent development. That was until chef Adam Aamann opened his eponymous restaurant in Østerbro in 2006 and followed it up with Aamanns Deli & Take Away next door.

"Smørrebrød had become less about satisfying hunger and more about culinary 'bling'," he says. "The rye bread had been scaled down and even replaced with white bread, and the portions of meat or fish had grown to an almost grotesque level. Garnish was piled on top just to add drama. I decided to take smørrebrød back to its roots and give it a contemporary overhaul. I made rye bread the key again. I think Danish rye bread works extremely well with very different textures and aromas. It can also be very beautiful."

Aamann bakes his organic sourdough rye bread on-site in a process that takes two days; it is essential to let the dough rest overnight before baking. "Rye bread is the backbone. It has malty, complex and bittersweet flavours, which really tie together all the toppings."

Hearing Aamann describe the process of making smørrebrød, it sounds as much like a construction job as it does cooking. "On top of the bread you have the savoury spread: butter or mayo, a well-seasoned vegetable purée or a protein made into a soft topping, such as fish or chicken salad. This adds body to the piece. If your spread is not the main ingredient, you top up the bread with slices of either cured or smoked fish, homemade cold cuts or thick slices of cooked vegetables such as potato or beetroot. A crunchy garnish – usually a pickle – is more than just decoration: it adds a contrast in texture, freshness and flavour."

The so-called King of Smørrebrød has also won plaudits for taking greater care in sourcing his produce; organic free-range meat from Grambogård on the island of Funen, for instance, and vegetables from Søllested on the island of Lolland. "We insist on making all the elements ourselves, from the mayo to our cold cuts," he says. "Smørrebrød is the Danes' only food claim to fame." — (M)
aamanns.dk

Recipe
Serves 10

Ingredients
1 x 2kg (4½lb) chicken
2 onions
5 garlic cloves, peeled
Small bunch of thyme
Small bunch of parsley
2 bay leaves
1 tbsp coriander seeds
1 tbsp black peppercorns
1 tsp salt
400g (14oz) root vegetables, peeled and diced into 1cm (½ inch) pieces
2 tbsps cold-pressed rapeseed oil
1 lemon, juiced
1 tbsp apple cider vinegar
400ml (1⅔ cups) mayonnaise
500ml (2 cups) crème fraiche
1 tsp curry powder
2 tbsps Dijon mustard
16 slices of bacon
10 slices of rye bread or toast
1 small apple cut into small pieces, to serve
Chervil, to serve
Runner beans, sliced, to serve
Green pepper, sliced, to serve
Salt and pepper

The method
To poach the chicken, place in a pot, cover with cold water and bring to the boil. Reduce heat to a simmer. Add the onions, garlic, thyme, parsley, bay leaves, coriander seeds, peppercorns and 1 tsp of salt. Cook the chicken for two hours, skimming the foam from the surface regularly. Remove and set aside for 30 minutes to cool, then remove all the meat.

Preheat oven to 180C (350F/GM4). Add root vegetables to a bowl with oil, lemon juice and vinegar. Season well. Place vegetables on a roasting tray and put in the oven to bake for 15 minutes, or until tender. Remove and set aside to cool.

In a bowl, mix vegetables with chicken, mayonnaise, crème fraiche, curry powder and mustard. Season to taste with lemon juice, salt and pepper.

Bake bacon in the oven for 5 minutes, or until golden and crispy.

To serve, place chicken mixture on rye bread or toast and top with bacon, apple, chervil, beans and pepper.

Bouchon, *Monte Carlo*
Steak tartare

Recipe

Serves 4

Ingredients
4 x 250g (9oz) quality beef fillet, minced
(ask your butcher to do this)
2 tbsps Dijon mustard
2 tbsps Worcestershire sauce
2 tbsps ketchup
1 tbsp Tabasco
100ml (7 tbsps) rapeseed oil
4 egg yolks
4 tbsps capers, chopped
1 small onion, finely diced
1 small bunch of parsley, chopped
Salt and pepper

The method
Place the mince in a bowl and add mustard, Worcestershire sauce, ketchup, Tabasco and oil. Season and mix thoroughly.

Place a 10cm (4-inch) cooking ring on a dinner plate and fill with mince. Press to shape.

To serve, remove the ring and arrange capers, onion and parsley around the mince. Place egg yolk on top.

"We wanted to give the restaurant that feeling of age, of a different period – a bygone era," says architect Emil Humbert, who travelled the Parisian and Niçoise flea markets on the hunt for furniture from the 1920s. He came away with marble tables, art deco lamps and antique mirrors decorated with cursive scribbles announcing the *menu du jour*. "It seems like the space has been around forever."

Serving traditional French brasserie food, owner Riccardo Giraudi has managed to create a laidback space on Monte Carlo's upscale Princesse Grace Avenue. "Its roughness contrasts nicely against the city's bling," says Giraudi. "We make simple food: the French classics with a refined twist."

"It's one of those places where people can while away a whole day," adds Humbert. "Some clients come to read the papers in the morning, stay for lunch and linger until the evening, meeting their friends for an aperitif."

Part of the reason for its cosiness is the familiar setting and design. "Everything was handmade by the best French and Italian artisans, from the tiled floors to the lamps' metalwork," says Humbert, who once followed a dodgy seller through a derelict garage to buy the vintage blue-glass bottles that adorn Bouchon's shelves. "I was scared in the beginning but when I saw what was hidden under a dirty blanket I was in awe; it was like finding Aladdin's cave." And

although the decoration gives the restaurant a homely feel, what is really alluring about the place is the uncomplicated food, headlined by its signature steak tartare.

The raw meat used for the tartare is trimmed Black Angus muscle; it's a sirloin cut from Kansas and imported by Giraudi's family, who have been in the meat business for more than 50 years. The fresh produce is minced rather than chopped, compacting the fork-and-spoon-mixed ingredients so that you get all the crunch of the onion, capers and parsley in one bite.

But if the diners prefer to have their meat chopped, executive chef Thierry Paludetto (*pictured*) is happy to serve it thus. At Bouchon guests have the final word and that's why the tartare is prepared at the table, letting them try the recipe along the way and decide whether it needs an extra dash of Tabasco or teaspoon of mustard. The dish is best enjoyed with red wine, which is sold in three categories – Drinkable, Agreeable and Incredible – to suit the palates (and pockets) of diners.

For that well-rounded finish Paludetto likes to serve crêpe Suzette. "If our customers are well behaved we might even let them flambé the Grand Marnier," he says with a smirk, just before setting the pan on fire and pouring the warm sauce over the translucent crêpes. — (M)
bouchon.mc

Bar Brosé, *Sydney*
Sea urchin spaghetti

Recipe

Serves 10

Ingredients
2 sea urchins
50g (3 tbsps) crème fraiche
20g (4 tsps) butter
50g (1 cup) panko breadcrumbs
360g (13oz) fresh spaghetti
40g (3 tbsps) cultured butter
½ lemon, juiced
20g parmesan
1 bunch of chives
1 bunch of fennel tops

The method
Cut open the sea urchins, scoop out flesh and pass it through a fine sieve into a bowl. Add the crème fraiche and whisk by hand until thickened (but not whipped). Set aside.

Heat a frying pan over medium heat. Add the butter and the breadcrumbs and toast until golden brown.

Bring a pot of salted water to the boil and drop the pasta in.

Meanwhile, place the cultured butter, lemon juice and a small ladle of the pasta cooking water in a small frying pan over medium heat until combined.

When the spaghetti is al dente, drain and add to the pan, along with the parmesan and chives.

To serve, sprinkle the pasta with the breadcrumbs and top with the sea urchin mixture and fennel.

NOTE *Sea urchin can be ordered from quality fishmongers. Cultured butter is created from cream using live bacteria and is slightly tangy. It can be purchased from specialist food shops.*

Chef Analiese Gregory (*pictured*) was always likely to want to travel. "I grew up at the end of the earth in a little town called Matamata in New Zealand and I was desperate to get out and see the world," she says. "My mum and I travelled around Australia for five years so I blame her for my inability to stay in one place for very long."

Gregory's wanderlust has also been fed by her success in the kitchen. She was a sous chef at Quay in Sydney for five years and worked in San Sebastián, London and Paris before returning to Sydney in early 2015. "When I came home I was living in Rushcutters Bay up the road from Acme," she says. "I'd been cooking in fine-dining restaurants for 12 years straight. My training is French so I'd never really learnt how to make pasta. I asked chef Mitch Orr if I could come in and just make pasta every day."

A stint presiding over the pasta machine quickly became a full-time gig and before long the pair were mulling over opening a new restaurant together. Owned by the team that founded Acme in 2014, Bar Brosé opened in March 2016 in Darlinghurst with Gregory in charge of the kitchen (ably assisted by four female helpers). Gregory designed the menu, which comprises elegantly simple dishes with European, Japanese and African influences that reflect her time cooking abroad and hint at the exacting nature of her role in and out of fine-dining establishments.

"We've long been enamoured with Analiese, with her skill and her talent," says Acme and Bar Brosé co-owner Ed Loveday. "When she came home and started working with us at Acme we were trying to decide what to do with this site and Analiese was trying to decide where and with whom she wanted to work with next," he says. "We were pretty determined to convince her to stay in Sydney and to keep her for ourselves."

Open five nights for dinner, the restaurant and wine bar inhabits a narrow and light space that was formerly a hotel breakfast bar. Now divided into three dining rooms, there are two kitchens. "One hot and one cold," says Gregory as she inspects a crate of sea urchins that have just arrived from Tasmania. She will use them in a sauce to dress spaghetti, which she makes from scratch.

"I am glad I know how to make pasta but I've always loved making desserts the most," she says as she handles a tub of buffalo-yoghurt sorbet destined to be served with kaffir lime-infused Italian meringue, dark maraschino cherries and fresh raspberries. "When I was cooking in Morocco I had to resort to camel milk. It's important to be able to use whatever is on hand and make it look and taste good." — (M)
barbrose.com.au

Ho Lee Fook, *Hong Kong*
Roast Wagyu short ribs

Recipe

Serves 4

Ingredients
1 set of Wagyu short ribs
25ml (2 tbsps) soy sauce
25ml (2 tbsps) shaoxing wine

Jalapeño purée
100g (4oz) jalapeño peppers
1 onion (1oz), diced
30g garlic
50ml olive oil
25ml fish sauce
5 spring onions, julienned, to serve

Kimchi paste
25g (5 tsps) Korean chilli powder
25ml (2 tbsps) fish sauce
25g (2 tbsps) sugar
25ml (2 tbsps) sesame oil
20ml (4 tsps) rice vinegar
5ml (1 tsp) chilli oil
¼ onion, diced
30g garlic
1 long red chilli, deseeded

The method
Put ribs in vacuum bag with soy sauce
and wine; cook in an immersion circulator
at 68c (154F) for 22 hours.

Preheat oven to 200c (400F/GM6).

Heat a frying pan over high heat. Add
jalapeños and onion and cook until
charred and blackened. Remove from pan
and set aside to cool.

Add garlic to the pan and toast until
browned and soft. Place in a blender with
the jalapeños, onion, oil and fish sauce
and purée. Remove from blender and
set aside.

Add all kimchi paste ingredients to the
blender and blitz until smooth.

Remove ribs from the immersion
circulator and place in a roasting pan.
Place in the oven and roast until crust is
browned (approximately 15 minutes).

To serve, toss shallots with kimchi paste.
Add purée. Serve.

NOTE *If you don't have an immersion
circulator, the jalapeño purée and kimchi
paste pair well with steak.*

A Chinese chef cooking Chinese food in Hong Kong isn't a rarity. But step into Ho Lee Fook (yes, you read that correctly) and you'll quickly realise that this restaurant is different from the noodle, barbecue and teashops that surround it. While the name may appear tongue in cheek to western visitors, the three characters actually translate from Chinese to "Good fortune for your mouth". Ahem.

"Different people's perceptions of what a Chinese restaurant is can vary," says Jowett Yu (*pictured*), Ho Lee Fook's charismatic Taiwanese-born chef who was raised in Canada before moving to Australia to start his cooking career. While working in Sydney, Yu partnered with Dan Hong, and the pair worked together for the Merivale Group. In 2014, a few years after their first meeting, Yu opened Ho Lee Fook in Hong Kong's Soho.

While most Chinese kitchens are hidden from diners, Yu's is open and positioned at the restaurant's entrance. Centred around two magnificent wok burners in which many of the staples are cooked, the kitchen also includes a barbecue oven from which Yu and his team can be seen removing whole roasted geese and ducks. Then there's the wall of fortune-bestowing golden cats that wave to customers descending the stairs into the low-lit dining room.

Since its opening, Ho Lee Fook has been packed every night. The menu is unpretentious and in true Chinese style the plates are put together with sharing in mind. Favourites include hand-wrapped pork-and-cabbage dumplings derived from Yu's mother's recipe. "We didn't have a food processor so she kept everything really chunky," says Yu. "A dumpling should have a bit of a bite."

The *char siu* (Cantonese-style barbecued pork) follows a traditional recipe but is made with Japanese Kurobuta pork, while the roast short ribs – a grand plate that arrives pre-sliced with accompanying bone – are made from Wagyu beef sourced from Canada.

"Here there's some Cantonese food, Taiwanese food and some Sichuan dishes," says Yu. "It's all the things I like to eat. That's what I love about Chinese food: it's so dynamic and encompassing. It is different all around the world."

Ho Lee Fook's menu encourages relaxed dining, with dishes such as steamed rice, seaweed and pork floss served alongside plastic gloves so that guests can shape their own rice balls. "I want people to relax, eat, have some drinks and share stuff. That's the whole Chinese experience. We get a bunch of food, get a group of people together and just go crazy," says Yu. "We are in no position to elevate Chinese food. I'm just adding something to the existing dialogue." — (M)
holeefook.com.hk

Smile To Go, *New York*
Roast chicken

Recipe
Serves 4 (as a light meal)

Ingredients
1.3kg (2¾lb) whole chicken, wing tips
trimmed and tied with cooking twine
1 small bunch of rosemary, leaves picked
1 small bunch of thyme, leaves picked
200ml (¾ cup) extra virgin olive oil
2 garlic cloves, roughly chopped
2 tbsps salt
1 heaped tsp finely ground peppercorns

The method
Preheat oven to 200C (400F/GM6).

Place the herbs, garlic and olive oil in a
blender and blitz on high speed until well
combined (about 30 seconds).

Place chicken in a baking dish, rub all
over with marinade and season.

Put chicken in the oven and cook for
approximately 1 hour, until skin is dark,
golden and crispy. Serve.

Grabbing a quick and healthy takeaway in
Manhattan is no easy feat. Every day during
lunchtime the streets of lower Soho fill up
with bicycles delivering food to hungry
workers because there are surprisingly few
options for quick and tasty dining. "There
are a lot of creative businesses in this area but
there was nowhere for them to grab a good
lunch," says Matt Kliegman, who opened
Smile To Go with partner Carlos Quirarte
in 2012. "We've enjoyed dining at takeaway
places in other cities so it made sense to open
one here."

Located on Howard Street, a peaceful
stretch in busy Soho, Smile To Go is the
duo's second restaurant. In 2009 they opened
The Smile a few blocks north on Bond Street
and hired Melia Marden (*pictured*) as head
chef, a Harvard art-historian-cum-chef who
catered for the art and fashion crowd with
her company Looking Glass until she joined
the team. Now Quirarte, Kliegman and
Marden divide their time between the
two restaurants.

Occupying the space of a former Chinese
bakery and bubble-tea shop, the café has
enough room for a few dine-in tables and
is open from morning till night every day
except Sunday. From scones and cookies –
baked on-site by pastry chef Rosanne Smith
– to daily specials that change according to
the season, Marden designs her recipes with
simplicity in mind. "I use as few ingredients
as I can to make something taste good. Our
food is home-cooked; we're not trying to be
a big fancy restaurant." Dishes are displayed
in bright Dansk Kobenstyle serving plates,
adding splashes of colour to the counter.

Marden sources meat from family-run
butcher Pino's Meat Market, vegetables
from the farmers' market and dairy from
Battenkill Valley Creamery. Her recipes mix
Mediterranean influences – inspired by her
European travels – with a US sensibility.

One of Smile To Go's staples is rotisserie
chicken, which was suitably inspired by food
counters at marketplaces in the South of
France. "I saw all of these portable rotisseries
in the street markets there," says Marden.
"The way we roast our chicken gives it a
unique taste – the fat drips off and leaves
the skin crispy and the meat tender." And
the unique blend of freshly chopped thyme
and rosemary, and the mix of white, pink
and black pepper, give it a mild smoky, spicy
flavour too.

"At Smile To Go the dishes are more
immediate," says Marden. "It's similar to how
I cook and develop recipes at home: I can
try something new, serve it family style and
see how people react. We get so many repeat
customers that I think they'd get bored if I
made the same thing every day." — (M)
thesmilenyc.com

Rose and Sons on Queen St, *Toronto*
Pork tenderloin, wild mushrooms with crème fraiche and tarragon

Recipe

Serves 4

Ingredients
5 tbsps olive oil
300g (10oz) wild chanterelle
or morel mushrooms
1 garlic clove, diced
1kg (1¼lb) pork tenderloin
1 sweetcorn cob
60ml (¼ cup) crème fraiche
2 tbsps butter
3 tbsps white wine
1 bunch of tarragon, chopped
Salt and pepper

The method
Heat a heavy-based frying pan over medium heat. Add two tablespoons of oil and sauté mushrooms. Add garlic and fry for a few seconds. Remove from heat, season and set aside.

Add two tablespoons of oil to the frying pan and heat over medium heat. Place pork in the pan and cook, turning regularly, until it begins to caramelise (approximately 15 minutes for medium rare). If pork is spitting, cover loosely with foil. Remove from heat and set aside to rest for at least 10 minutes.

Use a sharp knife to cut down the length of the corn close to the core, to remove the kernels. Heat remaining oil over a high heat in the same frying pan. Add corn kernels and cook for a few minutes.

Turn off heat and add the mushroom mixture, crème fraiche, butter, white wine, tarragon to pan with corn and season.

To serve, slice the tenderloin and spoon over mushroom and corn mixture.

According to chef Anthony Rose, being expelled from Montréal's Concordia University in the late 1980s for cheating on a cartography exam was the best thing that could have happened to him. "I wasn't a very good student," he says as he settles into one of the dusky red booths of his restaurant, Rose and Sons on Queen St, which opened in Toronto in 2015.

Since graduating from the California Culinary Academy in San Francisco's Tenderloin district in the early 1990s, Rose has become one of Toronto's most lauded restaurateurs, known for taking over what he calls the "dying lights" of the city's dining scene and illuminating them anew. "It is in our heart and soul to go to these places that have been such a big part of our culture," he says. "So when the Swan [as the restaurant was previously called] came up for business it really was a dream come true."

After 17 years and having become an institution, the Swan closed in 2015 due to financial issues. The outcry was palpable, especially from those who had spent leisurely mornings enjoying its famed eggs benedict or a glass or two of Toronto's beloved brunch cocktail, the Caesar. Eggs benedict is still on the menu but it is now served on homemade sourdough bread with a choice of wild mushrooms, stewed peppers or clothbound cheddar.

The wood-framed booths were removed, cleaned and reupholstered before being returned to Rose and Sons' long, dim dining room. A record player sits next to the kitchen and the shelves are heavy with records from Rose's vinyl collection. "It still has that little bit of dankness to it, that feeling of being old school," he says with relish.

Rose and Sons on Queen St is the fourth in Rose and business partner Robert Wilder's roster of restaurants and it takes a similarly thematic approach to its forebears. "At all the restaurants I really encourage the chefs to do what they want to do," says Rose, over the spatter of pork tenderloin being seared in the kitchen behind him by chef Sonia Marwick. "The way I see it with our restaurants is that we're not the cheapest, we're not the most expensive. But we offer very good, simple food and that really drives everything we do."

Rose's goal after graduating from cookery school was to open his first restaurant by the time he was 30. "But it didn't actually happen until I was 40," he says. "That's why I'm moving so fast now: I've just got so much in me that I've got to get out." — (M)
roseandsons.ca

Zum Schwarzen Kameel, *Vienna*
Wiener schnitzel

Recipe

Serves 4

Ingredients
4 x 150g (6oz) pieces of saddle of veal
5 eggs
200g (1⅔ cups) flour
200g (4 cups) fine breadcrumbs
250ml (1 cup) rapeseed oil
250ml (1 cup) clarified butter
Salt and pepper

The method
Place the portions of veal between two sheets of baking paper and hammer until very thin. Season well.

Crack the eggs into a wide, shallow bowl and lightly beat with a fork.

Place the flour and the breadcrumbs in separate shallow bowls.

Remove the veal from the paper and season again. Dip into the flour to coat evenly, followed by the egg mixture and then the breadcrumbs.

Heat the oil and butter in a large heavy-based frying pan over medium-high heat. Fry the breaded schnitzel until golden brown (approximately two minutes each side).

Serve with half a lemon or lime.

A venue with a history dating back to 1618 is a rarity, even in Old Europe. However, on the narrow Bognergasse in Vienna's Baroque Innere Stadt, Zum Schwarzen Kameel (loosely translated as The Black Camel) has been going strong since Johann Baptist Cameel established it as a spice retailer. Transformed into a dining establishment 200 years later, this is the place where nobility came to relax over comfort food, where Beethoven dined and where artists such as photographer Elfie Semotan still come for a drink. "From about 1830 until the First World War, Kameel supplied wines and spices to the imperial court – and the Habsburgs and other celebrities came here to eat and drink as well," says owner Peter Friese (*pictured*), whose parents took over the business in the 1950s.

The immediate postwar period was a low point for the venue but these days the Kameel is again a meeting place for well-to-do locals. In the bar a mixed crowd sits along a dark-wood counter or stands at chest-height tables sampling tiny sandwiches (introduced by Friese's late mother). In the restaurant the tiled walls, hanging half-moon lamps, classic vitrines and wooden panelling from the early 1900s are a shining example of original Viennese art deco.

In many ways Zum Schwarzen Kameel is a reflection of modern Austria: high culture and blue blood meets earthy pleasure and smiling hospitality (the moustachioed maître d', Johann Georg Gensbichler, is well known for his impeccable service). Viennese classics such as veal goulash and schnitzel are favoured, although vegetarian dishes also grace the monthly menu.

Seasonal ingredients are found close to home as much as possible. "You can define Austrian cuisine in a lot of ways," says the Salzburg-born chef de cuisine Sevgi Hartl. "It can be schnitzel, trout or dumplings. But as traditional as we are, we make sure we modernise to customers' tastes as they evolve. Not everyone wants to eat *schweinsbraten* [roast pork] every day." To prepare a perfect wiener schnitzel, she says, the 150g veal cut should be hammered thin, breaded, quickly fried until golden brown and plated up.

Serving about 100 covers a night, Kameel is a place where Vienna's mayor will dine with statesmen and come again with his family. "You can see them relax during the meal," says Friese of better-known customers. But Kameel doesn't eschew more common requests: "If a child wants French fries with ketchup, of course he can have French fries with ketchup," he says, laughing. After all, 400 years on, this place has seen it all. — (M)
kameel.at

Common Ground, *Hong Kong*
California burger

Recipe

Serves 4

Ingredients

500g (1¼lbs) minced beef
1 egg
½ red onion, finely diced
10g (1 tbsp) oatmeal
4 slices of cheddar cheese
4 fresh burger buns
4 slices of pineapple
1 small butter lettuce
Ketchup, mustard and thousand island sauce, to serve

The method

Place mince, egg, onion and oatmeal in a large bowl and mix by hand until well combined. Portion into 4 even patties.

Preheat oven to 200C (400F/GM6).

Heat a griddle pan over medium-high heat. Cook burger patties, flipping every 15 seconds for 6 minutes. Turn the heat off, place the cheese on top of the patties and allow it to melt for 20 seconds. Transfer patties to a plate and cover with foil to keep warm.

Slice the buns in half and place in the oven. Cook for 3 to 4 minutes, watching closely to ensure they don't burn.

Heat the griddle over medium-high heat and cook the pineapple for approximately 2 minutes on each side.

To assemble each burger, top bun with patty, lettuce and a slice of pineapple. Add ketchup, mustard and thousand island sauce to taste. Place the other half of the bun on top and serve.

Finding a peaceful café that serves a good cup of coffee and a tasty burger or simple salad alongside a wide selection of independent magazines might not be a hard task in cities such as Sydney, New York and London. But in Hong Kong, where western food can be overpriced and quiet neighbourhoods are hard to come by, a meal at Common Ground is a rare treat.

"We knew we had to do a place that served comfort food," says Joshua Ng who runs the restaurant with his twin brother Caleb (*both pictured, Joshua on left*). "Hong Kong lacks simple food; even something as basic as avocado toast is often done wrong. I want Hong Kongers to know that good food can be simple."

Tucked away on a set of stairs that connects Hong Kong's busy Soho district to the residential Mid-Levels, Common Ground's glass front can open up in warmer months. The 1945 building is in an old neighbourhood where the pace of life is relaxed. "We went to university in Los Angeles and we miss finding chilled-out cafés where you can spend a whole day reading a book," says Joshua. "We wanted to create a similar environment here as it's hard to find in Hong Kong."

Common Ground, formerly known as Protest Design, originated as a design studio founded by brothers Sean and Elias Lam in 2012. "The customers always wanted to hang out and have drinks so [Sean and Elias] decided to start a café," says Caleb. Having started out by importing wine from the Napa Valley and pairing it with home-cooked dishes at private kitchen events, the Ng twins joined forces with the Lams. In early 2013 the four turned Common Ground into a café that maintains a small retail offering on the side, selling everything from local hand-crafted jewellery to regional Man Cha tea.

The menu features classic burgers, scrambled eggs and simple soups; the coffee is made from three different beans, all roasted in Hong Kong. "Originally I used Ethiopian and Indonesian beans but it was quite acidic so I added Colombian beans to add chocolate to the taste," says Joshua. The café's burger patty is made fresh every day, mixing Hong Kong beef with US beef (and a touch of soy sauce) to bring depth to the flavour.

Common Ground is a hit with Hong Kongers as well as the large expatriate population. "We want to add on some more Chinese elements," says Caleb. "Something like traditional Hong Kong milk tea. We want to make our café like the store name: it's a common ground so both groups can exchange stories here." — (M)
+852 2818 8318

Lurra, *London*
Solomillo pork with pobre potatoes

Recipe

Serves 4

Ingredients

2 large potatoes, cut into ½ cm-thick
(¼ inch) half-moon shapes
½ medium onion, sliced
1 bay leaf
Few stalks of thyme
4 garlic cloves, cut in half
100ml (7 tbsps) olive oil
400g (14oz) solomillo (Ibérico pork fillet)
1 egg yolk
Salt and pepper

The method

Place potato in a bowl and add onion, bay leaf, thyme and garlic. Mix well.

Add oil to a heavy-based frying pan and heat over high heat. When oil is very hot, add potato mixture to pan and cook until golden. Remove potato from pan (discarding bay leaf) and transfer to a plate lined with kitchen roll to drain.

Heat a non-stick frying pan or a griddle over medium heat. Cook solomillo, turning occasionally, for approximately 10 to 11 minutes or until medium-rare (if you have a meat thermometer, cook pork until it reaches 56c/132f). Remove from heat and set aside to rest for a few minutes.

To serve, slice solomillo and place on a plate with potatoes. Drizzle with a little egg yolk and season.

Reprising a successful first restaurant is a tall order. But that didn't faze Melody Adams and Nemanja Borjanovic (*pictured*) when they decided to add a new space to bijou Basque joint Donostia, which they opened in Marylebone in London in 2012. They had set a high benchmark: Donostia's spare decor, small scale and faultless service (not to mention a menu that features delicacies such as hake *kokotxas pil-pil*) caused a stir when it first opened.

The pair's follow-up premises is also in Marylebone. Lurra – Basque for "land" – opened in 2015 and is a fitting sequel. The dining room is a whitewashed, marble-topped affair with pale wooden furniture and pistachio-green upholstery selected by Adams. A shelf of design books adds a homely feel, while the brass balustrade leading up the oak staircase, pointing to another 20 seats upstairs, is an elegant touch.

The kitchen is overseen by Tehran-born head chef Mahdi Seifi. He cut his teeth at Seville's Taberna del Alabardero and numerous other Basque restaurants, which exposed him to the region's food and culture. The ingredients and dishes at Lurra (roll the "r") have retained the simplicity of Donostia but the difference is the hardware: a heavy-duty robata-style grill in the centre of the open-plan dining room. According to Seifi, it's the heart of the kitchen.

"My cooking defines me; this is my life," says Seifi. "I started cooking at a really young age and haven't looked back since." Talk quickly turns to the colour, marbling and pH of his meat, and at what temperature you can expect the fat to melt (and the merits of grilling a turbot whole). Sourcing and cooking are a real passion; this shines through in the flavours of the grilled octopus with piquillo sauce and the 14-year-old Rubia Gallega prime rib.

"Opening a restaurant on the other side of town would have been obvious if we wanted to roll out a concept," says Borjanovic. "We don't want to be another chain," adds Adams. Like Borjanovic she worked in finance before a chance visit to San Sebastián ignited the idea of starting a restaurant. Opening a second space so close to the first was a happy accident; the couple fell in love with the new site as soon as they saw it. "Business-wise you don't want to cannibalise yourself but 80 per cent of our bookings at Donostia are still by word of mouth," says Adams.

Like Donostia before it, Lurra has a simple formula that is flawlessly executed: attentive owners and an obsessive chef are united in a mission to serve the best Basque produce they can find. — (M)
lurra.co.uk

Café Lisboa, *Lisbon*
Steak with Café Lisboa sauce

Recipe
Serves 4

Ingredients
2 tbsps olive oil
4 x 180g (6oz) eye-fillet steaks
40g (3 tbsps) butter
2 garlic cloves, finely sliced
3 sprigs of thyme
400ml (1⅔ cups) beef stock
80ml (⅓ cup) single cream
1 tbsp Dijon mustard
1 tsp lemon juice
Salt and pepper
French fries, to serve

The method
Preheat oven to 180C (350F/GM4).

Heat oil in a non-stick frying pan over high heat. Season steaks with salt and add to the pan. Cook for 1 minute on either side. Add 20g (1 tbsp) butter, garlic and 2 sprigs of thyme. Turn down heat to avoid burning the butter.

Move steaks to a tray (discard the thyme but retain the butter and garlic) and place in oven for 5 minutes.

For the sauce, add beef stock to the frying pan with butter and garlic and heat over medium-low heat. Add cream and mustard, stirring until well combined. Add remaining butter and thyme, stirring well again. Remove sauce from heat and add lemon juice.

To serve, place steaks in shallow bowls and pour over sauce. Serve with French fries.

Finding a perfectly cooked steak in the Portuguese capital can be tough, as many restaurants' menus revolve around fish and pork dishes. But the fact that beef isn't Portugal's strong suit hasn't stopped one of the Iberian nation's best chefs from dedicating his third restaurant to perfecting it.

"Three centuries ago Lisbon was among the cities that used to serve the most steaks in the world," says José Avillez, one of Portugal's most prominent authorities on the country's eating habits. "We had *tabernae* and cafés where artists and writers would get together and talk, have a drink – a coffee – or eat a steak. I wanted my restaurant to bring back this tradition in some way."

Café Lisboa is in the central district of Chiado and the restaurant shares a building with the city's opera house, the Teatro Nacional de São Carlos. It's a fitting host considering Avillez's appreciation of the classics. "We restored all the interiors, from replacing the gold leaf on the walls to installing a new bar. The restaurant has been open since 2013 but it looks like it has been unchanged for centuries," he says. Despite the building's age, the atmosphere is far from olde worlde and interior-design studio Anahory Almeida's flourishes provide a sense of freshness. There is also an outdoor terrace that draws a diverse lunch and dinner crowd throughout the week.

Steaks are the forte here and each is made from tenderloin beef from the reputable French Charolais breed, before being cooked sous vide the day before service with one of Café Lisboa's signature sauces.

Beyond its beef, Café Lisboa has brought back a few emblems from the capital's culinary past. "It took me three or four years to develop the recipe for our custard tart," Avillez says. Although the restaurant serves *bacalhau à Brás* (shredded cod, onion and potato with olives) and beef croquettes with turnip-topped rice, these staples have become unfashionable and increasingly hard to find elsewhere in Lisbon. "We have developed new techniques of preparing these traditional recipes, as we have with our steaks, which rest an hour after slow cooking before being reheated bain-marie style and then teppaned [cooked on an iron griddle] for a couple of minutes," he says.

"Our kitchen is small and very busy with up to 100 people being served in an hour sometimes," adds Avillez. "So when we conceptualise our menus it takes a long time for us to develop ways not only to produce plates but to deliver them as best we can in the restaurant." — (M)
cafelisboa.pt

Eventide Oyster Company, *Portland (Maine)*
Bloody Maria

Recipe

Serves 2

Ingredients
Ice
180ml (¾ cup) tequila
440ml (1¾ cups) tomato juice
2 limes, juiced
10ml (2 tsps) jalapeño pickle juice
10ml (2 tsps) rice-wine vinegar
1½ tsps sugar
1 tsp horseradish
1 tsp Tabasco
½ tsp Worcestershire sauce
Pinch of onion powder
Pinch of garlic powder
2 olives
2 slices of lemon
Salt and pepper

The method
Fill two pint glasses with ice and add 90ml (6 tbsps) of tequila to each.

Place the rest of the ingredients in a jug and stir to combine. Divide between the glasses.

To serve, garnish with a skewered olive and slice of lemon.

It all began in 2009 at Hugo's, one of Portland's finest restaurants, just after its owner Rob Evans won the James Beard award for best chef in the northeast. In the span of a year he hired the team that would ultimately create Eventide: Arlin Smith, Mike Wiley and Andrew Taylor.

"Hugo's was situated next door to a cookbook shop – one of the best in the world. It was amazing," says Wiley on a sunny morning in Portland. "We'd run out of the restaurant, dip in next door, flip through a cookbook and say, 'Oh, that's right – with agar!' and run back." When the owners of Rabelais Books decided not to renew their lease in 2012, Smith, Wiley and Taylor (*pictured, left to right*) seized the opportunity to take over the space and also buy Hugo's, which Evans had been keen to part with for some time.

Three months later, Eventide Oyster Company opened on the site of the bookshop. It was decided that the concept would be more casual than Hugo's (which the new owners vowed to keep unchanged): bar seating, no need for reservations and a menu revolving around simple dishes. But an unusual set-up guarantees the two restaurants' cohesion: they share a kitchen. "When we first opened our running joke was from *Jaws*, when they finally clap eyes on the shark and say, 'We're going to need a bigger boat,'" says Wiley.

The centrepiece of Eventide's space (and its menu) is the massive granite bed of oysters laid out on ice but few dishes rival the lobster roll, a staple of any Mainer's diet. The recipe for this sandwich stuffed with lobster and mayonnaise is traditionally simple but here it veers from convention – at the risk of angering a few locals.

"We're staying true to Maine history but we're also elevating it," says Taylor. Every morning in peak season about 400 to 500 lobsters are delivered to the restaurant, a few steps from Casco Bay. Unlike elsewhere, Eventide's lobster is blanched and prepared in a special oven before being served on handmade bread. "Putting a lobster roll on a steamed bun is definitely not tradition," says Taylor, who didn't like the mass-produced aspect of the classic toasted white roll. "They're steamed to order so they're like warm pillowy clouds that just melt away," says Smith.

The recipe, which tastes particularly good with a Bloody Maria, has made a splash on the food scene, which just goes to show that with a sprinkling of innovation, a local snack can become a universal classic. — (M)
eventideoysterco.com

The Hand & Flowers, *Marlow, UK*
Chocolate pots

Recipe

Serves 4

Ingredients

80g (5 tbsps) muscovado sugar
5 egg yolks
500ml (2 cups) double cream
2 vanilla pods, split lengthwise
200g (7oz) dark chocolate,
roughly chopped
Salt, to serve

The method

Place muscovado sugar and egg yolks in a large bowl. Mix well.

Heat a large heavy-based saucepan over high heat and add cream and vanilla. Bring to the boil. Remove from heat and pour over the egg mixture in the bowl.

Return the mixture to the saucepan and stir constantly over medium heat until it begins to thicken (the mixture will curdle slightly).

Place the chocolate in a large non-reactive bowl. Strain the cream mixture onto the chocolate and stir to combine (the cream mixture will melt the chocolate).

Pour mixture into small ramekins and place in fridge to set (for a few hours or overnight).

Sprinkle with salt and serve at room temperature.

What tapas bars are to Spain and bistros to France, pubs are to the UK. And while it's true that it's an institution in danger, with dozens of public houses closing every week due to rising beer taxes and changing tastes, Tom Kerridge isn't unduly concerned. He's the owner and chef at The Hand & Flowers in the well-bred town of Marlow, a 45-minute drive from London – and this is the first (and only) pub in the world to hold two Michelin stars.

"I spent most of my career at Michelin-starred restaurants and they're amazing places to work but not the sort of place where I would want to eat," says Kerridge. A man more fond of lager and ale than shiraz and malbec, it was only natural that he should open a pub that could offer first-class cooking at affordable prices.

Inside The Hand & Flowers kitchen, chefs swing pots and pans, dodging boiling stock and sizzling meat and cheering at the near misses, all under the watchful eye of Aaron Mulliss. The head chef has been here since 2007, a year after the pub was awarded its first Michelin star; his slick look and cocky attitude give him the air of a football captain. When Kerridge shouts, "Here we all work as a team, right lads?" the cooks stop for a second before uttering a resounding, "Yes, chef!" in unison. "That's why I became a chef: I love the camaraderie in the kitchen," says Kerridge.

"Food moves like fashion," he adds. "In the past it was the Spanish restaurants that were popular; recently it's been the Scandinavians. For a while in the UK we lost focus on our own food because we were trying to copy these trends. Fortunately we're slowly falling back in love with our own produce." The owner's enduring relationship with British cuisine means he prefers turnips, parsnips and carrots to Mediterranean tomatoes and aubergines. "Why serve a carpaccio when you can deliver a hearty soup?" he says, helping prepare the chocolate pot that Mulliss has whipped up in seconds.

Initially the simplicity of these dishes – with ingredients that can be found in any market and prepared without molecular methods – makes it hard to see how Kerridge has earned his multiple awards and rave reviews. However, just a spoonful of that chocolate dessert dispels any doubt. "When we opened we wanted to offer our patrons tasty, uncomplicated food – not earn Michelin stars," he says, sprinkling sea salt on the warm pots. "Winning them proves we've been doing things the right way. I'm not aiming for a third – but I definitely wouldn't want to lose my second one." — (M)
thehandandflowers.co.uk

Tadich Grill, *San Francisco*
Custard rice pudding

Recipe

Serves 4

Ingredients
590g (3¼ cups) cooked pudding
or arborio rice
6 eggs
2 oranges, zested
½ tsp cinnamon
1 tsp nutmeg
220g (1 cup) sugar
4 tbsps vanilla extract
120ml (½ cup) marsala wine
600ml (2½ cups) cream
2 tbsps honey
Melted butter, to grease

The method
Preheat oven to 170C (325F/GM3). Brush 4 x 1 cup ramekin dishes with melted butter to lightly grease. Fill each with cooked rice until it's full.

Place the eggs, orange zest, cinnamon, nutmeg, sugar, vanilla syrup, wine, cream and honey into a bowl and whisk until well combined.

Pour the mixture into the ramekins and sprinkle each with 1 tablespoon of vanilla extract.

Place in oven and bake for 35 to 40 minutes until the pudding is set. Remove from oven and allow it to cool at room temperature. Serve chilled with berries and mint.

At the Tadich Grill in San Francisco, tradition is king. Founded in 1849, serving rice custard since the 1920s and having a loyal staff of 36 (a Croatian called Tony Vrcic has been waiting tables since 1982) why would the Tadich change anything if its 110 seats are always full?

As the oldest restaurant in San Francisco this is a classic American dining room. There are seven mahogany booths where solicitous waiters wearing white jackets serve seafood dishes. In the centre, swivel chairs are stationed around a long bar. Tadich started out on a wharf as a coffee stand run by three Croatian immigrants and has moved eight times over the years, forced out by earthquakes and expanding building projects. It has been in its current location, a former bank in the heart of the financial district, since 1967. The restaurant is now in the hands of Mike Buich, whose grandfather bought it from its former proprietor, John Tadich, in 1928. That's a lot of history.

Head chef Barney Brown (*pictured*), who hails from Hawaii and previously worked at The Rotunda in Neiman-Marcus, sources the fish for his dishes from local suppliers that he calls each morning to make his order. Among these dishes is the restaurant's signature *cioppino*, a seafood stew said to have been invented in San Francisco during the 19th century when fishermen combined their catches of the day in a pot; Tadich serves approximately 32,000 bowls of it per year. All the produce is seasonal and the sauce is made fresh daily in an enormous steam kettle. Various chefs have honed the recipes over the years and Brown takes care to ensure that this tradition is carried on. "My philosophy with seafood is that I want to taste it," he says.

Another celebrated dish is the rice pudding, which has a distinguished lineage: "I know my grandfather and his brothers were making it," says Buich. Although Brown uses regular white rice, the results are never less than special. Robert Hass, the former US poet laureate, once recommended it on the radio after novelist Patrick O'Brian complained that there was no "decent pudding" in America.

Brown is in charge of a wide-ranging menu offering more than 75 starters, many of which are local catches – including sand dabs (a flatfish) and Dungeness crab – and he comes up with 12 specials daily. "At least half of this menu goes back 100 years," says Buich, which is around the time his grandfather took over the restaurant. "The most frequent comment I get from customers is, 'Please don't change anything.'" — (M)
tadichgrill.com

Karakoy Lokantasi, *Istanbul*
Kadaif with milky syrup

Recipe

Serves 10

Ingredients
250g (9oz) kadaif (Turkish dessert noodles)
100g (7 tbsps) butter
350g (3 cups) walnuts, crushed
500ml (2 cups) milk
300g (1½ cups) sugar
Extra milk, to serve

The method
Place kadaif in a bowl and carefully unravel strands. Preheat the oven to 160C (320F/GM2.5).

Place sugar and milk in a saucepan over high heat and boil for 10 minutes, stirring occassionally. Remove from the hob and allow to cool.

Add the butter to a pan and melt. Pour it over the kadaif, ensuring that the noodles absorbs the butter.

Place two small handfuls of kadaif in a cup, sprinkle with the walnut and compress firmly.

Turn the cup upside dowm on a tray to create an 'igloo' shape; repeat to make 10 desserts.

Bake in the oven for 20 minutes at 160C (320F/GM2.5). Turn the oven to 170C (350F/ GM3) and bake for a further 15 minutes.

Remove desserts from the oven and set aside for 2 to 3 minutes to cool. To serve, pour milky syrup over each kadaif dessert plus 1 to 2 tablespoons of cold milk. Sprinkle with crushed walnut.

Lunchtime in Istanbul has a particular bustle as bankers and builders pull up seats beside one another in the city's *lokanta* canteens. In these garrulous places, chefs serve well-oiled meat, bulbous aubergines and liberally stuffed peppers from vats. Plus there's an unspoken agreement among diners that it's fine to share a table with a total stranger. Even the Turkish for bon appétit – *afiyet olsun* – is said as an invitation to tuck in with gusto and without pretence.

"You find people from all different trades and with very different lives eating in the *lokanta*," says Aylin Okutan (*pictured*), who runs Karakoy Lokantasi with her husband Oral Kurt. Their restaurant is a subtle update on the *lokanta*, with crisp tablecloths and tiles the colour of the Aegean Sea, care of Turkish design firm (and regular diners) Autoban.

Freshly made cold starters and cool milk desserts sit alluringly in glowing fridges. Okutan runs her finger down the menu, pointing out the Sultan's Delight (tender lamb on a bed of aubergine purée), stuffed vine leaves and *manti* (Turkish ravioli), traditional stalwarts of the city's restaurants. "We change the menu every lunchtime because half of our customers come every day," says Okutan. Her husband agrees: "For the lunch crowd, this place is like a club."

Together they draw up a weekly menu plan according to the weather and what's available in the city's markets. Karakoy Lokantasi prepares its Turkish staples in a lighter and healthier way than most of their traditional stablemates. To be authentic, the food still needs to taste like it's come straight from a mothers' kitchen and Kurt's mother was enlisted as the restaurant's first head chef. She trained the cooks – many of them veterans of the canteen trade – to go easy on the oil.

Finding the right ingredients has been as important as what happens in the kitchen. A fisherman arrives at Karakoy Lokantasi's door at 05.00 every day without fail, with the morning's catch of bream, bass and octopus. "Then the *manav* [grocer] arrives with more fresh stuff," says Okutan. "We also work with specialist shops from all over Turkey. Our feta comes from Trakya and our tahini from Antalya. It's taken time to search out the best."

Come 18.00, the entire menu changes along with the lunchtime kitchen staff as Karakoy Lokantasi turns into a *meyhane* after dark, where mezes of cold starters and grilled fish are served to accompany a night of toasting with aniseed-flavoured *raki*. It's a constant trade in here but it's what gives the restaurant its bustle. "We know 90 per cent of our diners personally," says Kurt. "This place is a lifestyle for us." — (M)
karakoylokantasi.com

The Monocle menu

In keeping with our fuss-free take on all things culinary we've picked up a few time-tested recipes to suit every occasion, from informal suppers to must-impress lunches. Here are some unfailingly simple ways to elevate an evening meal or indulge in a decadent snack.
Do tuck in.

I.
Yoghurt flatbread with braised leek and burrata
Mediterranean-style bite

SERVES: 4
PREP TIME: 20 MINS
COOKING TIME: 30 MINS

INGREDIENTS

Braised leeks
6 leeks, well washed
1 tbsp butter
3 garlic cloves, finely
   sliced
150ml (⅔ cup) vegetable
   stock

Flatbreads
300g (2⅓ cups) bread
   flour
300g (1¼ cups) Greek-
   style unsweetened
   yoghurt
2 tsps baking powder
1 tsp salt
3 tbsps olive oil
1 garlic clove
1 tbsp mixed herbs
   (rosemary, thyme,
   parsley)

To serve
2 balls of burrata cheese
2 lemons, zested
1 tsp chilli flakes
Olive oil

METHOD

Remove the ends and leaves of the leeks to form six roughly equal-sized pieces. Melt the butter in a large, shallow frying pan over medium heat. Add the garlic and the leeks. Stir to ensure leeks are well coated with butter and cook until they begin to brown. Add the stock, cover and cook for 10 minutes. Remove the lid and continue to cook for 5 minutes, stirring occasionally. When done the leeks should be caramelised, and soft when pierced with the tip of a sharp knife. Remove from heat, season and set aside.

For the flatbread, combine the bread flour, yoghurt, baking powder, salt and 1 tablespoon of the oil in a large bowl. Using your hands, gently incorporate all the ingredients until a dough forms. Turn it out onto a lightly floured surface and knead for a few minutes until smooth. Divide into 4 even balls, cover with the bowl and allow to rest for 10 minutes.

Using a mortar and pestle, gently crush herbs and the garlic with the remaining oil (the consistency should be thin; add more oil if a paste forms).

Heat a griddle pan over high heat. Using your hands, gently flatten and stretch each portion of dough to form a flatbread approximately 10cm in diameter (4 inches). Place on the griddle and cook, in batches, for 3 to 4 minutes each side (the pan will smoke a little). Once done, remove flatbreads from pan and brush with herb oil. Top with braised leek and burrata and sprinkle with lemon zest and chilli flakes. Drizzle with a little olive oil and serve.

NOTE *Burrata is a fresh cheese from Puglia, Italy. If you can't get burrata, substitute with buffalo mozzarella.*

2.
Gruyère and speck toasties
Grown-up grilled cheese sandwich

SERVES 2
PREP TIME 5 MINS
COOK TIME 4 MINS

INGREDIENTS

4 slices of sourdough
  bread
100g (4oz) gruyère
  cheese, finely grated
4 slices of speck
2 tbsps kalamata olives,
  pitted and roughly
  chopped
1 tbsp honey
1 tbsp butter
Pepper

METHOD

Place two slices of bread on a chopping board.
Top with half the cheese, followed by the speck and
olives. Add the rest of the cheese. Drizzle with honey
and generously season with pepper (no salt). Close
sandwiches with the other slices of bread and butter
each side.

Heat a griddle pan over high heat. Add the sandwiches
and turn the heat down to medium. Cook for
2 minutes each side, pressing down on the toasties
with a spatula to ensure the cheese melts. Serve.

3.
Warm potato-and-pancetta salad with hazelnuts
Salad for all seasons

SERVES: 4
PREP TIME: 10 MINS
COOKING TIME: 30 MINS

INGREDIENTS

500g (1¼lbs) baby new
  potatoes, halved
1 tbsp olive oil
2 sweetcorn cobs
95g (4oz) pancetta
100g (¾ cup) raw
  hazelnuts, skin on
140g (5oz) rocket
140g (5oz) red chicory
125g (4oz) red grapes,
  halved
Salt and pepper

Vinaigrette
75ml (5 tbsps) extra virgin
  olive oil
25ml (5 tbsps) white-wine
  vinegar
1 tsp Dijon mustard
Pinch of sugar

METHOD

Preheat oven to 200C (400F/GM6). Place the potatoes on a roasting tray with oil and season. Place the tray in the oven to cook for 20 minutes (set the timer).

Meanwhile, use a sharp knife to cut down the length of the corn close to the core, to remove the kernels.

When the timer rings, remove the tray from the oven and add the corn to the potatoes. Place the tray under the grill and cook for a further 10 minutes. Remove and set aside to cool.

Turn the oven back on and preheat to 200c (400F/GM6).

For the vinaigrette, combine all the ingredients in a bowl and mix well. Season and set aside.

Heat a frying pan over high heat and add the pancetta. Cook for 4 to 5 minutes or until the pancetta is crisp. Remove from the pan and drain on kitchen towel.

Place the hazelnuts on a baking tray and cook in the oven for 7 to 8 minutes (watching carefully so they don't burn) or until the skins start to separate from the nuts. Remove from the oven, place in a tea towel and roll back and forth with your hands for a few minutes or until most of the skins have been removed. Discard the skins.

Arrange the salad by layering the potatoes, rocket and chicory. Add the corn, pancetta, hazelnuts and grapes. Drizzle with the dressing and serve.

4.
Asian-style omelette with crab and miso butter
The breakfast standby, reinvented for all hours

SERVES: 4
PREP TIME: 10 MINS
COOKING TIME: 5 MINS
(PER OMELETTE)

INGREDIENTS
8 eggs
4 tsps butter
200g (7oz) crab, mix of
    white and dark meat
75g (3oz) pea shoots

Miso butter
25g (5 tsps) sweet white
    miso paste
Thumb-sized piece of
    ginger, finely grated
60g (4 tbsps) butter

To serve
2 long red chillies, sliced
4 spring onions, sliced
1 small bunch of coriander,
    leaves picked
Salt and pepper

METHOD
For the miso butter, heat a small saucepan over
low heat and add the miso paste, ginger and butter,
whisking quickly until melted. Set aside.

Heat a medium-sized non-stick frying pan over high
heat until very hot. Add a teaspoon of butter and
gently shake to coat the pan.

Crack two eggs into a bowl and quickly whisk
together. Add the egg to the frying pan and slowly
swirl around until evenly distributed. Cook the
omelette for 1 to 2 minutes or until it starts to bubble.
Don't flip it. Slide it out of the frying pan and onto
a plate. Arrange the pea shoots and crab on one half
and fold the other side over.

To serve, garnish with chilli, spring onion and
coriander, drizzle with the miso butter and season.
Repeat for each omelette.

5.
Sesame soba-noodle salad with prawns and pickled cucumbers
Flavourful noodles that pack a punch

SERVES: 4
PREP TIME: 10 MINS
COOKING TIME: 20 MINS

INGREDIENTS

300g (10oz) soba noodles
1 tbsp sesame oil
6 spring onions, julienned
1 tbsp sesame seeds, plus
  extra to serve
1 large bunch of
  coriander, leaves and
  stalks roughly chopped
12 large tiger prawns,
  peeled, deveined and
  tails intact

Pickled cucumber
1 large continental
  cucumber
1 heaped tsp salt
200ml (¾ cup) cider
  vinegar
100g (½ cup) sugar

Dressing
2cm (¾ inch) piece of
  ginger, peeled and
  grated
100ml (7 tbsps)
  sesame oil
2 tbsps light soy sauce
5 limes, juiced
4 tbsps vegetable oil
2 tsps sugar
1 long red chilli, deseeded
  and finely chopped
2 tsps fish sauce

METHOD

For the pickled cucumber, use a mandoline or a very sharp knife to finely slice the cucumber into rounds. Place in a bowl and add the salt, vinegar and sugar. Mix well and set aside to pickle for at least 20 minutes.

Cook the noodles according to packet instructions. Add to a bowl and toss with sesame oil. Set aside to cool.

To make the dressing, combine all the ingredients and mix well. Add to the noodles along with the onions, sesame seeds and coriander.

Drain the cucumbers and use your hands to squeeze out any excess liquid. Pat dry with kitchen towel and place in a small serving bowl.

Heat a griddle pan over high heat. Add the prawns and cook for 3 minutes either side or until cooked through (when done they will turn pink and opaque). To serve, top the noodle salad with prawns and sprinkle with extra sesame seeds.

NOTE *To make a vegetarian dish you can omit the prawns.*

6.
Pearl barley with maple-roasted carrots, shallots and feta
Robust salad for cooler months

SERVES: 4
PREP TIME: 10 MINS
COOKING TIME: 45 MINS

INGREDIENTS

400g (14oz) banana shallots, peeled and halved (with the roots intact)
300g (10oz) baby carrots, topped and washed thoroughly
1 tbsp olive oil
2 tbsps maple syrup
250g (1½ cups) pearl barley
75g (½ cup) raw almonds, skin on

Dressing
100ml (7 tbsps) extra virgin olive oil
1 tsp maple syrup
1 tsp Dijon mustard
2 lemons, juiced
1 garlic clove, crushed
Salt and pepper

To serve
75g (3oz) Greek feta
1 tbsp flat-leaf parsley, chopped

METHOD

Preheat oven to 200C (400F/GM6). Place the shallots flat side down in a roasting tray and add the carrots. Drizzle with the olive oil and maple syrup and season. Roast for 40 minutes.

Cook the pearl barley according to packet instructions. Drain and set aside to cool.

Lightly toast the almonds in a frying pan over medium heat for 4 to 5 minutes or until they start to brown slightly. Set aside to cool, then chop coarsely.

For the dressing, combine all ingredients in a bowl, season and mix well.

Spoon the pearl barley onto a large, flat serving dish. Add the carrots and shallots and top with the almonds. To serve, crumble the feta on top, add the parsley and drizzle with the dressing.

7.
Roasted celeriac soup with cheesy toast and rocket pesto
Easy winter warmer

SERVES: 6
PREP TIME: 10 MINS
COOKING TIME: 50 MINS

INGREDIENTS

Celeriac soup

2 celeriac (approximately 1kg/1¼lbs), peeled and diced into 2cm (¾ inch) pieces
2 tbsps olive oil
1 heaped tbsp butter
2 leeks, sliced into 1cm-thick (½ inch) rounds
1 garlic clove, crushed
2 medium potatoes (approximately 400g/14oz), peeled and quartered
1.5ltr (6 cups) vegetable stock
300ml (1¼ cups) single cream
1 tbsp Dijon mustard
1 lemon, juiced
Salt and pepper

Rocket pesto

100ml (7 tbsps) olive oil, plus 2 additional tbsps
30g (1oz) parmesan cheese, finely grated
1 garlic clove, roughly chopped
50g (2oz) rocket
1 lemon, juiced
30g (3 tbsps) pine nuts
1 tsp salt

Cheesy toasts

4 slices of sourdough bread, toasted
1 tbsp butter
140g (5oz) gruyère cheese, finely grated

METHOD

Preheat the oven to 180C (350F/GM4). Place the celeriac in a baking dish. Drizzle with the oil and place in the oven for 45 minutes or until soft.

For the rocket pesto, place all ingredients in a blender. Pulse until a paste forms. Add a little warm water to loosen the mixture and pulse again. Stir through 2 tablespoons of olive oil, season well and set aside.

Heat a large stockpot over medium heat. Add the butter, oil and leeks and cook, stirring occasionally, for approximately 10 minutes or until leeks are soft. Add the garlic and sauté for 1 minute. Add the potatoes and stock and turn up the heat to high. Bring to the boil and then reduce the temperature to medium. Cover and simmer gently for 20 minutes or until the potatoes are soft. Add the celeriac and simmer for a further 5 minutes.

Remove from the heat and set aside for a few minutes to cool slightly. Using a blender, process the soup in batches until smooth. Stir through the cream, mustard and lemon juice. Season generously.

Butter the sourdough toast and place on a baking tray. Top with the cheese. Set the oven to the grill and place the tray under it. Watch toast carefully while the cheese melts and remove from heat once it begins to bubble.

To serve, ladle the soup into bowls, top with the cheesy toast and drizzle with the rocket pesto.

NOTES *Celeriac is at its best during autumn and winter. To save time it's possible to use a high-quality shop-bought rocket pesto, thinned with a little extra virgin olive oil.*

8.
Orecchiette pasta with courgette, sausage and chilli
Quick-fix weeknight wonder

SERVES: 6
PREP TIME: 5 MINS
COOKING TIME: 25 MINS

INGREDIENTS

25g (2 tbsps) butter
2 garlic cloves, finely
   sliced
2 medium courgettes,
   sliced into half moons
1 heaped tsp chilli flakes
6 × (approximately 400g/
   14oz) organic pork-and-
   fennel sausages
500g (1¼lbs) orecchiette
   pasta
1.5ltr (6 cups) chicken
   stock
200g (7oz) baby spinach
1 lemon, finely zested

To serve
Parmesan
Salt and pepper

METHOD

Place a large frying pan over medium heat.
Add the butter and garlic and cook until fragrant.
Add the courgette and cook, stirring occasionally, for
approximately 10 minutes or until soft and starting
to brown. Sprinkle with chilli flakes.

With a sharp knife, make a small incision in the end of
each sausage. Using your hands, gently push the meat
out of each casing and into the frying pan (so that
small meatballs are formed). Don't be concerned if
they break up a little. Repeat for all sausages and then
cook for a further 5 minutes, stirring occasionally, or
until the meat begins to brown.

Transfer to a bowl, cover and set aside.

Return the frying pan to the heat (without cleaning
it) and add the pasta and stock. Cover and cook for
12 to 14 minutes. Add the spinach and replace the lid
to cook for another minute.

Place the courgette and sausage back in the pan and
stir for a couple of minutes to combine (there may be
some liquid remaining but the pasta should be cooked
through). Add the lemon zest, generous amounts of
parmesan and stir well. Season and serve.

NOTE *Listen up: orecchiette means 'little ears' in Italian. It can be
substituted for any type of small pasta.*

9.
Rack of lamb with chilli-roasted fennel and butternut squash
Perfect roast for need-to-impress occasions

SERVES: 4
PREP TIME: 20 MINS
COOKING TIME: 45 MINS

INGREDIENTS

600g (1½lbs) butternut
   squash
4 fennel bulbs, fronds
   removed
4 garlic cloves, peeled and
   halved
1 tsp chilli flakes
1 tbsp olive oil
2 × 500g (18oz) racks of
   French-trimmed lamb
Salt and pepper

Yoghurt dressing
150ml (⅔ cup) natural
   yoghurt
2 tbsps pomegranate juice
1 tbsp maple syrup
2 tbsps mint leaves,
   chopped

METHOD

Preheat the oven to 200C (400F/GM6). Chop the squash into wedges. Slice the fennel into quarters and place on a roasting tray with the garlic. Sprinkle over the chilli flakes, drizzle with oil and season. Place in the oven to cook for 20 minutes.

While the vegetables are cooking, heat a frying pan over high heat. Season the lamb rack and add to the pan (turning to ensure all surfaces are sealed). Add the lamb to the roasting tray, balancing it on top of the vegetables. Return the tray to the oven and cook for 15 minutes. Remove the lamb from the oven, wrap in foil and set aside to rest. Cook the vegetables for a further 10 minutes.

For the dressing, combine all ingredients, season and mix well.

When the vegetables are cooked, remove from the oven and transfer to a plate. Slice the lamb, arrange on top and serve with the yoghurt dressing.

10.
Sea bass en papillote
Seafood, all wrapped up

SERVES: 4
PREP TIME: 10 MINS
COOKING TIME: 35 MINS

INGREDIENTS

650g (1½lbs) potatoes
(kipfler or charlotte)
Olive oil
4 whole small sea
bass (approximately
250g/9oz each), gutted,
scaled and cleaned
2 lemons, sliced into
thick rounds
1 large bunch of dill
100ml (7 tbsps) white
wine
400g (14oz) cherry vine
tomatoes
200g (7oz) green beans
60g (⅓ cup) kalamata
olives, pitted and halved
lengthwise
3 tbsps capers, drained
Salt and pepper

METHOD

Preheat the oven to 180C (350F/GM4). Slice the potatoes and place on an oven tray. Drizzle with oil and season.

Place each fish in the centre of a 30 sq cm (12 square inches) piece of baking paper and stuff with lemon and dill. Pour a quarter of the white wine over each, drizzle with oil and season well.

To enclose the fish, bring the edges of the paper running along the fish together and fold down to secure. Tuck the ends near the head and tail under the fish.

When the potatoes have been in the oven for 10 minutes, add the tomatoes to the roasting tray. Add the fish to the oven for a further 20 minutes or until cooked through.

Bring a pot of water to the boil. Top and tail the beans and cut in half. Blanch beans in boiling water for 2 minutes then remove from heat, drain and refresh under cold running water.

Place beans in a bowl with the olives, capers and 1 tablespoon of oil, and season well. Set aside.

Remove the vegetables and fish from the oven. Carefully unwrap the fish (beware steam when opening the parcels) and serve with the accompanying sides.

11.
Baked meatballs with cherry-tomato sauce
Homely Italian classic

SERVES: 4
PREP TIME: 10 MINS
COOKING TIME: 50 MINS

INGREDIENTS

Cherry-tomato sauce
2 tbsps olive oil
1 large white onion,
    finely sliced
1 garlic clove
1.2kg (2¾lbs) cherry vine
    tomatoes, washed, with
    vines removed
50ml (3 tbsps) balsamic
    vinegar
200ml (¾ cup) tomato
    passata
1 tbsp dark brown sugar

Meatballs
100ml (7 tbsps) milk
75g (¾ cup) breadcrumbs
500g (1¼lbs) pork mince
400g (14oz) veal mince
1 small white onion, very
    finely diced
1 egg, lightly beaten
1 tsp thyme leaves, finely
    chopped
2 tbsps olive oil

To serve
Basil leaves, chopped
Parmesan, grated
Crusty bread

METHOD

For the tomato sauce, place a large, heavy-based frying pan over low-medium heat. Add the oil and onions and sauté, stirring occasionally, for 8 to 10 minutes or until the onions are soft and transparent. Don't be tempted to rush this stage – the sweetness of the sauce depends upon it.

Add the garlic, cherry tomatoes and a splash of water to the pan. Turn the heat up to medium and cook for approximately 20 minutes, stirring occasionally, or until the tomatoes burst and the sauce begins to thicken. Add the vinegar, passata and brown sugar and season generously. Remove from heat and set aside.

To make the meatballs, place the milk in a large bowl and add the breadcrumbs. Add the pork, veal, onion, egg and thyme and season well, using your hands to combine thoroughly. Portion into golf-ball-sized meatballs.

Heat the oil in a large frying pan over high heat and add the meatballs. Cook gently in batches, turning occasionally, for 3 to 4 minutes or until browned all over.

Pour the sauce into a large ceramic baking dish and add the meatballs. Place in the oven for 30 minutes. To serve, spoon a portion of meatballs and sauce onto each plate and top with basil leaves and parmesan. Serve with crusty bread.

12.
Butterflied sumac chicken with warm aubergine and chickpea salad
Chicken with a Middle Eastern twist

SERVES: 4
PREP TIME: 5 MINS
COOKING TIME: 45 MINS

INGREDIENTS

Aubergine salad
6 tbsps olive oil
1 large onion, finely sliced
2 aubergines, diced into
  1cm (½ inch) pieces
1 tsp ground coriander
½ tsp ground cumin
1 garlic clove, crushed
1 large red chilli, finely
  diced
2 × 400g (15oz) cans of
  chickpeas, drained
2 lemons, juiced
2 tbsps sultanas
1 large bunch of flat-leaf
  parsley

Sumac chicken
1.8kg (4lb) chicken,
  butterflied (you can ask
  your butcher to do this)
150ml (⅔ cup) olive oil
1 tbsp ground sumac
1 tsp sweet smoked
  paprika
1 tsp ground cumin
Salt and pepper

METHOD

Preheat the oven to 200C (400F/GM6).

Heat a large frying pan over low heat and add the onion and 2 tablespoons of oil. Sauté, stirring occasionally, for 8 to 10 minutes or until onions are soft and transparent. Set aside.

For the chicken, combine the olive oil with the sumac, paprika and cumin in a bowl and mix well. Slash the skin of the chicken and massage with the herb mixture. Season well and place on a wire rack inside a lined baking tray (to catch the juices). Place in the oven and cook for 35 minutes or until cooked through, with the skin crispy.

Add the aubergine to the frying pan with the onions and the remaining oil and stir well. Turn the heat to medium, cover and cook for 15 minutes, stirring occasionally. When the aubergine begins to brown and soften add the coriander, cumin, garlic, red chilli, chickpeas, lemon juice and sultanas. Simmer on a low heat, stirring occasionally, while the chicken is cooking. Stir through the parsley, season well and serve alongside portions of the chicken.

13.
Asian fish burger
Korean comfort food

SERVES: 4
PREP TIME: 10 MINS
COOKING TIME: 50 MINS

INGREDIENTS

Crumbed fish fillets
480g (1lb) skinless cod
    loin fillet
2 eggs
150g (1 cup) flour
75g (1½ cups)
    breadcrumbs
1 small bunch of
    coriander, roughly
    chopped
2 limes, zested
100ml (7 tbsps) vegetable
    oil, for frying

Pickled onion
150ml (⅔ cup) apple
    cider vinegar
1 tbsp sugar
1 heaped tsp salt
1 red onion, thinly sliced

Gochujang mayonnaise
4 tbsps whole egg
    mayonnaise
3 tbsps gochujang chilli
    sauce
2 limes, juiced

To serve
4 brioche buns
1 butter lettuce
1 cucumber, cut into
    ribbons

METHOD

For the pickled onion, add the vinegar, salt, sugar and 200ml water in a small bowl. Whisk well then add the onion. Set aside to pickle for 1 hour.

For the mayonnaise, add all the ingredients in a bowl and mix until well combined. Set aside.

Slice cod into 4 evenly sized pieces.

Crack eggs into a large bowl and lightly whisk. Place the flour and the breadcrumbs in two separate bowls. Add the coriander and zest to the breadcrumbs and mix well. Dip the fillets in the flour, shaking off any excess. Dip in the egg and then in the breadcrumb mixture, pressing firmly to coat. Season well.

Heat the oil in a large heavy-based frying pan over a high heat for a few minutes, or until it is very hot. Add each fillet and cook for 2 to 3 minutes on either side until golden and breaking apart slightly. Carefully remove fish from pan and transfer to a plate lined with kitchen roll to drain.

Lightly toast buns under the grill or in a hot griddle pan. To serve, place lettuce on the base of each bun, top with the fish, cucumber, pickled onion and mayonnaise. Close with the other half of the bread and serve.

NOTE *Gochujang is a Korean chilli sauce. It can be substituted with sriracha or hot chilli sauce.*

14.
Lemon and ricotta cake with limoncello syrup
Tipsy bake with a touch of citrus

SERVES: 10
PREP TIME: 15 MINS
COOKING TIME: 70 MINS

INGREDIENTS
Lemon and ricotta cake
250g (1 cup, 2 tbsps)
  butter
150g (¾ cup) sugar
3 eggs
500g (2 cups) ricotta
3 lemons, zested
2 tbsps limoncello
1 tsp vanilla bean paste
150g (1 cup, 1 tbsp) flour
1 tsp baking powder

Limoncello syrup
5 tbsps limoncello
3 tbsps icing sugar

To serve
300g (10oz) mixed berries
Crème fraiche or double
  cream

METHOD
Preheat oven to 160C (325F/GM3). Grease and line a round 20cm (8 inch) cake tin that has a removable base.

Use an electric beater to beat the butter and sugar in a mixing bowl until light and fluffy (approximately 5 minutes).

Add the eggs, one at a time, to the bowl (beat well before adding the second).

In a separate mixing bowl, add the ricotta, zest, limoncello and vanilla bean paste and stir until smooth. Add this to the butter mixture and beat until thoroughly combined.

Sift the flour and baking powder into the bowl with the cake mixture and use a spatula to gently fold in the dry ingredients.

Pour the mixture into the prepared cake tin and use a spatula to smooth the surface. Place in the preheated oven and bake for 60 minutes. It is done when a skewer inserted into the centre of the cake comes out clean.

Remove from the oven and set aside for 20 minutes to cool. Release the cake from the pan and place on a wire rack to cool completely (the cake will fall a little in the centre).

For the syrup, heat a small saucepan over medium heat. Add the limoncello and icing sugar and cook for approximately 3 minutes, or until the sugar is dissolved. Remove from heat.

Top the cake with the mixed berries and limoncello syrup. Slice into pieces and serve with a dollop of crème fraiche or double cream.

15.
Rice pudding with poached rhubarb and gingersnap crumb
Delicious dessert, hot or cold

SERVES: 4
PREP TIME: 10 MINS
COOKING TIME: 20 MINS

INGREDIENTS

Rice pudding
500ml (2 cups) milk
250g (1¼ cups) arborio/
   pudding rice
1 tsp vanilla bean paste
4 tbsps maple syrup
1 tsp ground ginger
100ml (7 tbsps) single
   cream

Poached rhubarb
4 stalks of rhubarb,
   chopped into 5cm-long
   batons
3 tbsps sugar

To serve
6 gingersnap biscuits,
   lightly crushed
Maple syrup, for drizzling

METHOD

Preheat oven to 140C (275F/GM1). Place the rhubarb, 2 tablespoons of water and sugar in a small baking dish and mix well. Cover the dish tightly with foil and place in the oven for 30 minutes or until the rhubarb is very soft and falling apart.

For the pudding, place the milk, rice, vanilla bean paste and 250ml (1 cup) of water in a heavy-based saucepan. Bring to the boil over medium heat then reduce heat. Place the lid on the pot so it is half covered and cook for 15 minutes, stirring occasionally, until the rice is soft and creamy. Stir through the maple syrup and ginger.

To serve (either warm or cold), stir through the cream and place in bowls. Top with poached rhubarb, drizzle with maple syrup and sprinkle with crumbled gingersnap biscuits.

NOTE *The rhubarb can be substituted for berries during summer.*

Cook's notes

Ingredients

While it's not essential to use organic produce and free-range meat, it's good to be generous (whether you're entertaining or eating alone) and use the best ingredients you can get hold of. Plus, the flavour of many recipes will be improved by using fruit and vegetables while they are in season. Unless stated otherwise, our recipes use full-fat milk, salted butter, large eggs (average weight 65g), plain flour and unwaxed lemons and limes for zesting. Herbs are fresh unless specified as dried. For seasoning we use sea salt and freshly ground black pepper.

Measurements

Where relevant we have included both metric and imperial measurements in our recipes. The tablespoon measurement is 15g according to those used in the UK, US and New Zealand (Australian tablespoons are 20g). When measuring dry ingredients, level the top of the measuring device with the flat of a knife. Where a measurement is not given (olive oil, for example), the amount to be used is discretionary.

Ovens

Our recipes are tested in a conventional oven. If you are using a fan-forced oven we recommend reducing the temperature by 10 to 20C. For convenience we have listed temperatures in Celsius, Fahrenheit and as a gas mark.

PART 4.

The Directory

10.
Restaurants, Cafés & Bars

Where in the world to dine and drink

What do you really want from a restaurant, bar or café? While most recommendations are preoccupied with congratulating a clutch of lauded chefs (at the same few restaurants) or fawning over a so-called "mixologist" du jour, we've totted up the places that have been consistently good for decades – not to mention newer establishments with all the ingredients to become favourites. At its core, our list suggests that the drinking and dining experiences we treasure aren't about pageantry or affectation. Forget square plates, foams, emulsions and innovation for its own sake. Instead, our A to Z guide celebrates hospitality done well around the globe with simple, honest food and genuine service from chefs and restaurateurs with a stake in the business. From a smart seafood restaurant in Auckland to a coffee shop in Reykjavík and a wine bar in Warsaw, these are the places that pride themselves on being unpretentious and where the maître d' or person behind the counter will more than likely remember your name. Not forgetting, of course, the memorable dishes and drinks they create that you'll find yourself coming back for time and again.

The mess hall-style dining area is offset with comfy booths

Pink Moon Saloon is a narrow building with a broad fanbase

Osteria Oggi
Adelaide
Italian staples

For years Adelaide's Italian heritage could only be tasted in shabby old-school restaurants but by 2015 Simon Kardachi opened Osteria Oggi as an unashamedly modern outing. The menu finds harmony in an Antipodean take on classic Italian staples. The tunnel-like entrance follows a long deep-set bar, opening on to a large mess hall where diners can sit under a pergola-style central gallery or in the comfort of curvy booths. All the pasta and gnocchi is produced in-house and there is plenty of seafood on the menu. And with the Barossa Valley and Adelaide Hills vineyards nearby, an empty wine glass is an incendiary gesture. *osteriaoggi.com.au*

STAR DISH
Beef carpaccio: razor-thin slices of raw beef garnished with rocket, aioli, parmesan and a drizzle of olive oil.

Pink Moon Saloon
Adelaide
Wood-oven specials

The five friends behind this folksy bar and restaurant got themselves out of a tight spot (so to speak) by building their premises in a tiny alley between two existing buildings. The result is a laneway mountain cabin with a pitched roof, wooden planked exterior and cheerful sky-blue door – all surrounded, somewhat unceremoniously, by stonework. Inside, it's divided into three sections: the slender wood-hued saloon including a front bar; an open-air courtyard; and a restaurant out back. You can also enjoy a drink – and make the most of Adelaide's fine weather – by taking a seat on one of the outdoor benches. *pinkmoonsaloon.com.au*

STAR DISH
The availability of the wood-fired chops changes daily but the Pink Moon Club sandwich is a filling perennial.

Executive chef
Jo Pearson cooks
Italian with an
antipodean twist

As well as its
seafood, The
Oyster Inn
provides an
idyllic weekend
getaway

Ortolana
Auckland
Seasonal produce

Ortolana, in downtown Auckland, is a brick-and-timber pavilion with steel-framed windows opening on to a small courtyard. Half the tables are outside – with blankets and heaters for when the weather's brisk – and inside there are linen banquettes and timber tables. Much of the produce comes from the owners' farm in Kumeu, 25km outside the city. Head chef Gavin Doyle makes even the familiar exciting and the menu is ostensibly Italian but served up with antipodean flair. Service is reliably attentive and patrons have the option of dining indoors under a lofty pitched canopy outfitted with hanging spherical lamps or, if they prefer, alfresco on the veranda. *ortolana.co.nz*

STAR DISH
Beef short-rib agnolotti with mustard and Brussels sprout leaves – the pasta is handmade on site.

The Oyster Inn
Waiheke Island, Auckland
Casual seafood

When Andrew Glenn and Jonathan Rutherfurd Best returned to New Zealand in 2011 after years in London, they fell in love with Waiheke Island, an idyllic spot 35 minutes by ferry from Auckland. After buying a piece of land on a whim, they took on an abandoned restaurant and reopened it as The Oyster Inn. Across a fern-filled atrium they built a private dining room, a large event space, three airy guestrooms and a small shop. The restaurant serves a seasonal seafood-focused menu that is casual and unpretentious. Having a meal at The Oyster Inn is just half of the fun; some guests stay the weekend. *theoysterinn.co.nz*

STAR DISH
Fish and chips – line-caught Hauraki Gulf fish and triple-cooked chips never fail to delight.

Jarrett Wrisley works front of house; Paolo Vitaletti is the executive chef

Excellent coffee and the big breakfast are the stars of the show

Dizengoff
Auckland
Best for brunch

Dizengoff is a high-ceilinged space in a heritage building. It isn't the newest joint on the Ponsonby strip, nor is it the fanciest, but it's still the best. Crowded from morning until afternoon, the tables are small and cosy with a slightly retro edge: you can happily while away a few hours here or hold an important meeting. The coffee, from Kiwi supplier Allpress (*see page 36*) is as good as it gets (the flat whites come in a glass here) and the Jewish-inspired menu – salmon scrambled eggs, bagels and the excellent Israel plate – is comforting and moreish. *+64 9 360 0108*

STAR DISH
Dizengoff knows that if something works, there's no point in changing it: the menu doesn't alter very much and the coffee comes fast. The egg dishes are also uniformly delightful.

Appia
Bangkok
Classic Italian

Roman-style trattoria Appia succeeds by bringing simple regional Italian cuisine to a Bangkok culinary landscape previously dominated by haute-cuisine clichés and cream-heavy carbonara sauces. The menu gives jaded Bangkok diners a slice of executive chef Paolo Vitaletti's life as the son of a butcher in Rome's Testaccio district. There is roast chicken dressed in gremolata sauce, and porchetta stuffed with liver and rosemary, as well as an ever-changing roster of specials and a carefully selected wine list. With Jarrett Wrisley of Soul Food Mahanakorn working front of house, Appia balances rustic offerings with a relaxed atmosphere. *appia-bangkok.com*

STAR DISH
The oxtail stew with gremolata (a zesty herb salad) is Italian comfort food at its finest.

All of Err's dishes are blissfully free of MSG

AR Sutton's design is as meticulous as its expertly mixed drinks

Err
Bangkok
Southeast Asian meats

Hidden in a small alley between Wat Pho and the river, Err raises the bar compared to the food (and drink) found in typical Bangkok pubs. Opened in 2015 by the team behind Bo.lan, it's a casual spot that invites diners in from 11.00 and serves dishes that are made to share. Cured and preserved Southeast Asian meats are the speciality; order skewers of *moo ping* (spicy pork) and a plate of the tasty *look chin ping* (pork meatballs). There's also a range of spicy salads for those wanting something lighter. Alongside the beers and wine, Err's signature cocktails include options made using Nikki rice spirit and rum from Chaolong Bay. *errbkk.com*

STAR DISH
Chicken Movie: the deep-fried skin of a whole bird is served with Sriracha sauce.

AR Sutton & Co Engineers Siam
Bangkok
Cool cocktails

Ashley Sutton, designer of some of Bangkok's most popular drinking spots, has his own venture in the colonial-themed AR Sutton & Co, incongruously located on the ground floor of a large shopping centre. Despite its surroundings the bar evokes a different world from the moment you step onto its chessboard-tiled floor. The menu is pared down and leans towards the classic with its amaretto sour, negroni and dirty martini, while the drinking area boasts details that have come to characterise Sutton's style: high ceilings, copper stills and filigree balustrades punctuated by semi-hidden spaces for drinkers who put a premium on privacy. *63 Sukhumvit Soi*

TOP ORDER
The ever-so-briny dirty martini is a savoury revelation; the Vesper Martini, with Kina Lillet, is a sweeter discovery.

Patrons can sample dishes of Shiite, Maronite, and Armenian origin

The large communal table at the back is perfect for meetings or making new friends

Tawlet
Beirut
Regional plates

Beirut is a city where food is central to almost everything, from family to business. Kamal Mouzawak is a remarkable man who has used food to bring people together in an even bigger way: across the country's sectarian lines. He founded the city's first farmers' market, Souk el Tayeb, and in the process brought together everyone from Druze to Sunni.
Then he launched Tawlet in 2009, where every day different cooks bring produce to life in dishes that introduce local specialities you'd be hard-pressed to find in any other restaurant. The results are extraordinary. *tawlet.com*

STAR DISH
The ever-changing roster means a star dish isn't a concept that really works at Tawlet. The best strategy is to come for the weekend buffet spread.

Distrikt Coffee
Berlin
Morning glory

Having moved to Berlin several years previously, British-born Sophie Hardy realised her dream of opening a coffee shop in December 2014. The full-time science teacher and her German partner Hannes Haake have transformed the first floor of a pre-war building in Mitte into an airy space with exposed brick walls.
They offer organic food such as avocado toast, poached eggs and banana bread with caramelised nuts as well as top-notch coffee. "We source our beans from London, German, Sweden and Norway and serve food with a healthy slant, plus home favourites," says Hardy. *distriktcoffee.de*

STAR DISH
Buttermilk pancakes served with maple-berry preserve, citrus butter, crème fraiche, basil and granola.

The eccentric chef patron Cobo is as much a draw for guests as his menu

The bovine bust tells you you've come to the right place

Fischbänke
Bolzano, Italy
Aperitivo stop-off

The colourful decor outside Fischbänke in Bolzano, the bucolic capital of South Tyrol in northern Italy, makes the city's premier aperitivo spot a hard one to miss. It sprung up next to what was once the town's fish market, evident in the surviving white-marble counters that are now surrounded by the colourful signs, scribbles and artwork of the bar's eccentric and charismatic owner Rino Zullo. The artist-proprietor, known to all by his nickname Cobo, is perpetually on hand to offer recommendations and entertain his patrons beneath the pink-and-orange parasols and pendants that characterise this charming open-air haunt. *+39 340 570 7468*

STAR DISH
Cobo is a warm host and rustles up the best bruschetta in town.

Model Milk
Calgary
Comfort food

Spotting Model Milk is easy: above the former dairy's entrance in the Red Mile district is a white cow-head sculpture. With a capacity of 70 (20 more can be seated in the private dining room upstairs) the venue bustles with customers lured by the decadent Southern-style chicken and waffles, the calamari fricassée with edamame beans, or the succulent roasted pork – just a few of the recurring dishes on offer. A regularly shifting menu serves modern takes on comfort food made from high-quality ingredients, "without screwing them up before they hit the plate", says co-owner and executive chef Justin Leboe. *modelmilk.ca*

STAR DISH
Idaho rainbow trout is a crowd-pleaser, served with creamed spinach, new potatoes, trout roe and dill.

A farm-to-table ethos is at the heart of the restaurant

Michele Marques likes to keep ingredients regional – and delicious

Mercearia Gadanha
Estremoz, Portugal
Iberian delight

After setting up a grocery shop in Portugal's Estremoz, Michele Marques and business partner Mario Vieira expanded her establishment into a restaurant. Her creations are a rundown of the region's best ingredients. "Our cuisine takes advantage of the wealth of fresh produce the Alentejo [in central Portugal] has to offer," she says. Inside there are homely red-tiled floors, wooden furniture and whitewashed walls, and diners are treated as old friends. The lamb chops with asaparagus *migas* and the veal loin with ham and egg are a treat but those after something lighter will relish the *mil folhas de bacalhau e presunto*: bread, codfish, black-pork prosciutto, rocket and egg. *merceariagadanha.pt*

STAR DISH
Braised pork cheeks cooked slowly in red wine.

Babylonstoren
Franschhoek, South Africa
Straight from the garden

Babylonstoren mixes old traditions with contemporary Cape cuisine. The original Dutch farm dates back to 1692 and within its grounds owner Koos Bekker and his wife Karen Roos have created a sanctuary. From the heritage gardens to the farm-to-table recipes, Babylonstoren is an ode to simplicity layered with thoughtfulness and attention to detail. "The food is what the garden gives us," says Roos. "Every morning our chefs pick from the garden. Fresh, seasonal produce forms the heart of your plate." After a satisfying lunch and a browse in the farm shop, enjoy a stroll through the expansive grounds. *babylonstoren.com*

STAR DISH
Crispy pork belly that's been marinated overnight, served in satsuma-flavoured tom yum broth.

Marc Popper, owner of Paradiso

Sourdough is the bread of choice at De Superette

Paradiso
Geneva
Easygoing offerings

On the ground floor of a pretty townhouse on busy Rue des Bains is the charming café-cum-bar Paradiso. The light airy space is welcoming and cosy and it's pleasant to linger here with a strong espresso and the day's papers. If peckish, choose croissants and cinnamon rolls or more substantial fare such as a crunchy salad or avocado toast. They do a mean cocktail too. Luckily for residents and visitors, and unusually for the city, Paradiso serves up its successful blend of laidback cool on Sundays too.
cafeparadiso.ch

STAR DISH
The black-and-grey frontage gives little away but a dining room out back is the perfect place to enjoy the couscous salad with feta, cherry tomato, roasted almonds and red onions.

De Superette
Ghent
Somewhere to loaf

Housed in a one-time grocery shop, De Superette is a bakery and restaurant founded by Belgian chef Kobe Desramaults (also behind Flanders restaurant In De Wulf). Desramaults hired US-born baker Sarah Lemke to charge the wood-fired oven and Irish chef Rose Greene to look after the kitchen. Since it opened in 2014, the wholesome fragrance of freshly baked bread has been luring in passers-by. Customers can choose from a full range of products, including rye bread with beer, and honey-and-buttermilk loaves. All the wheat and grains are organic. In the evening the same oven that is used to bake bread churns out perfect pizzas. *indewulf.be/desuperette*

STAR DISH
The classic 'pomme boulangère' or potato gratin with onion and aged cheese.

German comfort food is the order of the day

If it's chicken on a skewer that you want, Yardbird is a preferable perch

Marinehof
Hamburg
Teutonic tucker

Marinehof has been cherished by residents and visitors alike since opening in 1990. Owner Astrid Wettstein learnt to cook northern German cuisine from her mother, and small but important skills (like letting peeled potatoes sit overnight before frying, lending them an unusually smooth texture) add up to sublime simplicity. The menu changes twice daily and features 35 dishes. To create a setting befitting the food, architect Hans Thalgot installed a spiral wrought-iron staircase next to the bar up to a mezzanine dining area. Large windows allow maximum natural light to flood the interiors and create a sense of airiness and space. *marinehof.de*

STAR DISH
Pollock – the pan-seared fillet comes with a fennel and apricot side salad, basmati rice and salsa.

Yardbird
Hong Kong
Chicken skewers

Yardbird has been packed since it threw open its doors in 2011 – and the atmospheric no-reservations *yakitori-ya* (a Japanese grilled-chicken-skewer outlet) remains a staple of the Hong Kong food scene. It's run by Canadian chef Matt Abergel, and the chickens arrive daily from farms in the New Territories outside the city. There's a bumper selection of sakés, whiskies and cocktails in the bar, and what follows is a menu of fresh skewers – using different cuts of meat – that sell out nightly. Scrummy sides, including Korean fried cauliflower, fly out of the kitchen almost as quickly as the chicken. *yardbirdrestaurant.com*

STAR DISH
Breast 'yakitori' is marinated in soy sauce and wasabi – and packs a serious punch.

With so much art on display, the bartenders have elevated their craft to compete

Livestock Tavern's offering helps Hawaii's native farmers

Duddell's
Hong Kong
Cocktail hour

This beautiful two-storey space designed by Ilse Crawford houses a Chinese restaurant, an art gallery and a salon for events. Above all it's a civilised spot for sundowners, especially the leafy terrace on the upper floor. The bar offers an impressive list of wines and spirits and a short-but-sharp selection of cocktails with playful Asian touches. The Herbalist's Mojito takes inspiration from traditional Chinese medicine and the Hong Konger – with plum wine – is the bar's own take on the New Yorker. You'll have to be a Duddell's member to reserve a table in the bar or on the terrace but the concierge will gladly find a spot for walk-ins when there is room. *duddells.co*

TOP ORDER
Beeb Wua Fizz, an Asian cocktail made with coconut milk, ginger-lemongrass soda and Tanqueray.

Livestock Tavern
Honolulu
Slice of Americana

Nestled on the corner of Hotel Street in Chinatown Livestock Tavern is emblematic of the neighbourhood's recent revival and, more broadly, the renewal of Honolulu's restaurant culture. It bills itself as US-inspired, which is a tough sell in a city where drive-in diners and mom-and-pop restaurants are firm fixtures. But unlike many chefs, Jesse Cruz's aim is to elevate US comfort food by using regional ingredients: grilled octopus made with critters netted off the Hawaiian coast and served on a bed of endives or prime-rib beef smoked for hours in his kitchen's kiln. *livestocktavern.com*

STAR DISH
The crispy sea bass or grilled octopus are both worthy catches.

Enjoy brunch or a cocktail – or stay long enough to enjoy both

Aheste means "slow" in Turkish, so take your time over the meze

Mangerie
Istanbul
Turkish delight

With its pretty wooden mansions and Bosphorus-side park, Bebek ("baby" in Turkish) is one of Istanbul's most well-heeled 'hoods. Offering traditional Turkish dishes as well as decent takes on western options, Mangerie is where the city's joggers like to brunch after a dash along the strait. The steep steps to the entrance provide a fitting warm-down and you can head up to the roof for a stunning view. Linger over coffee on the white-decked terrace or (if the sun has passed over the yardarm) pamper yourself with a refreshing fruity cocktail. Come evening you can sip martinis on the terrace and trace the dark outlines of supertankers on the Bosphorus. *mangeriebebek.com*

STAR DISH

Choose bacon, prosciutto, spinach or smoked salmon for your eggs benedict.

Aheste
Istanbul
Anatolian allure

The scrubbed firebrick interior of this former workshop provides a blank canvas for the proprietor, Iranian-born Sara Tabrizi, to riff on cuisine from her motherland, as well as Anatolia, Syria, Armenia and Lebanon. Each meze plumps for bold flavours and fresh produce from the city's organic markets. The tomato and goat cheese salad with pomegranate sour is a mouthwatering starter, while the tangy sea bass ceviche suits a balmy day (if you can't make up your mind, opt for the tasting menu). Filament lights, wrought-iron doors and artwork by Archive+Lab create a twinkling, romantic ambience – we're not the only ones in on the secret, so book ahead. *ahesterestaurant.com*

STAR DISH

Slow-roasted lamb shank cooked to perfection; the meat is so tender that it slides off the bone.

Four Letter
Word's Eylem
Ozkaya makes
a beautiful brew

The Indonesian
capital's best
coffee shop

Four Letter Word
Istanbul
Caffeine fix

Life on the Princes Islands is calm and car-free – all
that mainland Istanbul is not – and that brings with it
a slew of restaurants geared towards weekenders. Eylem
Ozkaya opened Four Letter Word, a kiosk-sized café on
Burgazada, with sommelier Ria Neri and entrepreneur
Kevin Heisner. On a peaceful side street near the ferry
station, a Giesen coffee roaster behind the counter roasts
Ethiopian Konga beans. Ozkaya returned to the islands
after running coffee shops in Chicago, and she pins
a note about the beans onto each bag she sells. "This
is a tea-drinking community," she says. "When you sell
coffee you have to sell your knowledge too." *4lwcoffee.com*

STAR DISH
*Beans from Diositeo Torres's El Mirador farm in Colombia
result in a well-balanced coffee with sweet apple notes.*

Kopimanyar
Jakarta
Full of beans

You don't hear about many architects opening coffee
shops but that's exactly what Andra Matin did in
the Jakarta suburb of Pesanggrahan in 2015. Working
with his wife Dite and two colleagues, Matin turned a
house opposite his studio into an alluring new space.
Kopimanyar (meaning "coffee on Manyar Street")
serves beans grown in West Java to Eastern Bali.
To furnish the ground floor and showcase Indonesian
craftsmanship, Matin chose chairs and tables made
by Jakarta companies, some designed by his own firm.
"And now we have our own space to hold meetings,"
he says. *+62 21 735 3932*

STAR DISH
*Packets of Kopimanyar's house-blended beans are excellent
take-homes.*

Gambrinus was named after the mythical king credited with inventing beer

Hanging plants recreate the feel of a Cypriot terrace right in the heart of London

Gambrinus
Lisbon
Perfectly Portuguese

The chefs at Gambrinus have been committed to traditional Portuguese dining since 1936, yet it's the high standards of service and classic decor that make the difference. The current look is the brainchild of architect Maurício de Vasconcelos who, in 1964, outfitted the establishment with its distinctive lamps and dark wooden furnishings. Gambrinus is named after the mythical king credited for having invented beer so an evening here is bound to be a jovial affair. Standout dishes include the partridge pie, fish stew and the crêpes suzette but also be sure to ask about the daily special.
gambrinuslisboa.com

STAR DISH
Ameijoas a Bulhao Pato – clams in a tasty coriander, garlic and olive oil bisque.

Lemonia
London
All Greek to me

Gems like this Greek taverna are hard to unearth; the sort that are always busy and run by penguined-up older waiters who carry out their duties with a healthy dose of wit and a seen-it-all-before smile. The food at Lemonia is homely and satisfying, and the service, though brisk by some tastes, is never rude. Go for the hummus and tzatziki to start, alongside calamari and the artichoke and broad beans; then plump for the slow-cooked lamb kleftiko or moussaka for mains. Even the Turkish delight they dish out is second to none. Enjoy your food in the interior courtyard, which is sheltered by a pitched-glass roof that fills the dining space with natural light. *lemonia.co.uk*

STAR DISH
Arni me bamies: lamb with okra in tomato sauce, packing a subtle cinnamon kick.

Top coffee
in the heart
of literary
London

Perfectly
prepared
Japanese fare
in the heart
of London

The Espresso Room
London
Pour thing

Inside this tiny Bloomsbury coffee shop, the pared-back Donald Judd-inspired interiors create a smart but homely feel for the patrons awaiting their morning caffeine hit. Founder Ben Townsend's coffee epiphany came while working in Melbourne in education, which he quit to train as a barista and coffee consultant before setting up in England in 2009. Tom Mullings and Chris Rahlenfeldt took over the petite Great Ormand Street café in 2015 and have expanded the business to include two more outposts in Holborn and Covent Garden. The coffee remains a neighbourhood staple. *theespressoroom.london*

STAR DISH
The baristas make a mean flat white using independent beans from Caravan Coffee Roasters and Assembly Coffee.

Dinings
London
Japanese gem

Marylebone's quieter western reaches revealed a sumptuous secret to the world when this Japanese joint moved into an unassuming Edwardian townhouse in 2006. The brainchild of four former Nobu colleagues, it's stark and set over two floors, with a raw bar upstairs and moody 28-cover dining area below. Expect precise and perfectly judged Japanese dishes made from fresh British produce including Cornish crab and Scottish scallops and salmon. The *donburi* (rice dishes) are delightful and the sashimi is tender, while the crisp Tar-Tar chips are a moreish morsel with which to start your meal. *dinings.co.uk*

STAR DISH
Deciding between the sea bass carpaccio and the beef with garlic lemon soy and yuzu is tough.

There's more to this classic pub than pies and pints, although they're pretty good too

The food at Broken Spanish is an 'authentically inauthentic' take on Mexican food

The Bull & Last
London
Pub grub

Located across the road from the grassy 320-hectare expanse of Hampstead Heath, The Bull & Last pub is the perfect spot for a post-ramble pint or an intimate dinner. Regulars at this 19th-century former coaching inn include food critics, families and north London liberals. Expect a cosy setting with rustic furniture, mounted bulls' heads and open fires come winter. The menu is consistently excellent, with an outstanding charcuterie board featuring a notable duck prosciutto. At weekends there's an elegant take on the British roast with North Essex Shorthorn beef, Yorkshire puddings, roast potatoes, carrots and horseradish sauce. *thebullandlast.co.uk*

STAR DISH
The fish board is the most popular pick all year round. It comes with a medley of salmon paté, potted crab and squid.

Broken Spanish
Los Angeles
Downtown delight

Ray García isn't trying to make authentic Mexican cuisine. In fact, he calls it "authentically inauthentic". But it's an utterly delicious and undeniably Angeleno take on the food of his grandparents. Broken Spanish is a vast space in LA's Downtown area. It's a gutsy move opening evenings-only in the centre – testament to the continued revival of the area – yet his restaurant has quickly become something of a destination. With lovely details – vintage portraits on the wall, ceramics and hanging plants – the food (from stewed rabbit to raw diver scallops) manages to be both hearty and refined. The homemade tortillas are simply unmissable too. *brokenspanish.com*

STAR DISH
A big hunk of pork, the chicharrón is re-envisioned with elephant garlic, radish sprout and picked herbs.

An earthy decor provides the backdrop to Celso y Manolo's colourful dishes

The bodega is a Madrid drinking institution dating back to 1892

Celso y Manolo
Madrid
Treasured 'tasca'

Traditional *tascas* (taverns) tap into a love for informal eating and are hugely popular in the Spanish capital. They're typically specialists in unfussy food – which is enjoyed at a tall bar – but can be loud, boisterous and often a little dated. Not so in this sharp-looking space, which is in the buzzy Chueca neighbourhood. Chef and entrepreneur Carlos Zamora serves a contemporary riff on the concept while still ensuring that a taste of heritage makes it into every dish. Needless to say the dishes are tip-top too, including *rabas* (small calamari) and a wonderfully simple but delicious *cata de tomates* (tomato tasting plate). *celsoymanolo.es*

STAR DISH
Deep-fried calamari baguette: this tasty classic is a favourite among Chuecans.

Bodega La Ardosa
Madrid
Age-old liberations

The Bodega La Ardosa dates back to 1892; a television among the dust-covered bottles is the only clue to the fact that the world has changed in the century since. The red, black and white façade provides a quaint gathering point for punters who spill onto the pavement, *vermut* in hand. Inside, find yourself a perch among the barrels or duck under the bar to the dining room before sating your appetite with simple staples paired with a heady rioja. The owners recently purchased the space next door; an impressive renovation has seen the Casa Baranda bar returned to its former glory. If La Ardosa is filled to capacity, this new neighbour is a convenient second choice. *laardosa.es*

TOP ORDER
The house 'vermut' (vermouth) is a fortified wine of macerated botanicals that is an almost mandatory order on entry.

From morning to night, chefs prepare sharing plates from the kitchen for the sparsely decorated but ever busy dining room

A home away from home for Melbourne's brunch crowd

Supernormal
Melbourne
Asian influence

Those who mourned the loss of Golden Fields – chef Andrew McConnell's cherished St Kilda restaurant and bar – have come to regard his 2014 venture as an institution of much the same standing. Some dishes at Supernormal have been carried over from its predecessor but the seasonal menu raises the game, with more Asian influences. There's a touch of China in the slow-cooked Szechuan lamb and a hint of Korea in the sour kimchi and tuna. And if the tofu and miso peppering the menu don't spell Japan clearly enough, the neon signage on Flinders Lane and the private karaoke booth should do the trick. *supernormal.net.au*

STAR DISH
New England lobster roll. There's a reason why this dish has been carried over from St Kilda: it's stupendously good.

Top Paddock
Melbourne
Community café

Nathan Toleman founded Top Paddock in 2013 in Melbourne's Richmond district. Built in a former car park, the 160-seat space is a collaboration with Six Degrees Architects. It quickly found its feet as a community café, not least because of chef Daniel Snooks. Under his supervision, the kitchen whips up some of the tastiest brunch options in the city including toast topped with chilli scrambled eggs, mushrooms and goat curd. Regulars come from nearby offices. "People use it as their kitchen or an extension of their office," says Toleman. "They're here for breakfast and lunch and sometimes coffee in between." *toppaddockcafe.com*

STAR DISH
Chorizo, pickled onions, green tomatoes and poached eggs on toast.

Bottled cocktails mean no bar snarl-ups – plus, you can buy them to take home

A homely interior is paired with an ambitious mix of Latin, Jewish and US comfort food

Heartbreaker
Melbourne
Bustling boozer

Michael Madrusan made a name for himself at Milk & Honey in New York, before opening Melbourne bar The Everleigh. He weighed up the prospect of opening a sister bar for three years before coming up with this departure from the iconic cocktail haunt for which he was known. Heartbreaker is raucous, with a jukebox, a pool table and a cherry-red neon sign. The cocktails come pre-mixed and batched in individual bottles, which makes for less theatrical bartending but means service is sharp and speedy. There's also an enticing selection of beers, and ciders from the US, Denmark and New Zealand as well as a lively soundtrack. *heartbreakerbar.com.au*

TOP ORDER
Cocktail choices come down to Madrusan's famous four: negroni, martini, old fashioned and manhattan.

27 Restaurant and Bar
Miami
Informal eats

There are plenty of flashy joints in Miami but 27 is an ideal counterpoint. Set inside a 1930s home, the atmosphere – thanks in part to New York design studio Roman and Williams – is inviting and unpretentious, with eclectic furniture and mismatched wallpaper. Despite the informal feel, the food is honed and the staff well drilled. Pick from a menu that mixes Jewish and Latin flavours with American comfort food; you can't go wrong with the daily-caught fish in coconut curry, or the tahini-kale salad with crispy chickpeas. If the restaurant is full when you arrive, head across the leafy courtyard to sister bar The Broken Shaker (*see page 306*), and lounge by the pool while you wait to be seated. *thefreehand.com/miami*

STAR DISH
Griot and Pikliz: starter of pork shoulder and spicy coleslaw.

Much of Mandolin's produce comes from its on-site garden

The Broken Shaker has attracted plaudits despite its location within a humble hostel

Mandolin Aegean Bistro
Miami
Mediterranean air

This small pocket of Hellenic cuisine is hidden behind a blue picket fence where the Design District meets the residential neighbourhood of Buena Vista in Miami. Mandolin's plant-filled patio and deckchair dining creates the feeling that you've wandered onto an Aegean island. The Greek-Turkish menu is rustic and flavoursome and includes *sucuk*, a type of sausage, and calamari with almond tartar dip, alongside a straightforward choice of grilled fish and meat skewers. There's also a lovingly assembled selection of items for sale in the on-site Aegean Market, including chilli sauce and Miami-made honey. *mandolinmiami.com*

STAR DISH
Grilled octopus with a squeeze of lemon juice and a drizzle of olive oil.

The Broken Shaker at Freehand Miami
Miami
Hostel environment

It's rare that a bar inside a hostel is much to brag about but The Broken Shaker has received high praise (and plenty of awards) despite its humble berth. It's the handiwork of partners Elad Zvi and Gabriel Orta, who use herbs and spices from the on-site garden to make homemade syrups, tinctures and sodas. The menu has been known to change but the staff will happily fashion something to order if you can't find it listed. Indoor seating is sparse but the patio has plenty of deck furniture beneath the trees, where you can enjoy the evening air or check out the pretty young things who frequent this relaxed and revered cocktail spot. *thefreehand.com*

TOP ORDER
A changing menu makes a staple tough to recommend but whichever classic you plump for will be sublime.

Nora Gray riffs on Italian food using Québecois ingredients

Diners can opt for either the teak-panelled dining room or the terrace

Nora Gray
Montréal
Quality in Québec

Rustic fare served consistently well is why Nora Gray keeps its place in our esteem. According to co-founder Ryan Gray the secret is straightforward: "We get the best local products and let them speak for themselves – just like they do in Italy." Under the watchful eye of co-owner and chef Emma Cardarelli, the kitchen turns out plate after plate of house-made pasta and other mains with Québecois ingredients. There is lots to love about the drinks menu too: it boasts an expansive selection of natural wines along with modern takes on classic Italian cocktails. For instance, a seven-year-old Havana rum takes the place of gin in its take on a negroni. *noragray.com*

STAR DISH
Again, a constantly evolving menu makes picking a standout meal tricky but all the handmade pasta dishes are excellent.

Bar Giornale
Munich
Go-to Italian

Hotelier and restaurateur Rudi Kull and architect Albert Weinzierl added some Italian swagger to Munich's tree-lined Leopoldstrasse when Bar Giornale opened in 2011. While Kull focused on creating an authentic Italian dining experience, Weinzierl redesigned the former Café Extrablatt with images of Milan in the 1960s. "It's got a special spirit and a young, fresh audience that instils vitality into traditionally conservative Munich," says operations manager Andy Slager. In the evening the space fizzles with energy and summer months see the sunny terrace packed with guests fully embracing the Italian art of *dolce far niente*: the sweetness of doing nothing. *bar-giornale.com*

STAR DISH
Beef served with Café de Paris butter sauce.

The humble egg is elevated to new heights by chef Nick Korbee

Maya and Dean Jankelowitz have spots in Soho and the West Village

Jack's Wife Freda
New York
All-day dining

Run by husband and wife Dean and Maya Jankelowitz, Jack's Wife Freda is a tribute to Dean's grandparents. With locations in Soho and the West Village, the café's menu features an all-day selection of satisfying dishes, including a sandwich with duck prosciutto and creamy cheddar béchamel. "Most of the items are personal favourites with a story [behind them]," says Maya. Patrons range from suited city sorts to younger families, all dining shoulder to shoulder around communal tables; this is, as Maya puts it, "everybody's café for any time of the day". *jackswifefreda.com*

STAR DISH
Green shakshuka, Jack's Wife Freda's take on the Middle Eastern breakfast dish of eggs, pepper and tomatoes.

Egg Shop
New York
New yolk state of mind

This welcoming café started with a simple idea: to serve up the perfect egg sandwich – balanced, healthy and reasonably priced. Co-owner Sarah Schneider's concept has been adapted and expanded with the help of executive chef Nick Korbee, who brings his skilful hand to the process. Korbee has created refined day and evening menus that include hearty meat dishes and fresh salads, all accompanied by the namesake ingredient. The casual atmosphere is comforting and friendly and has drawn a devoted following in the artsy neighbourhood of Nolita. Prices are reasonable so no need to shell out. *eggshopnyc.com*

STAR DISH
Yolk-stuffed burrata with crispy chickpeas, truffle toast and sweet and sour tomato agrodolce.

Above: Ignacio Mattos (left) and Thomas Carter in their perfect paradise

Café Altro Paradiso
New York
Italian influence

Restaurateur Thomas Carter and chef Ignacio Mattos opened this airy "other paradise" on Spring Street in 2016 following the success of their popular Nolita mainstay Estela. The seasonal menu pays homage to the Bel Paese with pasta dishes and grilled swordfish galore. And there isn't a fussy tablecloth in sight – just plenty of white oak, Carrara marble and brass. According to Carter, the hardest part is getting people to understand that Estela and Café Altro Paradiso are different offerings. Though they share the same convivial atmosphere, the aesthetic and the menu are indeed different, the newer erring towards scrummy Italian staples served in a pared-down space. *altroparadiso.com*

STAR DISH
Café Altro Paradiso's fresh home-made pastas, accompanied by seasonally changing sauces, are its calling card.

Greenpoint Fish & Lobster Co
New York
Seafood for all

Brooklynites know the green frontage on the corner of Nassau and Eckford conceals some of the best seafood in town. There's a reason the lobster roll at Greenpoint Fish & Lobster Co tastes so fresh: co-owner Vinny Milburn rises at 04.30 to buy each day's produce. Word has spread, and he and partner Adam Geringer-Dunn now sell around 90kg of lobster from their fishmonger and restaurant every day. Their lobster is seasoned with tarragon, lemon and a touch of mayonnaise and served on a grilled bun. There's only a limited number of high stools and bar spots so be prepared to order to go; nearby McCarren Park is a superb picnic venue. *greenpointfish.com*

STAR DISH
Manhattanites are known to cross the East River just to satisfy their craving for a lobster roll.

Fuglen's interior is a hymn to mid-century Norwegian design

There's no clowning around when it comes to finding your cutlery

Fuglen
Oslo
Fjord focus

Fuglen feels more like a well-loved living room than a café, furnished with the best of Norwegian 1950s and 1960s design – from Fredrick Kayser glassware to Kåre Berven Fjeldaa ceramics. The pace is slow – staff don't shout out orders or whip away your cup before you're done. All this is a deliberate decision by owners Einar Kleppe Holthe and Peppe Trulsen, who took over a 1960s coffee bar in 2008 (they were later joined in the enterprise by Halvor Skiftun Digernes). "Peppe and I wanted to preserve a little piece of Oslo's identity," says Holthe. The coffee is sourced from Norwegian ethical, fair-trade brands and all of the objects on display are for sale. *fuglen.com*

STAR DISH
Both Fuglen's original spot in Oslo and the newer space in Tomigaya, Tokyo, are open late and offer cocktails. Anything with the Norwegian spirit aquavit in it will do.

Le Clown Bar
Paris
Playful plates

This quirky bistro is decorated and named in honour of the clowns who would come here to eat and drink after performing at the nearby Cirque d'Hiver. Sven Chartier and Ewen Lemoigne opened Le Clown Bar in 2014 after giving it a makeover and tapped chef Atsumi Sota, formerly of Vivant, to take over the kitchen. The belle époque-era interior, with painted circus figures somersaulting across the mirrored walls, is a fitting arena for the culinary twists and turns that Sota performs in his kitchen. Meanwhile, sommelier Pierre Derrien has picked out some of the most delectable organic wines around to accompany the tasty plates being juggled by the waiters. *clown-bar-paris.fr*

STAR DISH
Fried 'bulot' snails (Normandy whelks) with spicy mayo.

A rare moment of calm in Le Baron Rouge

The waffles come with whipped cream and jam

Le Baron Rouge
Paris
Place for all punters

It can feel as if the entire neighbourhood of Bastille crams into this blue-collar bar on weekend afternoons and weekday evenings. Le Baron Rouge is a boisterous and pretention-free spot for a post-market glass of wine, a plate of cheese or charcuterie or, in winter, a dozen fresh oysters. Be prepared to elbow your way to a spot at the bar or simply crowd around a barrel or stack of crates (which double as tables here). If you can't nudge your way in, head outside onto the pavement alongside the other latecomers, who are happy using nearby window ledges and the bonnets of parked cars for an alfresco aperitif. *+33 (0)1 4343 1432*

TOP ORDER
Wine from the five prominent barrels is inexpensive, sold by the litre and eminently quaffable.

Mokka Kaffi
Reykjavík
Expert espresso

Sloping Skolavordustigur street is about as close as Reykjavík gets to having a busy thoroughfare, and this unassuming shopfront is a portal to another era. Founded in 1958, the sit-down espresso joint is a mid-century enthusiast's dream: think thick crockery, wood panelling and low-hanging copper pendants. Surrounding the banks of booths are dusky leather banquettes, and on warmer days, the crowds spill out on to street-side tables. Expect a selection of sandwiches, cakes and waffles as well as rotating displays of Icelandic art. This was the first place in Iceland to serve Italian-style espressos, and its old La Cimbali machine still turns out the capital's best. *mokka.is*

STAR DISH
The coffee is excellent but don't leave without trying the thick and crispy waffles served with jam and clotted cream.

Aprazível provides a cosy perch on balmy evenings

Jerad and Justin Morrison's Sightglass is a roastery and coffee bar

Aprazível
Rio de Janeiro
Carioca night

Sitting at the top of hilly Santa Teresa, Aprazível (literally "pleasant") is a Rio institution. Ana Castilho opened the restaurant in her house in 1997 to cater to visitors to the Arte de Portas Abertas cultural weekend. On the menu are imaginative Brazilian dishes inspired in part by Castilho's upbringing in Minas Gerais, the country's culinary heart. Most of the ingredients are painstakingly sourced from Amazon producers; Castilho likes to call it "roots cuisine", which is a fitting thing to serve in this treehouse-like space. The restaurant also brews its own beer, which is the perfect accompaniment for a walk in the nearby hills. *aprazivel.com.br*

STAR DISH
Try the Carioca rice made with prawns and ginger as you look out over Guanabara Bay.

Sightglass Coffee
San Francisco
Focus on filter

Jerad and Justin Morrison opened their spare, loft-style café and roastery after two years of renovating a 1914 warehouse, during which the brothers served coffee to their Soma neighbours from a kiosk outside. While they make a mean macchiato on their espresso machines (from La Marzocco and Kees van der Westen), their focus is on filter coffee, using beans by small producers (the brothers provide "taste notes"). "We roast for our own use and for wholesale clients in our German Probat roaster," says Jonathan. "And we treat each type differently. We try to let the coffee's terroir shine." *sightglasscoffee.com*

STAR DISH
The Blueboon blend has hints of milk chocolate and stone fruit and makes for a comforting filtered cup of coffee.

Chefs Nicolaus Balla and Cortney Burns run the kitchen

This casual and inviting bar is hidden away behind a 1960s shopfront

Bar Tartine
San Francisco
Bay area beauty

In the agricultural breadbasket of California, skills such as preserving and pickling can feel like a throwback. In 2005, baker Chad Robertson and his wife opened Bar Tartine in San Francisco to bring these techniques to the fore, along with other traditional approaches such as fermenting, making vinegars and infusing oils. Chefs Nicolaus Balla and Cortney Burns have given the food a distinct East European accent but influences range from Scandinavia to East Asia. Guests are welcomed into the cosy dining space, outfitted with wood-panelled floors and rustic furnishings. And don't turn down the bread when offered: Robertson's fresh and fragrant delights are renowned for being perfectly balanced. *bartartine.com*

STAR DISH
It's hard to look past those loaves.

28 Hong Kong St
Singapore
Speakeasy of sorts

When New Yorker Spencer Forhart launched this speakeasy-inspired bar with two friends in 2011, its location was an easily missed road on Clarke Quay. There's no sign, so the bar remains a somewhat hidden gem. Inside the 1960s shophouse doors, however, the service is warm and inviting. "We take a back-to-basics approach and focus on independent craft spirits with a cost-be-damned attitude to making drinks," says Forhart. On any given evening you can expect to find designers and globetrotting businessmen alike sipping cocktails and snacking on mac-and-cheese balls. *28hks.com*

TOP ORDER
The Five Foot Assassin: a rum-based cocktail infused with Southeast Asian flavours of pandan leaf and tapioca pearls.

PA & Co's
mantra: if it
ain't broke,
don't fix it

The chefs
decide on
a different
menu every
morning

PA & Co
Stockholm
Unchanged excellence

A confirmed classic of Stockholm's restaurant scene,
this small bistro has held on to its spot in the limelight
ever since it opened about three decades ago. The dark-
wood-and-chandelier decor and the menu are basically
unchanged, as are many of the customers. You won't
find Michelin stars or the latest in gastronomy here;
instead there are famous faces, a joyful, intimate vibe and
delicious Swedish *husmanskost* such as *råraka*, which is
a fried potato rosti topped with Kalix Löjrom (delicious
Swedish caviar), sour cream and finely diced red onion.
The glass chandeliers, candlelight and open, bottle-lined
bar are all high watermarks of unerring style. *paco.se*

STAR DISH
*The Gino pudding, made from baked strawberries, kiwis and
bananas with white chocolate, is Stockholm's finest.*

Ett Hem
Stockholm
'Holm cooking

A dinner at Ett Hem, a boutique hotel and restaurant
housed in a former private residence built in 1910, feels
like a family meal. "We have no written menu and the
guests don't ask for one either," says owner Jeanette
Mix. "In the evening we simply serve that day's dinner."
The chefs double up as waiters, stopping to chat as they
present the dishes to guests, who can choose to gather to
eat in the cosy kitchen, the lush orangery or the beautiful
library. The food, which is clean and unpretentious, is
served on large sharing plates. And if you're lucky enough
to be staying in one of the 12 guest suites, feel free to
help yourself to a snack in the kitchen whenever you're
feeling peckish. *etthem.se*

STAR DISH
With no menus to refer to, let's just say every dish is a star.

The line-up at
Sturehof won't
disappoint

The Greek
treats on offer
at The Apollo
are many and
magnificent

Sturehof
Stockholm
Catch of the day

In a city where almost every week sees a new restaurant opening, brasserie Sturehof is a safe haven of classic Swedish cuisine (with a little French grace to boot). Since 1897 it has served impeccable seafood dishes such as poached cod with prawns, horseradish and browned butter to a hip clientele. Most fish is sourced from the Stockholm archipelago, sometimes by the passionate owner PG Nilsson himself, and prepared in the kitchen or sold at the food market next door. Jonas Bohlin's playful but elegant decor – his pendant lamps resemble a ballerina's tutu – has remained unchanged for years but still works perfectly. *sturehof.com*

STAR DISH
All the fish is fresh but landlubbers will love the lamb from Välnäs Farm or the asparagus and potatoes from Gotland.

The Apollo
Sydney
Godly eats

Chef Jonathan Barthelmess and restaurant impresario Sam Christie opened this 90-cover Greek joint in Potts Point in 2012. The homely George Livissianis-designed space is decked out with curvy Thonet chairs and sculptural Artemide wall lights. There's also an intimate chef's table, beloved by the city's more discreet diners. Try the saganaki cheese dish with oregano, honey and lemon, which arrives at the table bubbling in a cast-iron skillet pan. The roasted lamb with Greek yoghurt and lemon is a moreish morsel, and the taramasalata with cod roe and pitta is also a pop-in-the-mouth pleasure. *theapollo.com.au*

STAR DISH
The grilled pork radicchio pomegranate, which is fired over wood and charcoal.

In dishes and decor, clean flavours are the order of the day

Owner Pasan Wijesena can also be found slinging bottles as Earl's head barman

Bills
Sydney
Top-notch tucker

Ever watched a film only to be informed by a bookish friend that the novel it's based on is even better? It's a fair analogy for Bill Granger's flagship space in Darlinghurst, the formidable restaurant on which the Aussie chef's successful international expansion was based (the Bills banner can be found everywhere from Tokyo to Honolulu, London and Seoul). Inside the tasteful whitewashed space, diners of all ages and creeds shake off hangovers by flicking through magazines over hearty breakfasts, strong coffees and plentiful fresh juices. Brunch is treated as seriously as a religion in Sydney and not visiting Bills is borderline blasphemy. *bills.com.au*

STAR DISH
The sweetcorn fritters with avocado salsa are filling but fluffy and a hallmark of the chef's lightness of touch.

Earl's Juke Joint
Sydney
Butcher turned bar

The King Street space that houses Earl's was once a butcher's shop and the façade, with bold red lettering, white curtains and pickle jars in the window, is almost unchanged. Owner Pasan Wijesena is an alumnus of the rowdy Darlinghurst bar Shady Pines Saloon, which he left in 2013 to set up this atmospheric yet roomy spot. The place takes its cues from a New Orleans bar and it's named after Earl Palmer, a Big Easy drummer credited with the beat at the heart of rock'n'roll. An eclectic crowd descends on the place at weekends to sample a classic cocktail menu featuring homemade syrups and juices. *407 King Street, 2042*

TOP ORDER
Phife Dawg, a rum-based concoction that includes lime juice and bitters, and is topped with a slice of bamboo.

There's a no-reservations policy so find a spot at the bar while you wait

The meat is slow-cooked over a parilla grill at Porteño

10 William St
Sydney
Wine and dine

A shared passion for natural wines, made without chemicals and with minimal intervention, led brothers Enrico and Giovanni Paradiso to open this wine bar in 2011. With an extensive list to sample – including a sizeable contingent of orange wines – the snug space also doubles as a bistro. "The wine and food have the same thought process and ethos," says Giovanni, who with Enrico previously turned Fratelli Paradiso into a Potts Point institution. Sample the fare (made with fresh ingredients and served with an Italian touch) at the window table or perch at the curved bar to enjoy the buzzing atmosphere. *10williamst.com.au*

TOP ORDER
The Italian flavour of proceedings here almost excuses plumping for a decent Tuscan but the Aussie reds are better value.

Porteño
Sydney
High steaks

It was the tapas restaurant Bodega that kick-started Sydney's love affair with chefs Elvis Abrahanowicz and Ben Milgate in 2006. The duo has since had a hand in some of the city's more exciting restaurant concepts but it's Porteño that takes the crown. Opened in 2010 this clever take on the Argentine steakhouse has a parrilla grill and winelist dominated by malbecs from Mendoza and Patagonian pinot noirs. The hacienda-style space is also a big part of the draw. It's so popular that the team doesn't take bookings for groups of fewer than five, so turn up early. *porteno.com.au*

STAR DISH
The slow-cooked pork and lamb each spend eight hours in the fire before hitting your plate. Both are highly recommended.

Taro Yamamoto's café is in a renovated 1970s wooden building

Akaoni specialises in sakés that are difficult to find elsewhere

Mimet
Tokyo
Quality comestibles

Taro Yamamoto was studying architectural design when he had an eye-opening moment at the eatery where he worked. "I discovered even a ¥500 (€4.20) lunch can make customers happy." At his café in a renovated 1970s wooden space, he and his staff serve hearty lunches and dinners. While off the main street, Mimet has become a place for hungry locals, and word of mouth brings new regulars. Quality comes first: fresh produce is sourced from trusted farmers across Japan, delicious bread is baked in-house, and there is a good wine selection from France and Japan. Mimet is a short stroll from Yamamoto's other bistros, Aruru and Urura, which share the same comfortable vibe. *puhura.co.jp*

STAR DISH
Quiche Lorraine slowly cooked in nambu-tekki ironware.

Akaoni
Tokyo
Heavens saké

Japanese have been brewing saké from fermented rice, koji yeast and water for more than two millennia. Also known as *nihon-shu*, the drink is marginally higher in alcohol content than wine. At Akaoni, a 38-seat izakaya in Sangenjaya, you will find an excellent selection from Japan's 1,500 breweries. Opened in 1982 by Satoru Takizawa, this restaurant has 80 types of premium saké and a fish menu that changes daily. There's no English menu but the friendly staff will guide you with recommendations for food-and-drink pairings. *akaoni39.com*

TOP ORDER
Akaoni serves hard-to-find products from Japan's best small breweries, including Takagi Shuzo's unpasteurised saké Juyondai Junmai Daiginjo Akaoni.

Chefs prepare dozens of pork varieties

The quality of the meat here is second to none

Butagumi
Tokyo
Cut above

Butagumi's exquisite breaded pork cutlets (*tonkatsu*) come from pampered breeds: it is not uncommon for pig feed to include sweet potatoes and soybeans, making for fine, rich pork. In an old wooden house in Tokyo's Nishi Azabu district, chef Satoshi Ohishi turns out dozens of pork varieties, such as Kurobuta (Berkshire) from Kagoshima, Nakijin Agu from Okinawa and Ibérico de bellota from Spain. Pigs from Gunma supply the umami-rich fatty belly served at lunchtimes, the meat aged for two weeks at subzero temperatures. His Tsunan Pork fillet from Niigata is a popular choice. *butagumi.com*

STAR DISH
Chef Satoshi Oishi's exotic pork cutlets are a must-try for curious carnivores.

Ningyocho Imahan
Tokyo
Best for beef

There are plenty of excellent *sukiyaki* restaurants in Tokyo but Ningyocho Imahan is a classic. Founded in 1895, it is set in a wooden building in the neighbourhood of Ningyocho. This is a family beef business and the menu – featuring teppanyaki, *shabu shabu* and *sukiyaki* – is not for vegetarians. Head chef Nobuyoshi Numata knows how to prepare beef; Wagyu is the order of the day, preferably from female black-haired cows. One thing to note: *sukiyaki* is pronounced "ski-yaki", never "sooky-yaki". The word was hijacked for the English version of a Japanese song in the 1960s and has been mispronounced ever since. *imahan.com*

STAR DISH
Ponzu-sukiyaki. The sliced beef is cooked in a vinegar sauce at your table and served with vegetables.

Customers chow down in a relaxed wooden interior

Paddlers Coffee has quickly become a community café for young and old

Life Son
Tokyo
Lively lunch spot

Judging by the busy lunch crowd, residents of the Sangubashi district have taken a shine to Life Son, the creation of owner-chef Shoichiro Aiba. Aiba worked in Florence, where he learned to appreciate the charms of a neighbourhood restaurant and the local cuisine, and came back to open his own version in Tokyo. Life Son serves hearty food with an Italian bent; highlights include chunky minestrone soup and perfectly cooked roast chicken and salad. The site is shared with Hayato Tarui's bakery, which supplies bread to the restaurant. Aiba has made an impression on this Tokyo neighbourhood with two other restaurants (Life and Babbo), both nearby. *s-life.jp*

STAR DISH
Spaghetti pomodoro is ideal for refuelling before embarking on an afternoon hike.

Paddlers Coffee
Tokyo
Coffee and comfort

Two years after opening his first coffee stand, Daisuke Matsushima moved into a permanent home in Nishihara. Matsushima's business partner Takehiro Kato is in charge of making the coffee using beans from Stumptown Coffee Roasters in Portland, Oregon. The wood-panelled café has a homely feel; Matsushima renovated the 40-year-old apartment space and filled it with antique furniture, vintage floorboards and old music equipment, including vinyl and a cassette player. The outdoor bench under a cherry tree is our favourite spot. *paddlerscoffee.com*

STAR DISH
Go for an Americano and a hotdog made with bread from nearby Katane Bakery and sausages from popular restaurants Shonzui and Libertin.

Arrive early in order to claim one of Cignale Enoteca's 18 coveted seats

Cignale Enoteca
Tokyo
Counter culture

Fans of Toshiji Tomori's seven-seat restaurant in Gakugeidaigaku knew he was destined for bigger things – and so it has proved. Last year Tomori moved Cignale Enoteca to a new location in Matsumizaka, where he increased the space to 18 seats but retained the counter-style intimacy. The cooking is Italian with a touch of Chez Panisse; Tomori, who spent four years cooking in Italy, still makes everything from the bread and pasta to the limoncello. Quality ingredients are key and the changing menu might include such delights as roast Kinka pork with Italian summer truffles or marbled sole ceviche. A good dinner is guaranteed; a reservation, sadly, is not. *cignale.jp*

STAR DISH
The food and thoughtfully chosen wines are first rate.

The Federal features a menu of rustic comfort food

The Federal
Toronto
Classic dishes

Walk past The Federal in Toronto's Dundas West neighbourhood on any given evening and you'd think it was a decades-old institution. Its rustic design and vintage furniture belie the fact that it was set up in 2012 by high school pals Zach Slootsky, Adam Janes and Duncan MacNeill. "We wanted to seem as if we had been here forever," says Slootsky. After initially offering only brunch, The Federal expanded its service to include dinner a year later. "We have an accessible menu of comfort classics, including fried chicken coated in a sweet cayenne crust," adds Slootsky. The Federal has quietly but surely cemented itself as a treasured gem. *thefed.ca*

STAR DISH
Eggs Federal is the restaurant's spin on eggs benedict and offers a choice of kale, bacon or both.

Barque's bottled marinades are a great take-home

Conversation is king in Sam James's friendly cafés

Barque Butcher Bar
Toronto
Meat feast

In 2015, barbecue maestro David Neinstein moved into a second location, Barque Butcher Bar, a few doors down from his flagship Barque Smokehouse on Toronto's Roncesvalles Avenue. His second outpost sells fine cuts by day and drinks by night. "The idea is to share knowledge about how to smoke meat and barbecue," says Neinstein. There's a cabinet filled with herbs and spices to make your own rubs, while meats are vacuum-packed and displayed in fridges. In the evening, bar stools are dragged out and wooden slabs are put on fridge tops to form a bar. There is wine, beer and cider on tap to wash down the hearty plates. *barque.ca*

STAR DISH
The dry-rub ribs burst with flavour – no additional condiments required.

Sam James Coffee Bar
Toronto
Coffee and conversation

Sam James opened his eponymous coffee shop in 2009 on Harbord Street and has since added four more on Bloor, Queen and King and Toronto. Cafés citywide are crammed with freelancers gawping at laptops but personal interaction remains the reason James keeps his spaces free from wifi. There isn't much to see at his outposts: a La Marzocco coffee machine, some pastries on the counter and a bench. Despite this, the cafés are lively, with many lured by coffee but staying for small talk. "My shops, by virtue of their size, initiate conversations between strangers," says James. "You don't need communal tables to be communal, just a space people feel welcome." *samjamescoffeebar.com*

STAR DISH
Sam James's other business, Cut Coffee, roasts superlative beans in Toronto.

Large windows
are perfect
for people-
watching over
breakfast

Beniamin
Bielecki is one
of Bibenda's
co-owners

Café Prückel
Vienna
Austrian original

Café Prückel is a hotspot for both well-heeled and bohemian sorts, who ritually fill its weathered banquettes from dawn till dusk. Designed in the colourful, dreamy style of Austrian artist Hans Makart when it opened in 1904, its interior was later updated by architect Oswald Haerdtl, resulting in the 1950s-inspired decor that is so beloved today. We recommend the traditional *wiener frühstück* (*see below*) and the apple strudel – and you can get stuck into a wide selection of newspapers. In the evening, dishes such as goulash and potato salad are sure winners, while frequent piano concerts keep guests entertained. *prueckel.at*

STAR DISH
Wiener frühstück: fluffy pancakes, a soft boiled egg and an assortment of preserves.

Bibenda
Warsaw
Polish purveyors

Cousins Beniamin Bielecki and Zbyszek Gawron founded their 50-cover downtown restaurant Bibenda with Katarzyna Majewska in 2014. Before opening the wooden-floored space designed by ADD, the cousins operated pop-up restaurants and supper clubs; "There's been a metamorphosis in people's interest in food," says Gawron. With an evolving menu according to what's in season, Bibenda relies on vegetable-heavy recipes. "That said, we want to give options to everyone: carnivores, vegetarians and vegans," says Bielecki. The philosophy that underpins everything, he adds, is "to comfort and surprise people". *bibenda.pl*

STAR DISH
In summer, try the squash blossoms deep fried in a prosecco tempura and stuffed with herbed ricotta.

The wine list sticks exclusively to French tipples

Olive is located on one of Wellington's hippest strips

Bistro Charlotte
Warsaw
Top table

This charming café by day and wine bar by night occupies a sunny slice of bustling Saviour Square. It is inspired by founder Justyna Kosmala's passion for all things French. "I wanted to show that French food can be an everyday affair," she says. Inside, a 20-seater custom wooden table takes centre stage. Every evening at 18.00 waiters raise the tabletop using an inbuilt mechanism, replace chairs with high stools and soften the lighting to create an intimate atmosphere. Customers move on to the colonnade-clad square outside in warmer weather; when the tables fill, the patrons spill out onto the pavement. *bistrocharlotte.pl*

STAR DISH
Croque madame: a baked roast-turkey sandwich topped with gruyère and a fried egg.

Olive
Wellington
Daylong delicacies

Olive is a venue that morphs throughout the day to match the atmosphere and the punters outside on Cuba Street, one of Wellington's trendiest strips. The kitchen serves classic breakfasts and brunches, hearty lunches and slightly fancier dinners. In between mealtimes, the café-cum-restaurant buzzes with people grabbing coffee, a snifter of dry Kiwi sauvignon blanc or a craft beer. The laidback vibe means you never feel you're taking up a table for the "wrong" reason, and the changing moods throughout the day keep the place from ever feeling staid or sedate. *oliverestaurant.co.nz*

STAR DISH
The food is simple and homely but the smoked ora king salmon and leek tart with crisps and watermelon radish is an excellent lunch-time speciality.

A unique ambience and exquisite service make a lasting impression

Sit back with an americano – or three if you're headed for 'break-up corner'

Kronenhalle
Zürich
Painter's palate

Where else can diners enjoy German-Swiss classics in the company of some of the world's greatest artists? Hulda and Gottlieb Zumsteg opened this elegant neighbourhood joint in 1924 with Picasso, Chagall and Matisse on its wood-panelled walls, courtesy of Hulda's art collector son Gustav. Using only the finest produce sourced from premium supplier Alfred Von Escher, chef de cuisine Peter Schärer stays faithful to traditional recipes such as *baleron* sausage salad. Remember to leave some space for dessert; the chocolate mousse is the perfect way to round off a meal. *kronenhalle.ch*

STAR DISH
The chateaubriand steak – thick medallions of beef tenderloin in béarnaise sauce – is a masterpiece to match the art on the walls.

Central
Zürich
Raising the bar

"We wanted something that could be relevant 20 or 30 years from now," says Kaspar Fenkart, one of the three owners of Zürich's Central. The trio's bar certainly dispenses with fleeting fashions, creating an intimate space with raw-wood panelling and blue-grey ceilings. "That's the break-up corner in the back," a bartender says. "First dates sit in the front." But across that arc your perfect negroni will taste the same year in, year out. This consistency is intentional. Central stocks only one kind of each spirit, such as absinthe from Switzerland and gin from the UK. "The best-made example from areas where producers have the most expertise," says Fenkart. *cntrl.ch*

TOP ORDER
Barrel-aged americano, crafted from Martinazzi (bitters) and red vermouth from Swiss maker Matter-Luginbühl.

BON APPÉTIT

Acknowledgements

Writers
Mikaela Aitken
Matt Alagiah
Liam Aldous
Chloë Ashby
Kimberly Bradley
Jessica Bridger
Megan Billings
Steven Bodzin
Michael Booth
Robert Bound
Ivan Carvalho
James Chambers
Annabelle Chapman
Melkon Charchoglyan
Maddison Connaughton
Jesse Dart
Linda Dyett
Pauline Eiferman
Jason Farago
Simon Farrell-Green
Josh Fehnert
Alastair Gee
Nolan Giles
Marianna Giusti
Torbjørn Goa
Nelly Gocheva
Bill Granger
Sophie Grove
Kenji Hall
Jessica Harris
Markus Hippi
Sahar Khan
Alicia Kirby
Kati Krause
Alice Lascelles
Tomos Lewis
Jason Li
Kurt Lin
Christopher Lord
Hugo Macdonald
Lisa Markwell
Aiden McLaughin
Kate McInerney

Marisa Mazria Katz
David Michon
Sarah Moroz
Tom Morris
Andrew Mueller
Elna Nykänen Andersson
Debbie Pappyn
Nathaniel Parish Flannery
Dan Poole
Carli Ratcliff
Amy Richardson
Chiara Rimella
Hannah Ritchie
Santiago Rodríguez Tarditi
Laura Rysman
Nathalie Savaricas
David Sax
Marie-Sophie Schwarzer
Aleksander Solum
Aisha Speirs
Ed Stocker
Syma Tariq
Junichi Toyofuku
Andrew Tuck
Jamie Waters
Fiona Wilson

Illustrators
Giacomo Gambineri
Gergo Gilicze
Satoshi Hashimoto

Photographers
Serra Akcan
Dustin Aksland
Sarah Anderson
Lacey Ann Johnson
Peter Ash Lee
Thom Atkinson
Simon Bajada
Mattia Balsamini
Sidney Bensimon
Aurélien Bergot
Karen Blumberg
Daniel Boud
Aya Brackett
Laura Braun
Lorne Bridgman
Jane Bruce
Rodrigo Cardoso
Earl Carter
Roger Casas
François Cavelier
Carmen Chan
Jesse Chehak
Terence Chin
Natalie Chitwood
Silvia Conde
Chris Crerar
Daniel Cronin
Ana Cuba
Bea de Giacomo
David de Vleeschauwer
Petros Efstathiadis
Thomas Ekström
Marius Ektvedt
Capucine Fachot
Muhammad Fadli
Andreas Fessler
Phil Fisk
Stuart Freedman
Stefan Fürtbauer
Daniel Gebhart de Koekkoek
Lucy Goodhart
Anders Gramer
Christoph Haiderer

Hideaki Hamada
Benya Hegenbarth
Mariano Herrera
Lutz Hilgers
Véronique Hoegger
James Horan
Anna Huix
Laura Hynd
Sayuki Inoue
Mika Ishikawa
Malte Jäger
Steven Joyce
Katie Kaars
Hubert Kang
Rachel Kara
Casey Kelbaugh
Drew Kelly
Dalia Khamissy
Amanda Kho
Rama Knight
Kensington Leverne
Jessica Long
Salva López
Lit Ma
Ehrin Macksey
Amanda Marsalis
Rebecca Marshall
Emma McIntyre
Benjamin McMahon
Trent McMinn
Renee Melides
Jason Michael Lang
Claudio Morelli
Justin Mott
Valerie Narte
Valeria Necchio
Alecia Neo
Hayato Noge
Tatsuya Ochi
Felix Odell
Baris Ozcetin
Krzysztof Pacholak
Satu Palander
Cristobal Palma

Ian Patterson
Kristoffer Paulsen
Kate Peters
Tony Potts
Heiko Prigge
Alex Pusch
Andrew Querner
Charlie Richards
Johannes Romppanen
Ewoud Rooks
Flurina Rothenberger
Greta Rybus
Carol Sachs
Ana Santl
Putu Sayoga
Jens Schwarz
Laura Sciacovelli
Jan Søndergaard
Ruedi Steck
Lauren Stonestreet
David Straight
David Sykes
Kohei Take
Peter Tarasiuk
Taro Terasawa
Brad Torchia
Gianfranco Tripodo
Nicole Tung
Andrew Urwin
Kerem Uzel
Jonathan van der Knaap
Marius W Hansen
Lukas Wassmann
Michael Wee
Weston Wells
Simon Wilson
Christopher Wise
Adam Wiseman
Virginia Woods-Jack
Andrea Wyner

Monocle

EDITOR IN CHIEF
& CHAIRMAN:
Tyler Brûlé

EDITOR:
Andrew Tuck

**The Monocle Guide to
Drinking & Dining**
EDITOR:
Josh Fehnert

BOOKS EDITOR:
Joe Pickard

ASSOCIATE EDITOR, BOOKS:
Amy Richardson

RESEARCHER/WRITER:
Mikaela Aitken

RECIPE DEVELOPMENT:
Kate McInerney

DESIGNERS:
Richard Spencer Powell
Kate McInerney
Jay Yeo
Sam Brogan

PHOTO EDITORS:
Matthew Beaman
Shin Miura
Faye Sakura Rentoule

PRODUCTION:
Jacqueline Deacon
Dan Poole
Chloë Ashby
Sean McGeady
Sonia Zhuravlyova

Chapter editing:

PART 1.
FOOD FOR THOUGHT

1.
Inspirational Producers
Nolan Giles

2.
How To...
Matt Alagiah

3.
My Last Meal
Jason Li

4.
Essays
Joe Pickard

5.
Local Flavours
Josh Fehnert

PART 2.
STOCKING UP

6.
Food Markets
Ed Stocker

7.
Food Retailers
Fiona Wilson

8.
Smart Packaging
Josh Fehnert

PART 3.
ROLL UP YOUR SLEEVES

Tools of the Trade
Josh Fehnert

How to Host
Robert Bound

9.
The Recipes
Kate McInerney
Marie-Sophie Schwarzer

PART 4.
THE DIRECTORY

10.
Restaurants, Cafés & Bars
Jason Li

Special thanks
Caroline Brewster
Ana Cuba
Pete Kempshall
Edward Kennedy
Ed Lawrenson
Gui Rebelo
Thomas Reynolds
Adam Richmond
Dara Sutin
Aliz Tennant
Ilse Viveros

Props
Another Country
Divertimenti
Georg Jensen
Goodfellow & Goodfellow
Japanese Knife Company
Makers & Brothers
May Studios
Minimalux
Riedel
SCP
Simple Shape
Skandium
Skultuna
31 Chapel Lane

Research
Mikaela Aitken
Melkon Charchoglyan
Ben Craik
Tina Haertel
Kurt Lin
Aliz Tennant
Charlie Young
Zayana Zulkiflee

Index

About Monocle

In 2007, MONOCLE was launched as a monthly magazine briefing on global affairs, business, culture, design and much more. We believed there was a globally minded audience of readers who were hungry for opportunities and experiences beyond their national borders. Today MONOCLE also has a 24-hour radio station, shops and cafés, a book-publishing team, films and events – and a great website too. We continue to grow and flourish and at our core is the simple belief that there will always be a place for a print brand that is committed to telling fresh stories, good journalism and the kind of experience that only paper delivers.

1.
Our team

Besides our London HQ we have seven international bureaux in New York, Toronto, Istanbul, Singapore, Tokyo, Zürich and Hong Kong. And as well as knowing how to land an interview with a prime minister or CEO, it turns out all our bureaux teams have become rather expert at spotting a good lunch spot or the perfect bar to take a contact to (you'll find their picks throughout this book).

Where our editors eat

1.
London: Il Blandford's
65 Chiltern Street,
W1U 6NH
ilblandfords.co.uk

2.
Singapore: Da Paolo
Pizza Bar
44 Jln Merah Saga, 278116
dapaolo.com.sg

3.
Tokyo: Pignon
16-3 Kamiyamacho,
Shibuya
+81 (0)3 3468 2331

4.
New York: Tacombi
267 Elizabeth Street, 10012
tacombi.com

2.
Monocle magazine

MONOCLE magazine is published 10 times a year, including two bumper double issues (July/August and December/January). We also have two annual specials: THE FORECAST, which is packed with key insights into the year ahead, and THE ESCAPIST, our summer travel-minded magazine. And all of these titles cover the world of food in-depth with recipes, reviews and our regular feature, My Last Meal, where someone we like tells us about their culinary and personal history.

3.
Monocle 24 Radio

Monocle 24 is our round-the-clock internet radio station (listen live at *monocle.com/radio* or download any show via iTunes, SoundCloud or from our own site). There's news, good music, magazine shows and, every Friday, there's a fresh episode of our food and drink show, *The Menu*. Hosted by Markus Hippi (*above*) it delivers a tasty takeaway of everything from brewing trends to interviews with the best chefs.

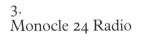

Tune in to The Menu: Fridays, 19.00

Listen up

1.
The Big Interview
Sundays, 09.00 London time

2.
The Globalist
Weekdays, 07.00 London time

3.
The Monocle Weekly
Sundays, 12.00 London time

4.
Monocle Café and Kioskcafé

We also have cafés in Tokyo and London serving Allpress coffee, great breakfasts and tempting lunches. And if you're passing through London's Paddington, be sure to visit our pioneering newsstand and coffee shop: Kioskafé.

Monocle Café Tokyo
B1F, Hankyu Men's,
2-5-1 Yurakucho, Chiyoda-ku
+81 (0)3 6252 5285

Monocle Café London
18 Chiltern Street, W1U 7QA
+44 (0)20 7135 2040

Kioskafé London
31 Norfolk Place, W2 1QH
+44 (0)20 3111 4242

5.
Monocle books

Since 2013 we have been publishing books – like this one – in partnership with Gestalten, as well as a series of city guides that are perfect for both seasoned travellers and first-time visitors. Our guides are designed to take you away from the well-beaten tourist path and show you the sites beyond the obvious (including the best cafés, bars and restaurants). The suite of guides includes London, Tokyo, Madrid, Bangkok, Miami, Sydney and Honolulu, with more titles to follow shortly. Buy today at *monocle.com/shop* or *shop.gestalten.com*.

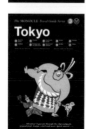

6.
Get involved

A subscription to MONOCLE is a simple way to make sure you never miss a copy and enjoy many additional benefits.

Our subscribers have special access to the entire MONOCLE archive, and also have priority access to selected product collaborations at *monocle.com*. Subscribers benefit from a 10 per cent discount at all Monocle shops, including online, and they receive exclusive offers and invitations to events around the world.

Delivery costs are included no matter where you are in the world, and we offer an auto-renewal service to ensure that you never go without.

Choose your package:

Premium one year
10 × Monocle
The Escapist + The Forecast
Porter Sub Club bag

One year
10 × Monocle
The Escapist + The Forecast
Monocle Voyage tote bag

Six months
5 × Monocle
The Escapist OR The Forecast

Subscribe now:
*monocle.com/subscribe or
subscriptions@monocle.com*

Subscribe and save 10 per cent online

Join us

There are lots of ways to be part of the ever-expanding MONOCLE world, whether in print, online or on the radio. We'd love to have you on board.

1.
Read the magazine

You can buy MONOCLE at newsstands in more than 60 countries around the world – or get an annual subscription at *monocle.com/subscribe*.

2.
Listen to Monocle 24

You can tune in to Monocle 24 radio live via our free app, at *monocle.com* or on any internet-enabled radio. You can also download our shows as podcasts from iTunes or SoundCloud to stay informed as you travel from nation to nation.

3.
Subscribe to the Monocle Minute

Sign up today at *monocle.com* to receive the Monocle Minute, our free daily news-and-views email. Our website is also where you will find a world of free films, our online shop and regular updates about everything we're up to.

MONOCLE – keeping an eye and an ear on the world

Thank you